UNDERSTANDING WRITER'S BLOCK

UNDERSTANDING WRITER'S BLOCK

A Therapist's Guide
to Diagnosis and Treatment

Martin Kantor

Westport, Connecticut
London

Library of Congress Cataloging-in-Publication Data

Kantor, Martin.
    Understanding writer's block : a therapist's guide to diagnosis
and treatment / Martin Kantor.
      p.   cm.
    Includes bibliographical references (p.) and index.
    ISBN 0-275-94905-2 (alk. paper)
    1. Writer's block. 2. Artist's block. 3. Creation (Literary.
artistic, etc.) 4. Writers—Mental health. 5. Artists—Mental
health. I. Title.
RC552.W74K36   1995
616.8'5—dc20   95–22005

British Library Cataloguing in Publication Data is available.

Library of Congress Catalog Card Number: 95–22005
ISBN: 0–275–94905–2

First published in 1995

Praeger Publishers, 88 Post Road West, Westport, CT 06881
An imprint of Greenwood Publishing Group, Inc.

Printed in the United States of America

The paper used in this book complies with the
Permanent Paper Standard issued by the National
Information Standards Organization (Z39.48–1984).

10 9 8 7 6 5 4 3 2 1

To M.E.C.

"God keep me from ever completing anything. This whole book is but a draught—nay, but the draught of a draught. Oh Time, Strength, Cash, and Patience!"

—Herman Melville, *Moby-Dick*

CONTENTS

PART I

DESCRIPTION

1

AN OVERVIEW

This is not a book about creativity, nor about the origin of creativity in madness. It is a book about creative, or writer's, block, one kind of "madness." Though this kind of "madness" affects romantic people, it is not a romantic disorder. It is not the kind psychiatrists and psychologists so often like to write about, the good kind where an unkempt creator with long hair spins beautiful poems from ugly delusions. It is the evil kind, the kind that cramps hands, stills voices, and empties hearts.

TERMINOLOGY: "CREATIVE BLOCK" OR "WRITER'S BLOCK?"

Although for purposes of convenience and to reflect popular usage the terms "creative block" and "writer's block" are used interchangeably, the term "creative block" is preferred here because it emphasizes how block affects the process of creating, not merely the act of writing, and can afflict all creative people.

Creative, or writer's, block is a relatively common disorder that affects the genius and the merely talented alike: the composer and the assembly-line worker, the painter of canvases and the painter of houses. Because of it Herman Melville writes comparatively little for thirty-five or so years; Antonio Vivaldi (to paraphrase a statement popularly attributed to Igor Stravinsky, among others) writes not five hundred concertos but one concerto five hundred times; and the head "cook and bottle washer" of the household instead of creating new dishes serves the same old ones each night to a progressively exasperated audience, his or her family.

Though creative, or writer's, block is both common and widespread there seems to be a general tendency at best to misunderstand and at worst to completely ignore it. The layman ignores block, thinking it merely troubles the lofty and the elite. The lofty and the elite ignore block, thinking it is inevitable, or their just punishment. And the scientific establishment, as typified by the fourth edition of the *Diagnostic and Statistical Manual of Mental Disorders* (*DSM–IV*) (American Psychiatric Association, 1994), ignores block because of a focus on other inhibitions deemed more important/profound, such as fear of going out of doors, or of eating in public. Though one would think there would be at least as many books on creative block as there are on creativity itself, data base searches using the key words "writer," "block," and "creative" turn up many works on creativity, especially on the relationship between creativity and madness, but few on creative block. It appears that the jacket notes of Zachary Leader's 1991 book, *Writer's Block*, are substantially correct in stating that his book is the first one to explore the phenomenon (at least this is true outside of the lay press).

Of course many works are de facto about blocked creators, describing various creative blocks without specifically identifying them as such. An exception to the rule is Ronald Hayman's biography of Tennessee Williams (1993) which describes several early periods when the author was unable to write at all and the fading final years when perhaps he wrote more than he said, and blames one of the early difficult periods on writer's block. Most texts follow the pattern of Stuart Feder's (1992) biography of Charles Ives, where we can find no mention either in the text or the index of the word block, even though the composer wrote little or nothing for approximately the last half of his life. Francis Toye (1987) calls Gioacchino Rossini's nearly forty-year silence the "Great Renunciation" (p. 166), which gives it an active, volitional quality, though I view it not as decision but as indecision, not as ease but as disease, and would prefer to call it not the "Great Renunciation" but something like the "Great Inhibition." And Albert Rothenberg (1990) completely overlooks blockage when he suggests that Jean Sibelius, who stopped writing at the peak of his career, had "no demonstrable mental illness" (p. 158). Finally, and perhaps not surprisingly, given the general confusion, other authors see block when it isn't there. For example, not so long ago musicologists said the composer Richard Strauss wrote little of value after his opera, *Der Rosenkavalier* (until, with the advent of the long playing record, they actually heard his later music) and viewed Igor Stravinsky's later neoclassicism so negatively that one got the impression that he wrote nothing at all worth hearing after *The Rite of Spring*.

THE USE OF PSYCHOBIOGRAPHY

Suggesting that Gioacchino Rossini might have been depressed, or Samuel Barber depressed and alcoholic may seem to be making diagnoses from things read about an artist or composer (secondary sources). Little of this text is drawn from original sources—interviews with the artist or his or her friends, family, or analyst. How valid is this material? Psychobiographers are known to commit errors. William A. Frosch (1992) notes:

> [P]sychobiography has, until recently, been the haunt of amateurs. Typically we (they) are trained in one of the fields, but not in the complementary one necessary to the scholarly work (if not to the occasional insight). . . . Freud's work on Leonardo is seriously marred by his mistranslation of the primary datum, and Slater and Meyers' understanding of Handel was led astray by their reliance on secondary and tertiary sources. (pp. 1741–1742)

Too often psychobiographers mix dynamic speculations with fact, for example saying that Rossini wrote no operas for the last half or so of his life because of oedipal conflict. They allow personal feelings to contaminate scientific conclusions, morality to influence aesthetics. And they select their material to prove a point already in place, as when one psychobiographer selected those major composers whose fathers were minor composers to prove a genetic recessive gene theory he had long favored, and when another emphasized how a permissive society was releasing for an artist who in fact liked control and needed to bear arms in the service of a cause, if (paradoxically) in the cause of freedom of speech.

But some objections to psychobiography are excessive. They are for reasons more emotional than rational. One artist who condemned all psychobiography was blaming others for invading artists' privacy as a projection of and a way to condemn her own voyeuristic tendencies, and for violating the sanctity of dead artists (whom she felt could neither explain nor defend themselves) as a projection of and a way to condemn her own guilt for having violated the sanctity of live artists when she was a critic.

Or the individual feels, perhaps too strongly, that studies of individuals are never of value, because the only studies of value are controlled studies of large groups.

Or the individual feels perhaps too strongly that studies of individuals are satisfactory only if primary sources (not what a biographer writes about an artist) are used.

As for the primacy of controlled studies, these too may be flawed. Rothenberg (1990) notes that Andreasen's study that found Affective Disorder rife in artists was skewed because it studied a select group of artists—those who had gone back to school, and were already depressed because in a sense they had failed in their chosen profession (pp. 150–151). And no less an authority than Christopher Perry (1992), in an article in *The American Journal of Psychiatry*, discusses some of the problems with the self-assessment tests on which many research projects rely (for example, self-reports do not adequately measure criteria that reflect objective phenomena, like restricted affect) and says that the clinical interview has a place in information gathering.

As for reliability, primary sources can be highly unreliable in their own way. For example, in some letters and diaries content obscures intent because the letters and diary entries are meant to be discovered and preserved for posterity and are more exhibitionistic than revealing.

Also, the artist on the analyst's couch is not necessarily more reliable than the artist on the psychobiographer's couch. Many artists on the couch display: poor insight; defensiveness; resistance; a tendency to repress; a tendency toward retrospective falsification, such as a need to distort the past to prove a present contention; an inability to distinguish a minor from major historical event or current stress; a need to emphasize deep over superficial motivation—as when the artist overlooks obvious causal factors of blockage like a troublesome marriage in favor of stressing arcane ones like oedipal guilt; a tendency to reserve the most important things for nonverbal communication, forcing the observer to infer what is going on; a need to say things to please, protect, displease, or hurt the analyst or other interviewer; an expectation of getting real gratification, such as a prescription for benzodiazepines; narcissism, so that the artist, always on stage, and decibel-dependent when it comes to applause, plays to the analyst like he or she plays to the balcony, to impress, presenting him or herself the way he or she would like to be, and expecting not treatment but approval, that is, good reviews; and depression, which creates distorted self-reporting based on a distorted self-image that is often dependent on external sources of approval or the outcome of inappropriate comparisons—as when a composer evaluates him- or herself in comparison to Mozart.

In telling the stories of their lives artists in particular tend to displace, overelaborate, and deny. In displacing, the artist might talk about a rejecting father when it was his mother's rejection that counted, suggesting an oedipal, when he had in fact a depressive block. One for example constantly complained that his father insisted he be the lawyer he didn't want to be, but he neglected to mention that while his father wanted him to be someone, the mother put all his ambitions down, undermining everything he wanted to do, and actually did.

In overelaborating, an artist makes more out of a situation than is merited. For example, when asked, "How was the driving to the clinic today?" one veteran answered, "Very bad," not because of the road conditions, but because the wind and the puddles reminded him of being back in Vietnam.

As for denial, so many artists overlook their human needs to the extent that they underreport real difficulties. They think, "I should not be affected by what affects normal people. I am on a higher plane." By overlooking the external in favor of the internal, they minimize or dismiss the real stress they are sometimes under.

Finally, the study of blocked artists is by definition the study of someone who has chosen silence as a defense—not the best platform from which to launch the balloon of self-exploration based on self-reporting.

Psychobiography is useful because it provides an overview not otherwise available. Few private practices can boast of many blocked artists as patients, and blocked friends won't do because they soon tire of being analyzed and seeing themselves (thinly disguised) in literary productions.

The problems associated with the use of secondary sources may be bypassed by employing them not for purposes of individual diagnosis but as clinical vignettes that are like legends, that is, they are twice-told tales that make a point, though they may not be historically accurate. Mozart may not have danced to keep warm, but the story that he did certainly tells us something about the plight of starving artists then and now.

Edward Gibbon (1776–1788) put it best in the *Decline and Fall of the Roman Empire*. He justified his study of the Romans through the medium of biography, saying, some facts of history "may be useful in drawing a partial conclusion, whereby the philosopher may be enabled to judge of the motives of an action, or some particular features in a character" (p. 7).

CLASSIFICATION

The one scientific text, the few lay works, and the dozen or so papers on creative block share a disturbing flaw: the tendency to partition the subject into separate, distinct entities. This creates a situation rather like the one that existed before catatonia, hebephrenia, and dementia paranoides were united under the overarching concept, Dementia Praecox. With creative block, the entities are: (1) writer's *block* of *emotional* etiology; (2) writer's *cramp* of *emotional* etiology; and (3) writer's *cramp* of *physical* etiology.

Artists with block of emotional etiology are believed to be intellectually impaired because of emotional problems. Artists with cramp of emotional etiology are believed to be physically impaired because of emotional problems, usually conversion disorder. And artists with cramp of physical etiology are believed to be physically impaired because of medical/neurological disorder, usually one given a medical sounding name, like carpal tunnel syndrome or dystonia.

There are two problems with this classification of creative block. The first is that it completely overlooks two other types of block: (4) writer's block of *physical* etiology, a possibility virtually ignored even in Leader's (1991) comprehensive text, *Writer's Block*, and (5) crossover phenomena, where physical and emotional factors combine initially to cause the disorder or because physical factors come into play after the disorder is formed for emotional reasons (or the other way around). Writer's block of physical etiology and crossover phenomena are discussed further below.

The second problem with this classification is that it virtually ignores how these so-called "separate" disorders are really all part of the same problem. Whatever the differences, they are minor compared to the similarities that exist. The most obvious of these similarities is that they are all blocks, and as such they all (without, for now, getting into a discussion of volition) have the same *intent*, that is, to stop creativity, and the same *result*, that is, they eventuate in the artist's working beneath capacity or not at all. True, the means to the end may differ. But the end itself is always depressingly very much the same. (Another commonality is mentioned below in the section, "Block as a Symptom of a Familiar Disorder.") We now explore these entities individually.

Writer's Block of Emotional Etiology

Writer's block is usually considered to be an emotional disorder that affects any or all aspects of creativity, ranging from initial inspiration to final perspiration. Here is a representative description of emotionally caused writer's block, taken from Lawrence H. Henning's 1981 paper entitled, "Paradox as a Treatment for Writer's Block":

> For professional writers, the fear that the creative well will suddenly run dry is equivalent to the singer's fear of losing the voice. For students, the severity of writer's block can range from an excuse to play tennis to the cause of academic failure . . . laziness was not the culprit. Some of these struggling people had spent hours and hours researching, sorting note cards, and deliberating endlessly, waiting for the first sentence to emerge. (p. 112)

Here is another, from Elliott P. Schuman's 1981 paper entitled, "A Writing Block Treated with Modern Psychoanalytic Interventions," which emphasizes "interference with functioning" (p. 113) including difficulty "completing writing for which . . . [one has] undertaken responsibility" sometimes, but not always, involving procrastination or "lingering" (p. 114) as when a "student . . . never gets his thesis completed" (p. 115).

Writer's Cramp of Emotional Etiology

Otto Fenichel and Gion Condrau are two of the authors who see writer's cramp as a physical manifestation of an emotional problem. Fenichel emphasizes the spasm and contracture and discusses the psychodynamics of both (the discussion is presented in chapter 5).

Condrau, in his 1988 paper, "Daseinsanalytic Therapy with a Patient Suffering from Compulsion Neurosis and Writer's Cramp," describes a patient whose conflicts about "human communication . . . disclosing . . . to others . . . and openness to the world" (p. 215) were expressed in his writer's cramp: "Having grown up under the most trying circumstances as the son of a chronic alcoholic, the patient had developed a compulsive personality and an extreme, neurotically inhibited disturbance of relationships. He also had developed a writer's cramp which seriously compromised his occupation as an accountant" (p. 211).

While Conversion Disorder is probably the most commonly cited emotional cause for writer's cramp, there are at least two other causes more common than usually supposed:

1. Pathological identification/merging, such as that found in Borderline Personality Disorder. Did the pianists Byron Janis and Gary Graffman develop pianist's cramp because of pathological identification/merging with their mentor, Vladimir Horowitz, who is rumored to have had a pianist's cramp of his own? It is likely that Horowitz did suffer from pianist's cramp, despite how, according to Glenn Plaskin (1983), his wife Wanda Horowitz protested that, "It is absolutely untrue that his illness affected either his mind or his hands, as some rumors have it" (p. 183). (Borderline Personality Disorder is discussed further in chapter 9.)

2. The delusional beliefs of schizophrenics and patients with a Delusional Disorder. Delusions can command the hand to cramp just as they can order the patient to kill or commit suicide. (Delusional Disorder is discussed further in chapter 2.)

Writer's Block of Physical Etiology

Few if any authors discuss the physical causes of writer's block, probably because few writers on the topic are physicians.

Perhaps the most familiar example of writer's block of physical etiology is also the most overlooked: writer's block that results from the organic brain damage due to addiction, alcoholism in particular. It seems that when it is a question of alcoholism our morality combines with our awe and our protectiveness of artists and we overlook the obvious. For example, Robert Layton (1992), one of Sibelius's biographers, suggests that Sibelius's final block, occupying approximately the last half of his life, was due to such factors as alienation and the Sibelius cults' expectation that he be a second Beethoven (p. 60). Yet it is likely that alcohol-induced dementia was at least one factor in his block, and a Substance-Induced Persisting Amnestic Disorder associated with confabulation could explain why he told some people he had written an eighth symphony when, as far as anyone knows, there were at most a few sketches. (Physical causes of writer's block are discussed in chapter 11.)

Writer's Cramp of Physical Etiology

While most authors view writer's block as an emotional disorder, writer's *cramp*, a spasm of the hand and related muscles, tends to be attributed, possibly overattributed, to physical causes. As Leader (1991) says, "Fenichel is not the first investigator to see writer's cramp as a psychological condition, but he is one of only a very few" (p. 2). Another is Wilfred Abse (1959), who stated that "occupational cramp . . . is a progressively severe disability due to spasm of the muscles employed in finely co-ordinated movements essential to the fundamental skills of the particular occupation of the patient. *Writer's cramp* is but one example. Occupational cramp often yields to psychotherapeutic intervention when the hysterical nature of the symptoms becomes apparent" (p. 279). Also, Rothenberg (1990) states that "when actual muscle cramping or paralysis of the hands occurs in writers, the cause is usually a so-called hysterical paralysis" (p. 175).

A more typical (and typically quaint) description of writer's cramp, from Ellis Bindman and R. W. Tibbetts' 1977 paper, "Writer's Cramp—A Rational Approach to Treatment?" follows:

> Writer's Cramp also known as craft palsy or craft neurosis, can be described as a muscular spasm of the fingers and hand of the writing arm, often spreading to muscles of the lower and upper arm, and even to the shoulder girdle with consequent incoordination and discomfort, leading to weakness, pain, and often tremor. The cramp occurs only when writing or during some similar activity such as typing or counting votes. The pen is grasped more and more firmly and the writing becomes more jerky and forcible, until the pen may be pushed through the paper and writing eventually becomes impossible. Distortion of the writing position occurs, with the hand supinated or over-pronated, sometimes with the pen grasped between the middle and ring fingers. (p. 143)

C. D. Marsden and M. P. Sheehy in their 1990 paper, "Writer's Cramp," describe the characteristics of writer's cramp in ninety-one patients as follows: "difficulty in writing; progression to involve other manual acts; pain; carpel [*sic*] tunnel syndrome; tremor on writing and/or postural arm tremor" (p. 148).

H. B. Gibson in his 1972 paper, "Writer's Cramp: A Behavioural Approach," sees the origin of writer's cramp in "occult neurological defect" (p. 374). He notes (in an apparent contradiction to the neurological theory of causation) that "the disorganisation is generally fairly specific to the skill—sufferers from typist's cramp need not have any disability in writing, and sufferers from writer's cramp may generally use manipulative instruments in delicate work without trouble" (p. 373).

Marsden and Sheehy (1990) put their case for organic causation somewhat more forcefully:

> Writer's cramp has been recognized for over a century, and originally was construed as a physical motor disorder. However, an unfortunate use of the descriptive term "professional neuroses" to describe this and other similar task-specific conditions, coupled subsequently with fashions in psychiatry, led to the mistaken belief that writer's cramp was due to psychic rather than motor pathology. Evidence has accumulated in recent years showing that writer's cramp is a real focal motor disorder, with a close relation to dystonia. (p. 148)

Crossover Phenomena (Disorders of Mixed Etiology)

In crossover block both physical and mental factors are operative. For example, in stage fright it can be difficult to tell if hormonal discharge is causing the anxiety, or the anxiety is causing the hormonal discharge. As Agatha Christie put it in her autobiography (1977), "I can describe what . . . [stage fright] seemed like by saying that I could not control my *physical* reaction" (p. 152). In some depressions the so-called emotional disorder is really due to a chemical imbalance. Some observers believe that chronic substance abuse begins as a physical (for example, genetic) problem, and certainly chronic substance abusers can go on to develop neurological stigmata of their abuse, sometimes when they are still very young. The difficulty in distinguishing Conversion Disorder from dystonia is partly because of the rapid onset of physical changes in the musculature in cases that begin as Conversion Disorder, or the rapid appearance of emotional overlay in cases that begin as dystonia. In cases of Postconcussional Disorder, there is often a blend of organic and emotional signs and symptoms. The organic thread consists of confusion and inability to concentrate. The emotional thread consists of the self-defeating behavior that originally may have provoked a needed accident, the posttraumatic symptoms attributable to the trauma that caused the concussion, and, on occasion, the exaggeration, or outright malingering, of some or all of the symptoms for gain.

According to Gillian Gill (1990), Agatha Christie's biographer, Agatha Christie blocked and couldn't write anything for some months after her mother died and her husband left her for another woman. The block, which seems to have begun with her Great Disappearance (discussed further in chapter 5), would seem to be a straightforward example of a dissociative episode, were it not for the possibility that she sustained a head injury when she crashed her car at the very beginning of her flight.

Arbie Orenstein (1991), Ravel's biographer, says that Ravel's final block was of some six-years duration. While "his mind was replete with ideas . . . when he wished to write them down, they vanished" (p. 107). At first glance this looks like a purely physical problem. A taxi collision in which Ravel "suffered several facial wounds and chest bruises" (p. 104) seems to have ushered in a period when his "health took a sudden turn for the worse during the summer of 1933 . . . he found himself incapable of coordinating his motions when swimming and encountered unusual difficulty in writing. The physicians who were consulted spoke of ataxia, the inability to coordinate voluntary muscular movements, and aphasia, involving difficulty in speech and a partial loss of memory" (p. 105). "Incapable of notating . . . [a] score . . . [he] dictated the transcription" (p. 107).

However, can we ignore that Ravel had previous serious, probably emotional, blocks early in his career? Orenstein (1991) describes how, after his mother's death in 1917, Ravel suffered a block that was complete and lasted for about three years in "virtual silence with regard to composition" (p. 75). According to Harold Schonberg (1981), twelve years before Ravel stopped writing completely he said of his work, "I have torn all of it out of me by pieces . . . and now I cannot do any more" (p. 488).

BLOCK AS A SYMPTOM OF A FAMILIAR DISORDER

A previously suggested overarching similarity of most if not all creative blocks is that they really are not disorders in their own right. Instead they are in effect symptoms of another, familiar, *DSM–IV* disorder such as depression or phobia. Like fever or most other symptoms, then, creative block may be said to have a differential diagnosis.

Turning this inside out, a perusal of the *DSM–IV* reveals that many of the mental and physical disorders described in its pages have one or more symptoms that are in effect creative blocks.

Ten categories of symptomatic block according to the disorder of origin are distinguished below. Each one will be taken up in a separate chapter (chapters 2–11).

1. *Schizophrenic Disorder block.* This may be characterized by *absences* resulting from the negative symptoms of schizophrenia, such as anhedonia. It may result from specific thought *process* disorder, such as the idea that thoughts are being pulled from the head, or from specific thought *content* disorder, such as the paranoid delusion that the FBI is ordering the artist not to write but to keep secrets, or from the somatic delusion that a pianist's hand has turned to stone.

2. *Affective Disorder block.* This is characterized either by the marasmic silence of depression or by the logorrheic tendency of the hypomanic to say too little by saying too much.

3. *Anxiety/Phobic Disorder block.* This is characterized by the use of block as avoidance to deal with the real and imagined anxiety

associated with creating. (All writer's blocks/cramps are partly phobic, containing as they do elements of stage fright and fear of success.)

4. *Conversion Disorder block.* This is characterized by the use of the somatic defense of conversion to resolve conflict about the creative process or product. The result is interfering motor paralysis (cramp), sensory deficit (anesthesia or paresthesias), or disruptive psychophysiological conversions such as severe constipation or tension headaches.

5. *Obsessive-Compulsive Disorder block.* This is characterized by creative paralysis due to withholding (from stubbornness) or recanting (from guilt). Often intellect is used to withhold feeling, resulting in ponderous academic art lacking depth and spontaneity. (Affective Disorder block is likely to be the culprit when feeling is used to withhold or retract intellect.)

6. *Posttraumatic Stress Disorder block.* This is characterized by disruptive traumatic recurrence appearing during and as a consequence of the creative act or as a consequence of the difficulties inherent in being a creative person. Such blocks are difficult to distinguish from Adjustment Disorder blocks that result from external *stress* (as distinct from *trauma*). In both there is often a contribution from personal hypersensitivity to stress and trauma.

7. *Sexual Disorder/Paraphilia block.* This is characterized by channeling creative energy into pseudosexual pursuits such as compulsive cruising, or pseudoerotic pursuits like fetishism or exhibitionism, and by contaminating the art with those conflicts that created the sexual disorder/paraphilia.

8. *Personality Disorder block.* This is characterized by channeling creative energy into persistent, disruptive interpersonal defensive behaviors like shy withdrawal, abject dependency, or compulsive professional rivalry, and by contaminating the art with those conflicts that created the Personality Disorder. In either event, art becomes attitude, as happened when one individual bought a big computer not to compute mathematically or word process but to consciously impress neighbors and friends with the size of his bank account, and unconsciously with the size of his genitalia.

9. *Substance Use Disorder (Addiction) block.* This is characterized by substance abuse that inhibits work either directly, by causing organic defect, or indirectly, by causing interpersonal difficulty, or both.

10. *Organic Disorder block.* This is characterized by a discrete, underlying physical/neurological basis for blockage, such as hypothyroidism or stroke.

Among the many advantages of viewing writer's block not as a syndrome unto itself but as a symptom of another disorder are: (1) It puts creative block into what I believe to be its proper position in mainstream psychiatry, allowing it to proudly, so to speak, take its place alongside such other familiar symptoms of emotional and physical disorder as obsession and depression, and (2) It suggests a specific treatment approach. For example, if an artist blocks because he or she is schizophrenic, then block can be treated using methods proven safe and effective for treating schizophrenia. If the artist is schizophrenic, avoid uncovering techniques when the patient is delusional or excessively hostile. If a disorder is reactive, that is, due to the problem an artist is having with his or her finances, audiences, and critics, anticipate that self-exploration alone will be inadequate and ask the artist to take control of his or her life and suggest steps to make the change.

A patient who lived in a small town where he had no colleagues couldn't make his teddy bears and watched helplessly as his finances dwindled until he was threatened with losing his house. Insight psychotherapy merely directed to his conflicts between passion and guilt was ineffective. One day, the therapist noticed how isolated he had become and recommended that he attend conferences in the Big City and rejoin his colleagues both socially and professionally. His new contacts inspired him to start working again and stirred up new ideas for his work. These in turn became grist for the mill first, for his art, and second, for his psychotherapy.

STAGES OF BLOCK: ACUTE VERSUS CHRONIC

Block in its acute, formative stages (early or preblock) can be distinguished from block that is chronic (well-developed).

Block in its acute, formative stage is little more than a pure *DSM–IV* symptom. As a result, acute symptomatic block tends to appear and disappear in step with the underlying generative disorder or syndrome. For example, Michael Kennedy (1987), in his biography of Sir Edward Elgar, describes a number of occasions when the composer seems to have blocked when he was depressed and unblocked when his depression lifted.

Block however loses its symptomatic "purity" when it occurs too often or lasts too long. Gradually it wears the artist down, becomes the subject of vicious cycling (say between block, anxiety about being blocked, and more block) and creates secondary complications ranging from reactive depression to alcoholism. This is chronic block.

Chronic block is blockage that has settled in. It loses many of the characteristics of its disorder of origin. It no longer precisely rises and falls with relapse and remission of the underlying disorder. And it develops new characteristics directly attributable to the chronicity itself. As a result sooner or later all blocked artists begin to look alike. All are in effect under- or unemployed, poor, lonely, and suffering from low self-esteem. (Chronic block is discussed further in chapter 12.)

COVERT OR HIDDEN (VERSUS OVERT) BLOCK

Chapter 13 discusses block that is covert or hidden. When block is covert or hidden the observer and/or the artist fails to recognize its presence. One of the most important tasks for therapists is to uncover block from its various hiding places, to avoid misdiagnosing or missing it entirely. According to Bernard Holland, writing in the *New York Times* (1994), Murray Perahia stopped playing the piano supposedly when he cut his thumb, developed an infection, and "surgery followed infection." That he doesn't remember cutting it is suspicious, as Holland says: "Mr. Perahia's current medical tribulations began nominally with a cut, but one can't help wondering if its roots are elsewhere" (p. C16).

Two of the various ways block can be hidden and missed have already been mentioned. Block can be hidden because:

1. It presents itself as a symptom of a familiar disorder, so it is perceived as anhedonia, delusion, or chronic fatigue syndrome. In personality disorders, it is common for block to be hidden in behavioral disguises such as plagiarism, and in compulsive acting-out that detracts from working.

2. It is in its late, chronic stages, and overripe—it has lost its distinctive, hard-edged, discrete quality, having blended into an artist's life and pathology.

Other reasons why block is hidden (discussed more fully in chapter 13) include:

1. It is in its early stages (what we call preblock), and so is not yet fully formed.

2. It appears in the art but not in the artist; for example, in the joyless academic musings, what Oscar Thompson's *The International Cyclopedia of Music and Musicians* (1964) calls "complicated" and "cumbersome" (p. 1761), found in some of the works of the composer Max Reger.

3. It affects the so-called nonartistic professions, such as science. Think of Freud's winning the Goethe prize for literature to realize how spurious the distinction between science and art can really be.

4. It is rationalized, as when it is cleverly blamed on reality. This often happens around retirement, when people have many seemingly plausible reasons for giving up their work. They say it is "too much aggravation," or "I want to devote myself to fishing," when they

mean, "I want to abdicate in favor of a younger person," "punish myself for being a survivor," or "punish the boss for what he or she did to me by in turn depriving the company of my valuable presence."

FALSE (VERSUS TRUE) BLOCK

Chapter 15 describes false, as distinguished from true, block. In false block the creator falsely believes he or she is blocked for one of two reasons:

1. He or she is a "normal" workaholic—someone who does quite enough work but thinks he or she should do more.
2. He or she is lazy. Some lazy people think they are blocked when they are in fact do-nothings. They call themselves blocked because they prefer to view themselves not as slothful, but as sick.

Therapists must not treat the patient for a problem that does not exist. In particular, preferential hard work must not be confused with compulsive workaholism. If it is, and the patient's career is interfered with on that account, block is not being removed. It is being created.

2

SCHIZOPHRENIC SPECTRUM DISORDER BLOCK

SCHIZOPHRENIA

If Robert Schumann were schizophrenic, his schizophrenia seems to have spared his creativity, at least until the end of his life. It is as if the two phenomena, schizophrenia and creativity, were parallel manifestations, occupying what we might call separate but equal compartments in the mind.

If Sylvia Plath were schizophrenic, her schizophrenia seems, at least sometimes, to have translated into effective, even extraordinary poetry. The same may be said of Emily Dickinson who, according to Susan Kavaler-Adler (1993), expressed "her inner psychic upheaval . . . through poetry, with inchoate sensation becoming articulated representation" (p. 228).

But most schizophrenics are not so fortunate. For most schizophrenics, schizophrenia neither spares nor causes creativity. Instead, in most cases, schizophrenia causes the opposite of creativity: creative block.

Block-Inducing Aspects of Schizophrenia

A perusal of the *DSM–IV* (1994) reveals how many signs and symptoms of schizophrenia are in effect creative blocks. In general, schizophrenia is characterized by failure to function either because of a failure to achieve a certain level, or because of a regression to a lower level of functioning. The result, an impoverishment of functioning, is in effect a form of block.

Negative symptoms such as avolition and anhedonia. Avolition refers to the relative or absolute inability to start or complete a task. *Anhedonia*, according to Dorland's *The American Illustrated Medical Dictionary* (1951), refers to a "loss of feeling of pleasure in acts that normally give pleasure" (p. 96).

Thought content disorder (specific delusions and/or hallucinations). Menacing or forbidding delusions, or intrusive hallucinations such as hearing an intrusive musical note in the mind (as may have happened to the composers Schumann and Rossini) can cause block, producing their effect either *directly* or *indirectly*.

Schumann (who may or may not have been schizophrenic) seems to have suffered from the *direct* effect of delusions and hallucinations. Schonberg (1981), in writing of the last years of the life of Schumann, notes that:

> as his mind became progressively unbalanced, Schumann withdrew into his own world. He kept hearing in his inner ear an incessant A that prevented him from talking or thinking. Always taciturn, he said less and less, and visitors could not get a word out of him. . . . Early in 1852 he went through an entire week during which he said that . . . devils in the form of tigers and hyenas were threatening him with Hell. (pp. 180–181)

Schizophrenic delusions and hallucinations must be distinguished from similar experiences that are not due to schizophrenia but that are a part of the flooding and controlled regression, or "regression in the service of the ego" (Ernst Kris in *Psychoanalytic Explorations in Art* as quoted by Peter Giovacchini 1984, p. 439) that sometimes accompany creativity in the normal. For example, Bonnie Friedman (1993), who does not appear to be suffering from a psychosis, in *Writing Past Dark*, describes a transient interfering feeling of "dissolving like an aspirin tablet" (p. 115), a somatic delusion that is quite different diagnostically from the kind that is consistent with schizophrenia.

Sometimes the effect of delusions and hallucinations is an *indirect* one. Delusions and hallucinations are often draining, preoccupying, and disruptive of the artist's interpersonal life. They cause the artist to lose touch with the outside world and miss the practical and emotional support that comes from other people.

Thought process disorder. In *thought withdrawal* thoughts appear to be pulled from the head. There might be an underproductivity of thought and speech or what Jules R. Bemporad and Henry Pinsker (1974), in their article on schizophrenia for the *American Handbook of Psychiatry*, call "aberrations in conceptual processes" (p. 533). In *ambivalence*, according to the revised third edition, *Diagnostic and Statistical Manual of Mental Disorders* (*DSM–III–R*) (American Psychiatric Association 1987), a partial or complete cessation of goal-directed activity occurs because of an inability to decide among alternative courses of action (p. 189). In *perseveration* repetitiveness is seen. Perhaps a variety of perseveration, what might be called "rhythmic perseveration," is why many of Emily Dickinson's poems can be sung to the tune of "The Yellow Rose of Texas": "As One does Sickness over/In convalescent Mind, his scrutiny of Chances/By blessed Health obscured . . . " (poem quoted by Kavaler-Adler 1993, p. 231). In *dwelling on abstractions*, preoccupations block, such as "preoccupations with time, the nature of life, [and] solutions (or supposed solutions) to political and social problems" (Bemporad and Pinsker 1974, p. 534). Bemporad and Pinsker write:

> [Such an] individual may appear deep or intellectual to his neighbors, but if he records his thoughts in notebooks, as is often done, it can be seen that the ideas are usually lacking in depth or systematic approach, tend to be expressed in dramatic or cryptic but inconsistent phrases, fraught with significance only for the writer. Mark Twain described a youth who memorized thousands of verses of Scripture, received a gold medal, then went mad. Today a young person with similar problems, instead of memorizing Scripture, might contemplate for months his own inner experiences and relationships. (p. 534)

Those unfamiliar with psychiatric diagnosis tend to attach too benign labels to this malignant, schizophrenic dwelling on abstractions, calling them obsessions or (terms used too loosely by Victoria Nelson [1985] in her book *Writer's Block and How to Use It*) "note-taking disease" being an "archetypal note taker" or "thesis block" (p. 99). This can overlook how the problem is really too severe and crippling to be neurotic. By minimizing the patient's difficulty conceptually, these labels invariably minimize the severity of the problem, and, in effect, suggest a wrong treatment approach.

George Eliot's Mr. Casaubon, as portrayed in her novel *Middlemarch* (1872), was probably the true obsessional Nelson (1985) suggests he was. Nelson calls this quintessentially blocked author "fussy, rigid, and anal retentive" (p. 99). And in the story itself, Casaubon's wife, Dorothea, is sensitively portrayed as reacting to her husband in a fashion consistent with the diagnosis, that is, in much the way real people react to blocked obsessionals. She loses patience, blows up in a controlled fashion, and hands out what we might call an implied fish-or-cut-bait ultimatum: "All those rows of volumes—will you not make up your mind what part of them you will use, and begin to write the book which will make your vast knowledge useful to the world?" (p. 98).

Nelson (1985) suggests that the following real-life case is also obsessional, but this patient seems to be one step closer to psychosis than poor Mr. Casaubon:

> A man . . . [was] driven by compulsive fears that he had failed in life and always would. Accordingly, he set out to master every scrap of learning material that came his way. He quickly fell under the spell of two books he was assigned in literature classes, those talismans of the sixties, *Lord of the Flies* and *Steppenwolf*. Immersing himself in these works, he devised

an elaborate theory that explained both the books and his own relationship to the universe. At term's end, however, he found himself completely unable to convey this complex tangle of interlocking ideas in the medium of two five-page reports. He was unable, in fact, to set down a single sentence from his well-thumbed stack of index cards. . . . [and] tortured himself nightly for several years poring fruitlessly over the books and his notes, hopelessly blocked. (p. 19)

This case of mine seems the closest to psychosis of all three: A writer couldn't concentrate on her work at all. She regressed into dependent inactivity because of an "obsession" with death associated with a "compulsion" to count her heart beats, and subtract each from the total the books said she was allowed for a lifetime, all the while recalculating how many days, years and months she thought she had left to live.

Positive Aspects

A number of authors, Kavaler-Adler (1993) among them, have implied or quoted others who have implied, that schizophrenia is good for creativity. For example, quoting Henry Wells, Kavaler-Adler notes that "his view acknowledges Dickinson's psychopathology and at the same [time] the interaction of madness and creativity as artistically profitable" (p. 228).

The lives of Sylvia Plath and others like her do suggest that in fortunate cases the symptoms of schizophrenia can be artistically pro-creative. Thought content disorder such as paranoid and grandiose delusions can be inherently interesting. The thought process disorders of circumstantiality, tangentiality, and loosening of associations can facilitate the artistic development and elaboration of idea. Sometimes spillage of unconscious material looks like, and probably is, good poetry. (In turn, the ability to spill unconscious material is one reason some schizophrenics are both attracted to and good at writing poetry.) Primary process emergence can result in creative twists, such as those that are the effect of what Rothenberg (1990) calls Janusian thinking. Janusian thinking is a kind of primary process thinking which he defines as a form of thought where:

multiple opposites or antitheses are conceived simultaneously, either as existing side by side or as equally operative, valid, or true. In an apparent defiance of logic or of physical possibility, the creative person consciously formulates the simultaneous operation of antithetical elements or factors and develops those formulations into integrated entities and creations . . . a leap that transcends ordinary logic. (p. 15)

Hallucinatory voices can facilitate the creative process when they act much like the good, supportive little voices of normals. One of my patients said, "They are as helpful, reassuring and soothing as my mother's voice that, long after she is gone, warns me not to burn myself with hot dishes ('Careful, use a pot holder.') and boiling liquid ('Pour fast, so that it doesn't spill.')." The voices, instead of criticizing him unmercifully and holding him back, supported him personally and spurred him on. When he was afraid, they told him to, "Relax, don't worry. Now, or ever, is not the time to panic." And when a good idea popped into his head, they warned him, "You'll not remember it, write it down," so that he, unlike many writers, rarely forgot what he was about to say. Also, he countered paranoid voices from the superego that warned him that the consequences of doing art were castration and dissolution, with grandiose voices from the same superego that assured him that he was omnipotent and, no matter what, nothing could harm him.

Even the hostile withdrawal, so characteristic of schizophrenia, can be the stuff of which not blockage, but art, is made. As one patient put it to me, "Craziness and isolation works for me like it did for Marcel Proust."

An underlying schizoid or schizotypal personality, or personality disorder, can protect as much as harm. While in one schizophrenic patient, block resulted from a paranoid hypersensitivity to criticism, in another, more fortunate, case, remoteness made the individual insensitive to criticism. Effectively and helpfully oblivious to her behavior's effects on others, she was detached from their possible negative responses to her behavior—the "certain indifference to the humiliation of defeat" that William I. Bennett (1994), quoted in the *Harvard Medical Alumni Bulletin*, says Jerome Kagan called a "precondition of creativity and effectiveness in life" (p. 13). (Schizoid and Schizotypal Personality Disorder are discussed further in chapter 9.)

Rothenberg (1990) sums up the negative and positive aspects of schizophrenia in these observations: He notes that Sylvia Plath's poetic works "in large measure display the conflicts and disturbances of . . . [the author and become] failures as artistic creations and subversions of self-creation" (p. 77), and "For some poets, it appears that illness does feed and nurture their gift" (p. 58).

Therapeutic Implications

There are at least two pressing therapeutic reasons to diagnose schizophrenia and schizophrenic block when present: (1) schizophrenic blockage can be, and often is, made worse with uncovering/anxiety-provoking therapies; and (2) schizophrenic blocks and schizophrenic blockers often require, and respond to, pharmacotherapy, usually a helpful supplement to verbal and behavioral forms of treatment.

The ideal outcome is removing the symptoms that block the patient while leaving intact those that promote creativity. Of course, pharmacotherapy or shock therapy doesn't distinguish between pro- and anticreative symptoms. This is the job of supportive psychotherapy, particularly the kind that fosters a positive relationship between the patient and the therapist. (Aspects of therapy of block are discussed in chapter 18.)

DELUSIONAL DISORDER

In Delusional Disorder, block either represents a response to *nonbizarre* delusions or is a product of an underlying Paranoid Personality Disorder.

A Response to Nonbizarre Delusions

The pianist who can't move one of his hands (the problem affects mostly males) because of the false belief that he suffers from nerve damage has a nonbizarre delusion because paralysis of the hand due to nerve damage *can* occur in real life. If, however, the pianist thinks he can't move his left hand because it has turned to stone, not possible in real life, his delusion is bizarre, and his diagnosis is not Delusional Disorder but a form of schizophrenia (see also the differential diagnosis of pianist's cramp, discussed below).

As with schizophrenia, delusions can dictate blockage *directly*, by commanding block, or *indirectly*, by causing interpersonal retreat and isolation. The nonbizarre delusions may be of the grandiose, somatic, or persecutory (paranoid) type.

Grandiose delusions are characterized, according to Kaplan and Sadock (1985), by "exaggerated conception of one's importance" (p. 501). While grandiose delusions can inspire and motivate, on balance they interfere, especially with the quality of the product. For example, they can produce unrealistic logorrheic, or longueur blocks if the author thinks his or her production is too good and important to need rewriting and editing.

Kavaler-Adler (1993) describes longueur block in Edith Sitwell, saying that she often "failed to bring any objective reflection to a first draft" (p. 287). Probably there is a relationship between Wagnerian operatic longueurs and Wagner's well-known, and well-documented, personal grandiosity. Grandiosity may account for why so many dull stretches survive in many of the works of Hector Berlioz. Felix Mendelssohn hinted at this possibility when, according to Schonberg (1981), he said Berlioz's "assumption of genius in capital letters, is insupportable" (p. 158). Schonberg himself refers to *Les Troyens*, one of the Berlioz operas, as a "monster" (p. 166). And Francis Madeira, a former conductor of the Rhode Island Philharmonic Orchestra, suggested that Hector Berlioz's grandiosity led to a lack of discipline; as a result he did not edit out long uninspired stretches, where, because melodic inspiration is lacking, the effect is one of "all bottom and no top" (personal communication, 1953).

In more serious cases, logorrheic blocks are characterized not merely by hypomanic production (discussed in chapter 3), that is, by overproduction, but by overproduction of psychotically tinged material.

There are two main categories of blocking *somatic delusions*. The first involves the gastrointestinal tract, when the artist becomes preoccupied with his or her health and, convinced that he or she is sick, feels too debilitated to work. As described further below, the pianist Vladimir Horowitz withdrew from the stage because he felt that he had chronic appendicitis. A pianist patient complained of, and was treated for, a colitis that kept her off the concert stage, a colitis that was actually due to a secret (delusional) conviction that tapeworms were eating away her insides. The second kind involves the hand and results in delusional writer's *cramp*. More than one pianist and violinist has had a performance cramp due to the delusional conviction that one hand has become dysfunctional, say because of muscular weakness. Such delusions can be a product not of Delusional Disorder but of Major Depression (discussed below).

Persecutory delusions can cause block because they make what could be cooperative into adversarial relationships and pursuits.

I suggest that persecutory delusion may explain block in the composer Charles Ives. According to Feder's (1992) biography of Charles Ives, around the time of the onset of his musical block (he wrote little to nothing for the last thirty-six or so years of his life):

Ives . . . vent[ed] his spleen . . . in an eighty-four page tract. The central verbal document of this period in Ives's life, *The Majority* [is a] groping, rambling, often irrelevant text, which is meant to be humorous, [but] is painfully unfunny [with] disarrayed thinking [and] various titles and subtitles . . . crossed out . . . he scribbled, "This is just to show how a man should write who considers himself a nice author and who everybody else considers crazy." . . . He attempted to bind in words grandiose ideas, the impulse that gave rise to them, and considerable aggression—all now threatening to dominate mental life. (p. 299)

Some so-called phobias are dynamically and structurally paranoid. For example, erythrophobia, the fear that others might see us blush, is often really the suspicion that others can read the forbidden thoughts that make us blush. Pseudophobic paranoid ideas or delusions can be the reason for one form of stage fright. Peter Gammons (1992), in *The Throes of Tossing a Baseball*, describes a ball player who "felt as if I were climbing up a rock on a mountain, and when I approached the top there was a rattlesnake" (p. 145). Another player had this recurrent dream: "[I throw] a ball in the bullpen that is wild, gets out on the field and the game is stopped while the ball is retrieved and everyone looks at [me]" (p. 138).

Nonbizarre delusions that are part of Delusional Disorder must be differentiated from delusions in major depression and delusions that are the result of a folie à deux (Shareo Psychotic Disorder).

Delusions in Major Depressive Disorder. Somatic delusions of colonic stasis and related delusions may be symptomatic not of Delusional Disorder but of

Major Depressive Disorder, severe, with psychotic features. Though it cannot be proved, major depression might have been the reason for Horowitz's first "nervous breakdown":

> In September 1936, Horowitz was suffering extreme abdominal discomfort, and suddenly decided to have his appendix removed. . . . Horowitz insisted that his appendix was the cause. The trauma of the operation and its aftereffects caused a nearly complete collapse of body and mind. . . . Since his mother's death after a delayed appendectomy, he had worried about the state of his own appendix. . . . [though] leading surgeons [said] . . . "There's nothing the matter with you or your appendix. You don't have to have it taken out. For heaven's sake, forget it." By 1936, though, Horowitz was plagued by pains both real and imagined, and had become convinced that his appendix was to blame. . . . Thinking . . . of his mother's death and fearful for his own life, Horowitz had the operation in Paris. (Plaskin 1983, p. 182)

Folie à deux. Here delusions are created not de novo but by a process of assimilation. A healthier individual identifies with, and develops the delusions of, a sicker companion. The individual who does the identifying is often not psychotic. Rather the process involves (1) borderline merging, (2) hysterical wanting to get attention by belonging to the crowd, or (3) identification—either passive dependent identification or identification with the aggressor. Identification can result in a student picking up his or her master's symptoms as a way to be the cooperative, good student. This professed cooperation often covers the reverse—the wish to be uncooperative and bad. It is a way to deny angry competitive fantasies directed to the successful professor. The goals are to avoid committing the ultimate (oedipal) crime of surpassing the professor and the intolerable guilt that comes with it, the "burden, created by surpassing, prevailing, even surviving, [that] hangs in mental life like a debt that cannot be repaid and that steadily accrues interest over a lifetime" (Feder 1992, p. 289).

As mentioned in chapter 1 and above, Vladimir Horowitz seems to have inspired those around him to share what may have been his delusions in a folie à deux. It may not be coincidental that two of his pupils, Byron Janis and Gary Graffman, developed problems with their hands. Again, their pianist's cramp may have been imitations of the rumored problems Horowitz had with his own hands—a fitting companion to the legendary problems Schonberg (1981) says he had with his appendix.

A Product of an Underlying Paranoid Personality Disorder

Artists with a Paranoid Personality Disorder tend to block due to paranoid cognitive errors. An example of a block-inducing, often paranoid, cognitive error is "If they don't love me for this, that is, completely, then they hate me for everything, that is, altogether." Another is the idea that similar things are the same thing. In one case this resulted in a degree of circumspection of paranoid proportions.

A writer/composer, as a consequence of thinking similar things were the same thing, confused self-expression with self-revelation and, overlooking that he refined and censored, disguised as much as revealed, he became excessively fearful that he was his characters, even in works that were only partially, or not at all, autobiographical. Now he became extremely circumspect and anonymous to avoid the humiliation, or further humiliation, that would result if others knew too much about him. To avoid what he considered to be excessive exposure, he refused to write in the first person, and, in whatever he wrote, he employed a minced, wimpish, inoffensive, uncommitted style. Or he used one emotion, like satirical anger, to hide another, like loving sexual/homosexual feelings, or the other way around. The result was a diatribe when love, or loving when a diatribe, was meant. Because the abstract hid the concrete, we got what he himself called a peculiar elitist, "British gentry," "gossamer veil," or "glockenspiel" art, in essence what the program guide (1994) for Benjamin Britten's opera *Death in Venice* refers to as too much Apollo and too little Dionysus (p. 18). (See also chapter 9.)

The next two examples of excessive circumspection, the first taken from Humphrey Carpenter's (1992) biography of the composer Benjamin Britten, and the second from Vera Stravinsky and Robert Craft's (1978) book, *Stravinsky in Pictures and Documents*, are illustrative of a principle only, and are not meant to imply that either man was paranoid.

Carpenter (1992) mentions over and over how others comment on Britten's thinness and unemotionality and praise Britten's skill but complain that his scores fail to say something. For example, Carpenter quotes Peter Evans as saying that a piece of Britten's music "almost entirely excludes any representation of some of Britten's most intense sentiments" (p. 278).

Many have implied that Stravinsky's music, particularly his later twelve-tone works, was lacking in feeling. According to Stravinsky and Craft (1978) the conductor, Ernst Ansermet, said, "You place too much emphasis on your technical powers and on your knowledge and not enough on . . . your instincts" (p. 450). Referring to Stravinsky's later works, in like manner, the novelist Michel Butor is quoted as having written that "in this third period . . . structure itself becomes the composition's most powerful element" (p. 449).

Block also comes from excessive projection. Leader (1991) emphasizes the origin of block in projection without actually using the term. He says block occurs when "the world is invested with needs or drives that are ultimately greedy or aggressive" (p. 155). The artist often projects one of three things: (1) his or her *greediness* toward *others*, (2) his or her *aggressiveness* toward *the self*, or (3) his or her *aggressiveness* toward *others*.

As a result, the artist comes to feel victimized by a world that uses, devalues, and abuses him or her. Feeling used, devalued, and abused are cornerstones of what is charitably called "artistic temperament," or "artistic vulnerability," but is, at least in some cases, really a paranoid hypersensitivity. Artists are famous for it, and it is sometimes benign. But more often it is serious and leads to block.

For example, block appeared in one case when a hypersensitive artist paid her critics too much mind; heard not what had been said but what she thought was meant; read between the lines when no hidden agenda was intended, or was intended but was intended to remain hidden; and, becoming angry and vengeful, stopped working, as she said, just "to show them they can't treat me that way." (Caution must be observed in employing the term paranoia as a term of approbation just because artists object to being treated badly in fact).

Positive aspects. Paranoid *sensitivity/hypersensitivity* can enhance creativity. Paranoid sensitivity/hypersensitivity and literary insight have much in common. For a sensitive person can look about and see things we do not all see, or see but ignore, and creatively use material most of us would consider slim pickings. Paranoids identify feelings they have that others would overlook. This, as we say, "puts them in touch with themselves," and empathy with others often follows. For example, one individual recognized, "If I react this way, so does everybody else." Instead of merely noting how depressed he got reading Barbara B. Heyman's 1992 biography, *Samuel Barber*, he took the next step and diagnosed Barber as depressed. He thought, "If I merely get depressed reading about his life, think of how depressed he must have gotten actually living it."

The positive virtues of *grandiosity* are well known. Grandiosity can simultaneously motivate, sustain, and protect. Block is essentially unknown in artists grandiose enough to truly believe that everyone is waiting for them to produce. As one artist put it, "if they don't like what I do, well, that's too bad—not for me, the artist, but for them, the world."

3

AFFECTIVE SPECTRUM
DISORDER BLOCK

Affective spectrum disorder blocks are categorized as depressive or hypomanic. There are three types of depressive blocks: (1) Dysthymic Disorder and Major Depressive Disorder, (2) Complicated Bereavement, and (3) Postpartum Onset Depression.

DYSTHYMIC DISORDER AND MAJOR DEPRESSIVE DISORDER

Depression is characterized by a number of symptoms that are in effect creative blocks. The patient, according to Robert Cancro (1985), experiences "depressed mood, including feelings of hopelessness . . . [and] the triad of reduced capacity to experience pleasure (anhedonia), reduced interest in the environment (withdrawal), and reduced energy (anergia) . . . a loss of interest or pleasure in . . . [one's] usual activities . . . [is] key" (p. 761).

Leader (1991), quoting Pat Rogers, describes a kind of depressive block in the poet William Collins, consisting of "feelings of inadequacy . . . [and] depression of mind which enchains the faculties without destroying them" (p. 120). Leader also writes of Samuel Taylor Coleridge "that Coleridge is here blocked, as well as depressed, is admitted explicitly in stanza 2. His dreariness is of a sort 'which finds no relief/In word, or sigh, or tear'—as if he had tried to utter it but could not. The beauty of the night sky is infected with the poet's deadness" (p. 199).

Dynamics

Guilt, associated with masochism and self-destructiveness. Joseph J. Schildkraut, Alissa J. Hirshfeld, and Jane M. Murphy (1994), writing in *The American Journal of Psychiatry* on mind and mood in modern art, studied a group of abstract expressionist artists of the New York School. They found that "over 50% of the 15 artists . . . had some form of psychopathology, predominantly mood disorder and preoccupation with death, often compounded by alcohol abuse. . . . Many . . . died early deaths, and close to 50% of the group (seven of 15) were dead before the age of 60" (p. 482). A quote they give from Robert Motherwell, an abstract expressionist artist, suggests a possible reason: "We . . . [know] damn well the black abyss in each of us . . . the demons of guilt . . . that largely destroyed in one way or another the abstract expressionist generation" (p. 485).

Some artists, like the painter Mark Rothko and the composer Jaromir Weinberger, actually committed suicide, while others instead "merely" neglected their physical health, injured themselves with addictions, or had, or perhaps "caused," an accident. Accidents seem to occur more than is explainable on the basis of chance alone. For example, citing just composers, Carl Maria von Weber ruined his singing voice by mistakenly drinking nitric acid; Jean-Baptiste Lully hit himself in the foot with his conducting stick, causing a fatal infection; Cole Porter fell from a horse; Ernest Chausson rode his bicycle into a wall; and both Caesar Frank and Edward MacDowell were hit by (and possibly walked into the paths of) moving vehicles—Frank after the success of his D Minor Symphony, and MacDowell after a disagreement with the administration at Columbia University, where he taught.

In a typical sequence, anger is a potent source of guilt, and in turn guilt over anger prompts the artist to internalize the anger. Not a few artists start off as angry young individuals, rebellious souls who function as elitists, or worse, as bigots, until later in life when they regret the adolescent rebelliousness and pay themselves back with depression and depressive block. This process can have a favorable outcome—to cite one such instance, it may have led the healthy Poulenc to turn from writing nose-thumbing satirical music to writing religious works. But in unfavorable cases, the progression from anger to guilt can cause perhaps less healthy artists to turn away from creating and become blocked.

According to Schonberg (1981), Arrigo Boito began his career as "one of the Young Turks of Italian music" (p. 266). He seems to have gone from criticizing Italian opera, to writing one, to writing librettos for his rival Giuseppe Verdi, to putting down his writing pen completely. In what Schonberg calls "one of the strange psychological blocks in musical history . . . he could not write music, and toward the end he was unable to write so much as a letter" (p. 267).

Orenstein (1991), Ravel's biographer, implies that Ravel criticized others unmercifully before turning his sword upon himself. In his early years he called

Wagner's influence "pernicious" and "disastrous." He "once told a young colleague that d'Indy's teaching was false because it was based on Beethoven. My teaching, he explained, is based on Mozart. Beethoven . . . was judged 'annoying,' and the *Missa Solemnis* was called an 'inferior' work. . . . Ravel's complex attitude toward Beethoven and Wagner would appear to combine elements of respect, awe, and jealousy, coupled with marked rejection [of the composers under discussion]" (p. 123).

According to Heyman (1992), Barber, also before the time of his final blockage, thought it amusing to call the composer Rene Liebowitz "Mr. Ztiwobeil" to his face, saying his name backwards to satirize how Liebowitz varied his tone-rows by writing them in retrograde (back to front) fashion (p. 319). Barber also appears to have been an arch-enemy of Ives—so much so that, according to the jacket notes of Barber's *Songs*, after stating "I can't bear Ives" he left rather abruptly after Aaron Copland (somewhat preemptorily it would appear) announced that Ives was a "great composer" (p. 5).

Boito, Ravel, and Barber suffered from severe, almost total terminal block. A factor in their terminal blocks was an element of destructive abuse of others converted into destructive self-abuse, along similar lines, and for similar reasons, with guilt over hostility changing the direction of the anger from others toward oneself.

Being a survivor is another potent source of guilt. I postulate that Ravel, who drove an ambulance in World War I, may have blocked during the war (about three-years duration) and toward the end of his life (about six-years duration) in part because he suffered from survivor guilt. Is this the same survivor guilt we see in World War II veterans who, as they get older, go from killing others to killing themselves, that is, from being homicidal toward others to being homicidal toward themselves, because they are depressed about being the ones still alive?

Grief over loss, associated with feelings of isolation and separation. Leader (1991), discussing Coleridge's depressive block, refers to his "radical sense of insecurity that resulted from . . . feelings of alienation from his mother" (p. 192), leading to a "sense of isolation and abandonment" (p. 193).

Feelings of insecurity, alienation, isolation, and abandonment are provoked by events that remind the artist of his own "separation . . . [as a] child from the . . . mother's protecting or nurturing functions" (p. 65). Though assertion is a basic part of the creative process, assertion is forbidden partly because it "involves separation" (p. 69), that is, "whenever individuals assert themselves [they feel separated], with the mother's role being taken by any number of opposed 'others' " (p. 71).

Kennedy (1987), in comparing the poet Lord Alfred Tennyson and the (often blocked) composer Sir Edward Elgar, notes that both were "liable to fits of almost demented grief over the death of friends" (p. 195). He adds that both had an excessive need for love in the form of the "admiring approval of friends and colleagues" (p. 185).

We don't usually think of Agatha Christie as blocked. But Gillian Gill (1990), Christie's biographer, describes a definite period of blockage around the time of Christie's Great Disappearance, following two losses. First, Christie was melancholic following the death of her mother. Then when "Archie [her husband] now at last came . . . [to see her], it was to admit to Agatha that he had fallen in love with Nancy Neele and wanted a divorce as soon as possible." Then "Agatha began to lose her identity, even forgetting her name when she came to write checks" (p. 105). Subsequently, there appears to have been a transient hypomanic episode just before the Great Disappearance, when she "sung a few songs, joked with Rosalind [her daughter]," gave "an hysterical [and seemingly inappropriate] laugh," angrily "complained about her novel—'These rotten plots. Oh, these rotten plots!'—and said she was feeling less depressed" (p. 108).

Then there was the Great Disappearance itself. (The amnesic aspects of this disappearance will be discussed under dissociative block in chapter 5.)

Then "over the next seven or eight months, Agatha was to experience a nervous breakdown. . . . She . . . withdrew into herself, and mourned" (p. 104). She was "physically weary, emotionally unsupported" (p. 105). She was unable to work for almost a year. She was unable to complete *Blue Train* for her publisher until, "conquering the writer's block that had plagued her in 1926, Agatha grimly completed two potboilers. . . . The first of these, *The Big Four* . . . [having been] written . . . with the help of her brother-in-law" (p. 118).

Jerome Weinberger in his paper, "A Triad of Silence: Silence, Masochism and Depression" (1964), emphasizes silence (a prominent characteristic of block) as a symptom of depression and suggests that the silence, like the underlying depression, is due to an angry regression brought about by adult losses that remind one of earlier, childhood losses.

> Wherever I have observed . . . [the] triad of . . . silence, masochism and depression . . . there has been a loss of status occurring between 18 months and the third year of life in relationship to a change in attitude or illness of the mother. . . . At the age in question, with the establishment of object relationships, neither speech nor the emotional resources for communication are adequate to express the sense of loss of status and the feelings of injured self-esteem. In situations where there are *no substitutes or compensation for this loss of the unique status with the mother*, a pattern is established of easily injured feelings expressed through silence, masochism as manifested in suffering and withdrawal from emotional contact with others, and depression. (p. 304)

Weinberger emphasizes the defensive role of the silence/block that develops in these cases: "Symptoms prevent further feelings of injured self-esteem and in a passive way serve unconsciously to restore the lost unique relationship to the mother. . . . It becomes a restitutive, defensive adaptation to the anxiety of new experiences, in which the old loss is threatened again in fantasy"(p. 304).

Narcissism and hypersensitivity. Artists are likely to be narcissists who take rejections, either by faint praise or overt criticism, both personally and seriously, and block as a consequence. Weinberger (1964) notes that the revival of old traumatic losses "appears characterologically in the individual's relationship to others . . . as intense sensitivity to any disappointment in his narcissistic demand for acceptance, approval, and love" (p. 304).

Artists sensitive to rejection often create, and welcome, depressive block as a defense against being hurt. In a typical sequence one of my patients began not to read her published works so that she did not see the typographical errors in them. She progressed to not reading her reviews so that she did not hear about her supposed personal and professional flaws. And she ended up by avoiding negative criticism entirely by doing no work at all, that is, by doing nothing to provoke it.

Passivity/passive-aggression/overt aggression. Some cases of depressive block are in effect a passive-compliant abdication to the artist's critics, both real and imagined.

In a typical sequence creators take everything that is bad that people say about them to heart, and instead of saying, "You don't know what you are talking about, and if you do it's only one person's opinion anyway," "Don't talk to me that way," or "Go to hell," they let their critics punch them around and hurt them. Believing their beating deserved and thinking that standing up for themselves will only make things worse, they don't fight back, but instead sullenly withdraw. According to legend, Beethoven did not withdraw when his teacher Albrechtsberger said he "never has learned anything and never will" (Nimet, 1995). But Francis Thorne, a contemporary American composer, did withdraw, under similar circumstances. In a speech given at the American Composers Orchestra concert on December 5, 1993, Thorne says he became a navy officer and composed nothing for almost twenty years because of what Paul Hindemith, his teacher at Yale, did to him. He tells of how whenever he brought a work to Hindemith, the composer would rip it up, then, sitting down at the piano with a blank page and red pencil, he would rewrite it, saying, "*This* is the way it should go." Then, at the end of each lesson, Hindemith would tell Thorne that he should compose, not professionally, but as a hobby.

Passive-aggressive individuals use passive compliance as a weapon for vengeance—as Weinberger (1964) says, the silent ones, "in addition to controlling and punishing the mother in fantasy, similarly frustrate her surrogates in everyday life" (p. 304). In essence they treat others badly—as badly as they treat themselves—to pay them back for their rejection by depriving them, and the world, of their creations. They beat the world up with their own body, bloodied especially for the occasion.

Still others become openly aggressive. Refusing, as one said, "to take it anymore," they finally decide to "set limits on being a punching bag" and "go on the attack against my critics." Many of these soon return to their compliant ways, having found that it was too late, both because they are used to being cowed and ashamed, and because others in their circle have gotten used to, and so come to expect, the passivity and compliance manifested so far.

Fall in self-esteem. Depression and depressive block are characteristically associated with feelings of low self-esteem marked by an unrealistically negative view of one's worth as an artist. In the less severe cases, the low self-esteem may be manifest as little more than an excessive modesty, which even protects the artist by keeping him or her from taking him- or herself too seriously.

According to her autobiography, Agatha Christie (1977) was so modest that she left her masterpiece, *The Mysterious Affair at Styles*, at her publishers for nearly two years without inquiring after it (p. 262). The autobiography itself mainly describes her life, and mostly downplays her art, to hide her high status as an artist, from herself as much as from others. She says that she wrote as a sideline, not as a career, taking pains to proclaim that her status, and occupation, was as a "married woman" (p. 418).

In severe cases, the artist feels personally worthless, believes his or her works are the flawed product of a defective person, then loses or tears them up, or withdraws from working entirely. One artist viewed his art both as less valuable than that of his rivals and as completely valueless compared, as he put it, to the "real work that needed to be done in the world." He stopped working to "avoid competing with my betters" and to do "something worthwhile—humanitarian endeavors that help relieve all the pain and suffering on this poor, sad little planet."

Low self-esteem causes block indirectly by affecting the artist's relationships with others, relationships he or she needs to function effectively. Others read the excessive modesty/low self-esteem not as neurotic self-effacement but as a realistic self-evaluation by one who should know. They then treat the artist as badly as he or she thinks is deserved, shattering more of what is left of the artist's self-esteem, starting a vicious spiral downward, into complete block.

Grandiosity. Depressives can block ultimately not from excessively low, but from excessively high self-esteem. In fact, low self-esteem can be little more than a breakdown product of high self-esteem, that is, it can be born in disappointed grandiosity. To illustrate, the individual who says, "I am down because I can't match up to my self-expectations" is commenting, however indirectly, on the elevated nature of the self-expectations he or she has, and cannot meet. According to Orenstein (1991), Ravel, who was later to suffer from severe terminal block, appears to have compared himself to Mozart (p. 123) and later there are hints that he thought himself entirely worthless because he didn't match up to Mozart, a standard that few, even Ravel, could match. Similarly, what was Rossini's self-esteem before his terminal block if, though he wrote forty or so operas, he still, as legend suggests, viewed himself as lazy?

One composer was not content to turn out beautiful things. His self-esteem depended on writing his music without having to erase and rewrite much of it. He got depressed when he couldn't write forward but had to stop, go back, and make corrections. Now he felt indistinguishable from composers who were mere mortals of lesser ability and standing.

Often block results from the poor judgment associated with excessively high self-esteem. Grandiosity can make the artist sufficiently offensive to some to isolate him or her politically and personally from those in a position to advance his or her career and cause. Or (as with some pacifists or communist sympathizers) it can get the artist into political and legal trouble he or she might better have avoided.

Excessive, hysterical, emotionality. This personality factor is found in most or all artists on some level, for artists generally speaking have a theatrical and excessively melodramatic streak. This is one reason they fail to make the nice, healthy distinctions we all must make to avoid concocting and becoming the victim of depressing cognitive distortions. For example, many artists think, melodramatically, that finishing a work is like giving birth, forgetting that it is also unlike giving birth. Now, upon completion of a magnum opus, the artist develops a Postpartum Onset Depression due to an entirely gratuitous separation anxiety. (Postpartum Onset Depression is discussed further below).

The reality of the creative life. Janet Malcolm (1993) says, "almost every writer I know has severe depressions. . . . It's part of the work" (p. 122). It is unclear if she means that to be creative it helps to be depressed, or that depression is an inevitable result of creativity, or both. Depression may result from the internal reality associated with being creative. As we create we can find out too much about ourselves, more than we intended to learn, and more than we wanted to know. However, external realities associated with creativity may themselves cause depression and depressive block. Victor Hugo (1982) said in *Les Misérables* that "genius invites hostility" (p. 995). And in *Sibelius*, Layton (1992) says, "greatness attracts the malice of the mediocre" (p. 62).

Certainly in today's society creativity often does little or nothing for the artist practically, that is, financially. The artist has to earn a living as best as he or she can. And often in earning a living he or she instead earns society's contempt. For example, Schonberg notes that Sibelius was called a "dated bore," an artist who, just because he wrote the popular "Valse Triste," was too uneven to be "taken seriously" (p. 411).

Poverty alone is bad enough. What makes it worse is that artists tend to equate money with love and view poverty as proof that they are not wanted—making them feel, as Weinberger (1964) would put it, that they have in some way lost "an especially close relationship with the mother . . . but not the mother herself" (p. 304).

Today's society does little or nothing for the artist emotionally. Artist abuse seems the order of the day. Society treats artists, among its most valuable resources, as if society is their castrating father or cruel, depriving mother. The narcissistic audiences of society, acting like feeding babies, ask the artist What have you done for me lately? and What can you do for me today? more often than they ask What can I do for you? Audiences want immediate gratification, can be reluctant to pay for what they get, at least to pay what it is worth, and readily express their displeasure when they don't get it in the amount and on the terms they expect. Sometimes, as one artist put it, "it seems as if they have about as much loyalty to their artists as tenants have to their landlords, buyers of gasoline to a filling station, fast food habitues to a hamburger, or some primitive animals to their young—and for essentially the same reasons."

Narcissistic critics add to the problem when they write reviews that are little more than personal temper tantrums disguised as professional aesthetic pronouncements. So often a critic gets side-tracked from reviewing the artist onto expressing his or her feelings and his or her need to build self-esteem. Instead of evaluating the artist, the critic tells his or her audience how the critic is smart, paying attention, not suckered in by all the glory, and carrying the standard of the critical profession aloft. For example, John Simon (January 3, 1994) reviewing *My Fair Lady* in *New York Magazine* seems to have been fanning his personal feathers, when he should have been bird-watching: "Yet splendid as this Lerner and Loewe musical is, it has one blemish that has always bothered me, even though Kenneth Tynan beat me to it at getting it into print (for which I've never forgiven him): the solecisms that Lerner put into the learned Higgins's mouth—*hung* for *hanged*, 'equally as . . . than,' for 'equally . . . as,' both of which are pretty gross" (p. 63).

Very personal vendettas emerge because the artist becomes a transference figure—the equivalent of a parent or a psychotherapist. One critic damned artists if they did and if they didn't the way she damned her parents in much the same way and for much the same reason. If her parents told her to follow her own star they didn't care enough about her to guide her themselves. Yet if they guided her, they were controlling her and telling her what to do. She had in effect identified with her own parents, and in her reviews had become like an evil parent to other artists. She found fault according to arbitrary and shifting standards primarily established to serve a pre-existing need to attack. Composers who wrote good tunes weren't paying sufficient attention to harmony, while composers who were long on harmony were short on melody. Sibelius, Bruckner, and Wagner, who couldn't, she believed, write as well in the short as in the long forms, were condemned as discursive. On the other hand, Chopin, whom she believed couldn't write as well in the long as in the short forms, was condemned as a miniaturist.

Another critic used essentially the same technique in picking on Agatha Christie for her superficiality of characterization. Isn't characterization pretty difficult to do while making intricate plots, at least if the work is to be kept to a manageable length? Isn't this like saying, "Einstein's theories are all intellect, but no soul?"

Instead of giving artists (whom she calls "diffident creatures") the little "encouragement" (p. 506) that Agatha Christie (1977) says they need, critics, often just to blow off a little steam, arbitrarily destroy in moments what the artist sometimes took years to complete. And they often do so without pity. If critics would consider their social responsibility more and indulge their smirking destructiveness less, all those beautiful works never written might be in the world today.

Sibelius

The following pastiche from Robert Layton's *Sibelius* (1992) illustrates depressive block in Sibelius, especially its origin in the negative attitude society so often took toward him. To illustrate some of the principles that hold in depressive block, the pastiche has been deliberately loaded to emphasize the events that caused Sibelius to get depressed and give up composing. Nothing has been changed; only the filler has been left out. This can be done safely because depressives do the same thing when evaluating their own lives. As with Barber, it is difficult to read about Sibelius's life without getting depressed—an indication of how he must have felt living it.

According to Layton, Sibelius had at least two early miniblocks, a period when he "was relatively unproductive" (p. 29), which Layton dismisses as the result of "swings of creative fortune that afflict all artists at one time or another" (p. 30), and another "singularly fallow period" between 1914 and 1922, where the "creative fires" do not "burn with their old intensity" (p. 49). But each time he rallied—until the last thirty or so years of his life, when, according to some accounts, he wrote little or nothing at all (according to others he wrote some things but tore them up). He developed a terminal writer's block that matched or surpassed the terminal blocks of Gioacchino Rossini, Edward Gibbon, Herman Melville, E. M. Forster, Dorothy Sayers, Samuel Barber, and Sir Edward Elgar, among others.

Sibelius seems to have suffered from labile mood with mood changes ranging from a "playful exuberance" (p. 14) or "periods of elation" (p. 44), to the "deepest melancholy" (p. 14). One "depression [was] after the *Piano Quintet*" (p. 22), another about some "operatic sketches" (p. 29), a third struggling with the Fifth Symphony until he was "plunged . . . into the blackest depressions" (p. 43), while a fourth, in 1919, followed his close friend Carpelan's death, when he wrote, "How empty life seems. No sun, no music, no affection. How alone I am with my music" (p. 36).

He often complained of "the closeness of death and an overwhelming feeling of isolation" (p. 42), and felt, "How terribly alone we all are. Alone and misunderstood. And then afterwards, who knows what happens to us?" (p. 45).

Though Sibelius was a composer of a high "level of mastery" he was nevertheless "plagued by self-doubt." He could be ashamed of pieces he wrote, and even "beautiful and subtle piece[s] . . . suffered from . . . [his] excessive self-criticism" (pp. 6–8). The attacks of self-doubt occurred when he "felt his standing threatened" (p. 35), which happened especially toward the end of his life, when he witnessed the wane of his fortunes. The "acute self-criticism . . . [eventually was] an inhibiting factor" (p. 56) and became an interference with his daily work. For example, once, "panic stricken" after delivering a manuscript to his publisher Breitkopf, he demanded they return it for "extensive deletions" (p. 57). Self-doubts arose from his being "vulnerable to slights, imagined or otherwise" (p. 60).

He suffered from bouts of "tinnitus" (p. 24) and general ill health including hoarseness caused by a throat tumor which eventually required surgery. In addition to real worries about his tumor and his hearing, his anxieties about his health amounted to hypochondria (pp. 38–41). He seems to have suffered from "nerves [that] took the form of a metallic taste in the mouth, accompanied by a tremor" (p. 16). As Sibelius himself said, once I was "in such a temper . . . that I smashed the telephone. My nerves are in a terrible state" (p. 46).

Sibelius had many real-life problems. He had problems with the press, both from a press that was too good—inflated "claims made by Constant Lambert . . . [and others that] cannot have made his task easier (p. 64),"—and that was too bad, so that Layton, quoting Martin Wegelius, wrote "Mahler . . . was hailed as music's saviour and Sibelius was dismissed in a few lines!" (p. 25). He was denounced as "ultra-modern" and actually "hissed" (p. 44), and in Sibelius's own words " 'abused in a scurrilous fashion' " (p. 46).

Finally, Sibelius drank heavily throughout his life. More than once he was described as "withdrawn and confused" (p. 55) due to drink. He himself blamed his creative problems on "excesses *in Venere or in Baccho*" which he said "have produced a spiritual paralysis" (p. 30).

Elgar

The distinct impression from Kennedy's (1987) biography of Elgar is that the composer was intermittently depressed throughout his life, and that his intermittent block was a product of this depression. According to Kennedy, Elgar writes, "Lumbago better, rheumatism bad, temper evil, disposition venomous, mind—vacant" (p. 190). Later he writes to his close friend, Jaeger, "Everything is dull & goes slowly: & I am tried very much liverwise & am wofully short of money. . . . Such is life & I hate, loathe & detest it" (p. 198).

Elgar blamed his depression in part on the "practical side of music" (p. 192) saying, "the more one has to do with [it] . . . the more awful this life becomes. I am so sick of it all!" (p. 192). And in part he blamed it on an abusive society, saying, "England ruins all artists" (p. 200).

Rossini

Rossini seems to have ground to a halt after the death of his mother in 1827. He wrote two more operas, *Le Compte Ory* and *William Tell*, then stopped writing operas (and most everything else) and entered the period usually called the Great Renunciation, which lasted until his death in 1868, a renunciation probably maintained and intensified by new losses. According to Oscar Thompson's (1964) *The International Cyclopedia of Music and Musicians*, "In January 1838 Rossini's nerves received a severe shock when the Theatre Italien was destroyed by fire and his friend Severini, the director, was killed." His father's health began to fail about this time and he died in 1839. His grief was intense. In May 1843 Rossini had a "serious urethral operation." In 1852 his "health went from bad to worse, and he was finally reduced to such a condition of neurasthenia and hypochondria that he seemed to be on the point of going out of his mind" (p. 1837).

According to Toye (1987):

> After 1852 . . . his condition became steadily worse. . . . It is possible that Lombroso exaggerated somewhat when he asserted that Rossini became definitely mad, that he suffered from the delusion of being completely ruined and used to beg for charity from his friends. . . . In 1854 . . . his neurasthenia had reached its most acute stage. . . . His face was pale, his eyes tired and sunken, his head bent and his cheeks withered. He had lost the faculty of taste and was unable to assimilate food. Worst of all were the tortures caused by lack of sleep. For three and a half months . . . he never closed an eyelid. Sometimes, standing before a mirror, he would upbraid himself for his lack of courage in not committing suicide. "To what am I come," he pitiably exclaimed, "and what am I doing in this world? And what will people say when they see me reduced, like a small child, to having to rely on a woman?" (pp. 202–203)

COMPLICATED BEREAVEMENT

Complicated Bereavement is, according to the article, "Complicated Grief and Bereavement-Related Depression as Distinct Disorders: Preliminary Empirical Validation in Elderly Bereaved Spouses," by Holly G. Prigerson et al. (1995), is grief associated with "enduring functional impairments" (p. 22). The block that is part of Complicated Bereavement is difficult to distinguish from the block that is part of Dysthymic Disorder or Major Depressive Disorder. In part this happens because Complicated Bereavement results from one or more real losses, then shades into pathological grief/major depression because (1) the artist's grief sensitizes him or her to the next loss. Already vulnerable, the artist overreacts, becomes more vulnerable, and so on, and (2) the grief inhibits functional capacity, making new loss more likely.

Historical Cases of Complicated Bereavement

Elgar

Elgar's composing, according to *The Cyclopedia of Music and Musicians* (1964), declined after his wife died.

Following the death of Lady Elgar in 1920, Sir Edward was numbed and silenced. Not since 1909 when his great friend and adviser A. J. Jaeger died, had he suffered such a loss. How much Elgar owed to his wife's companionship, practical help and belief in his powers, can be realized from one simple fact, namely, that all the works that proclaim his genius at its highest were composed during his married life. The beginning of the last phase of Elgar's life, though restless, was not unproductive. . . . [But even] honors, though he was proud of them, could not set flowing again the former tumultuous tide of his creative force. It had not dried up, however. Occasionally it emerged. (p. 596)

Tchaikovsky

While Peter Ilich Tchaikovsky seems to have composed to the end, he often complained about being temporarily unable to work, possibly a consequence of his depressions. In his biography of the composer, his brother, Modeste Tchaikovsky (1973), notes that Peter Ilich himself complained of "alternations of light and shade succeed[ing] each other with . . . regularity . . . the depression which darkened his last years" (p. 702).

Also, according to Modeste Tchaikovsky (1973), Peter Ilich Tchaikovsky seems to have become more severely depressed after his patroness broke off their relationship, which, though there were other factors, he seems to have interpreted solely as a rejection. In 1890, "Tchaikovsky received a letter from Nadejda von Meck [his patroness], informing him that . . . she . . . [could] no longer . . . continue his allowance" (p. 611). Tchaikovsky, reminiscing, noted that "I should certainly have gone out of my mind and come to an untimely end but for your friendship and sympathy, as well as for the material assistance" (p. 612). He "began to persuade himself that her last letter had been nothing 'but an excuse to get rid of him on the first opportunity'; that he had been mistaken in idealising his relationship with his 'best friend' " (pp. 613–614). He suffered an "agony of wounded pride" (p. 614) from this cruel blow; he felt this "situation lowers me in my own estimation" (p. 615), and his pride was "profoundly injured" (p. 616).

Rachmaninoff

Serge Rachmaninoff seems to have blocked partially following his friend Scriabin's death in 1915.

Thompson's (1964) *The Cyclopedia of Music and Musicians* tells us that this death exerted a profound influence on Rachmaninoff's career. "Standing at the grave of his great contemporary, he resolved . . . at that moment . . . to make a concert tour of all the larger towns and play only the pianoforte works composed by Scriabin. The importance of this decision rests in the fact that it turned Rachmaninoff's skill to the interpretation of music other than his own" (p. 1725). The last half of Rachmaninoff's life was less productive than the first. With a few exceptions, such as the Paganini Variations, most of the works we know him for today were written before Scriabin's death, in the pre-war period (p. 1726).

Ives

Ives stopped composing after he lost his father. Feder (1992) notes that "Ives's creative decline tracks the decline in George's life in an uncanny way, for it is an unconsciously lived-out revival of the sensitive boy observing the decline in his father's esteem that lay behind the manifest changes in his life" (p. 288). He also may have stopped due to a straightforward prolonged unresolved grief because of the loss. According to Feder, a late song, "Remembrance," arranged in 1921 from an earlier work, is a reminiscence of his memories of his father, who died some years previously. For it, Ives wrote the lyric: "A sound of a distant horn, Oe'r shadowed lake is borne, my father's song" (p. 2). Then Ives fell silent. Did Ives leave music to devote himself full time to his insurance business in order to avoid the further reminders of his grief that a continuing association with music could only provide?

Sidney Zion

According to Richard Perez-Pena (1994), the journalist and writer Sidney Zion said that following his daughter's death he "couldn't work for a year. . . . I would sit and stare at the typewriter and just cry. I'd go crazy. You never totally get over it" (pp. B1, B3).

Agatha Christie

In her autobiography (1977), Christie says it most simply and directly: "Ever since my mother's death I had been unable to write a word" (p. 341).

POSTPARTUM ONSET DEPRESSION

In many cases of block due to Postpartum Onset Depression, the artist blocks after finishing, because finishing creates anxiety. The next time, the artist blocks before finishing in order to avoid the anxiety. Finishing creates anxiety because the artist feels:

- Birth pangs
- Empty because "I don't have it in me any more"

- Parental resentment of the "child's" independence, and resents the creation "for going its own way and leaving me behind"

- Parental envy and jealousy of a new work that, like a new child, is "young while I am old, and has its whole life before it"

- Parental fear of a new work that, like an oedipal child, will rise up, kill, and consume the "mother," the person who created it. (Was this why Rachmaninoff became unable to bear his Prelude in C-Sharp Minor? Was he wreaking revenge on it as if it were competing for attention with the composer himself?)

- Parental possessiveness, so that to avoid the possibility that a new work would be taken away by others (in one case it was the "butchers who rewrite it as a popular movie"), the artist refuses to share his work, and withdraws or destroys it, saying in effect, "If I can't have it, no one else can." (The spiritual analogue of Nicolo Paganini's excessive watchfulness over the parts of his Fourth Violin Concerto—to the point that he hid it and it was almost lost—can be seen in a recent murder case in New Jersey where a man killed both of his children because his ex-wife was about to take them away from him.)

Edward Gibbon (1776–1788), developed what sounds just like a Postpartum Onset Depression after he finished writing the *Decline and Fall of the Roman Empire*. Dero A. Saunders says in his preface to Gibbon's book that Gibbon wrote to his friend Lord Sheffield in 1785:

"After laying down my pen [I experienced] . . . my first emotions of joy on recovery of my freedom . . . [but] . . . a sober melancholy was spread over my mind, by the idea that I had taken an everlasting leave of an old and agreeable companion, and that . . . the life of the historian must be short and precarious."

The completion of the *Decline and Fall* emptied his life [writes Saunders]. . . . [Gibbon says that] "my habits of industry are much impaired, and . . . I have reduced my studies to be the loose amusement of my morning hours, the repetition of which will insensibly lead me to the last term of existence." . . . It is always a question which is the more tragic, to fail in one's great ambition, or to succeed. (pp. 20–21)

POSITIVE ASPECTS OF DEPRESSION

Does it help an artist to be a bit or even seriously depressed? In other words, is creativity a positive manifestation of depression, with depression a kind of pathological ennobling?

Many authors, among them Arnold M. Ludwig (1994) in "Mental Illness and Creative Activity in Female Writers," which appeared in *The American Journal of Psychiatry*, emphasize how Affective Disorder is innate in creative persons and suggest that the creative process is a product of the Affective Disorder (pp. 1650–1654). In effect he, like many, views the artist's emotional pain and suffering as catalyzing and broadening.

Certainly depression can enhance creativity in ways ranging from the pedestrian to the grand. As for the pedestrian, some artists write, and push to get published, as a way to enhance their self-esteem. As for the grand, depression can make for art whose greatness is the product of excess, dross made into drama employing the hysterical and masochistic "romantic" touch that is one part of what Schildkraut et. al (1994) call the "inexplicable mystery that lies at the heart of the 'tragic and timeless' " (p. 482).

Many authors, among them H. B. Lee in Peter Giovacchini (1984), have noted that creativity can be part of a healing process following loss or depression. Conversely, creativity can decline when depression *improves*. Howard Gardner (1993) notes about T. S. Eliot:

When he finally separated from Vivien, consolidated world fame, and married Valerie, Eliot seems to have achieved a measure of peace and satisfaction. These achievements coincided with a clear decline in the power of his literary work, a decline occurring at a time of life when artists like Graham, Yeats, Picasso, and Stravinsky were still in their prime. Even as Eliot's singular attainments emerged when his marginality was its peak, a further accumulation of triumphs might have necessitated a continuing marginality that he neither wanted nor could sustain. (p. 260)

Treatment

Depressed artists need a supportive holding environment, especially in the acute phase. They often feel worthless, defective, and rejected by friends, family, and society. Probing them analytically or cognitively, or changing them behaviorally, at these times can, in some cases, do more harm than good. It is very easy for them to misread analytic interpretations as criticisms, cognitive corrections as being given an argument, and behavioral therapy as being pushed around. Patient hand-holding by all concerned is, at least in the beginning, often one of the most helpful things the therapist can do to tide the artist over what can be, in even some of the worst cases, a self-limited disorder. (Diagnosing and treating depression is a complex matter, and a full discussion is beyond the scope of this text.)

MANIA/HYPOMANIA

Episodes of mania are euphoric mood disturbances that tend to be severe enough to cause, according to Cancro (1985) not heightened but "diminished productivity" (p. 761). The mood disturbance can cause blockage directly, by making the creator too high to work, or indirectly, by causing bad judgment, of the kind that leads writers to feel that fragmentary works deserve publication, as one publisher complained (in a personal communication) about medical authors.

Four types of manic/hypomanic block can be distinguished according to four "mechanical models," or paradigms. The first type of manic/hypomanic block, what Nelson (1985) calls "logorrhea" (p. 142), an inverted block, and what Truman Capote (according to legend) called not "writing" but "typing," is manifest in increased production that is bombastic and empty. The mechanical model is the hose turned too high that sprays and soaks all unfortunates in its way. There is art, but it is, as Shakespeare says, "full of sound and fury, signifying nothing" (*Macbeth*, 5.5). The artist is blocked not because he or she doesn't speak, but because he or she speaks without saying anything, to avoid saying anything, or to say anything.

Type one manic/hypomanic creators often speak in words characteristically empty, devoid of idea, thin, and routine—what one artist called "the equivalent of painting by numbers." They often create prolifically to avoid their feelings. They produce art that is superficial or comic to avoid producing art that is deep or tragic. They tell jokes not to be funny but to avoid getting close, or, if they are among the more hostile hypomanics, they stun, shock, and antagonize audiences to avoid wooing and seducing them. Some are entirely too narcissistic and grandiose for the good of their art. Too caught up in themselves to give first consideration to their audiences' needs, they produce something no one can listen to, or read. In particular, they choose topics according to what they want to say, not according to what others want to hear, then complain that no one is listening.

Though their thoughts are too rapid and plentiful to constitute an artistic whole by themselves, proper capturing, containment, sorting, and editing is not the order of their day. Secretly they are "leaving it to mother," acting like infants who feel they deserve to be loved simply because they are there. The composer Alexander Borodin might have had this kind of relationship with the composers Nicolai Rimsky-Korsakov and Alexander Glazunov, passively leaving it to them to finish and orchestrate his sketches. John Cage's pseudocreativity also belongs here: especially toward the end of his life, he turned out a superabundance of aleatoric works, each of which, in spite of an often impressive title, amounts to little more than an unelaborated concept and a set of instructions/orders to others on how and when to do his work for him.

The second type of manic/hypomanic block results from what Leader (1991) calls, referring to Woolf's *A Room of One's Own*, a "work full of . . . vertiginous . . . proliferating possibilities" (p. 250). It is characterized by forward movement stalled due to lateral expansion. The lateral expansion often results when barriers are erected because of conflicts about, and so fear of, producing. The mechanical model is the kinked hose, and the net effect is a swelling in the middle, sometimes to the point of bursting. For example, the plot in Melville's *Moby Dick* (1851) seems to trace the pattern of the body of a whale—a little head (beginning), a little tail (ending), and a big, swollen middle that, as Dr. Richard Wagman says, tells us more about the whale than we need to know. Melville, who was to block essentially completely afterwards, may have sensed this in himself, and in his work, when he said in *Moby Dick*, "God keep me from ever completing anything. This whole book is but a draught—nay, but the draught of a draught" (p. 139).

Bonnie Friedman (1993) describes a case of lateral expansion, possibly due to a fear of what one's critics might say, in *Writing Past Dark*:

> [A professor] had been awarded permission to write the official biography of a certain towering literary critic. How many years have elapsed since then! And still his book has not appeared. . . . This professor labored over his paragraphs, stuffing them fuller and fuller of gratuitous erudition, references for their own sake (or, rather, for his own sake), refusing to let them split into other paragraphs . . . until each paragraph was at least two pages and so crammed it was virtually unreadable. Flow? The poor man himself could hardly breathe under the pressure of it all! (p. 108)

The third type of manic/hypomanic block also expands laterally, not because of stenosis, but because of primary diffusion. The mechanical model is a river delta, where a once strong forward-moving river dissipates into side channels. In these cases the effect is of too many talents waging war in the head, and who and what wins isn't always clear. The conductor thinks he or she should be writing until he or she writes, then he or she thinks he or she should be conducting, and so on.

There is grandiosity, but not the disdainful type so often associated with the first two categories of block. In fact, the artist tries too hard to please the audience, who at first finds him or her appealing, a Renaissance "man," but eventually rejects him or her as an unsatisfying dilettante. This the audience is in part justified in doing, for instead of focusing, the artist blurs—often as much in his or her works as in his or her life—and in blurring weakens resolve, diffuses interest, drains energy, and dissipates productive tension. In spite of multiple talents, the artist in effect treads water, that is, ideas multiply without a proportionate increase in fertility. When competing talents prevent the artist from reaching the top in any one field, the artist, good at much, but not great at anything, becomes the one cook who spoils too many broths.

The fourth type of manic/hypomanic block is really obsessive-compulsive workaholism. Here the hose is on high and productively waters the lawn. All is well unless the water bill becomes prohibitively expensive. While in the first three types of block, production is enhanced but quality diminished, here both production and quality are enhanced, a "healthy" hypomania. The artist rises early and goes to work. He or she works hyperactively but effectively. The means justifies the end, as hard work is rewarded. Exhaustion, and the resultant block, is the only negative consequence. Both the composer Robert Schumann and the writer Georges Simenon seem to have been workaholics until the end, when apparently both collapsed, seemingly under their own weight.

Treatment

The first three types of hypomanic blockers need someone to take them in hand, rein them in, and, where indicated, encourage them to stop putting water in the creative soup—dissipating energy in side channels of subspecialties—and instead organize themselves by picking one field of endeavor, doing one work at a time within that field, and sticking with, controlling, and mastering it.

As for workaholism, preferential workaholics neither desire nor need treatment. And compulsive workaholics usually do well until they overwork and exhaust themselves, when, theoretically at least, they could use therapy. But practically speaking, in most cases recovery is spontaneous following a brief period of rest, and no treatment, at least no extensive treatment, is necessary.

4

ANXIETY/PHOBIC DISORDER BLOCK

Virtually all artists have a degree of phobic block because they attach imaginary fears to the creative process, making it into a "phobic" trivial prompt, like Friday the thirteenth, or a black cat crossing one's path. Every creative act becomes an occasion for anxiety beyond what the actual circumstances warrant. Predictably, the artist deals with the anxiety by avoiding its presumed source—creativity itself. The artist hesitates or refuses to venture out into the world of art just as the agoraphobic hesitates or refuses to venture out into the world of life.

The extent of the damage from phobic block depends on at least three factors: (1) the degree of the anxiety, (2) the artist's ability to tolerate the anxiety, and (3) the artist's willingness to struggle with and fight back against the anxiety. Most often, neither creativity nor abdication to anxiety about creativity prevails in the struggle. This makes most artistic careers into a mixture of approach and avoidance, a compromise between talent manifest and talent withdrawn. Few artists give up completely, at least in the beginning. More are like the typical sufferers from stage fright who force themselves to get on the stage, knowing they will feel fine once they get started, their career mostly unaffected, but their lives mostly compromised. Like these early stage fright phobics, artists can get to work, but it is torture. They can go, but they have to force themselves to go; the trip is agony, a white-knuckled drive over high bridges or ride in deep subway tunnels, every inch of the way an occasion for fear, every second a moment of terror that they might lose control of themselves or be trapped in a closed space, stifle, and die.

Two levels of neurotic solution are available to handle creative phobias that seem too much to bear. First, the artist makes him- or herself comfortable by tithing—satisfying a sense of guilt by limiting the scope or depth of creativity. Often artists use partial failure to permit partial success. Sometimes they accomplish this by developing a psychosomatic disorder or an addiction, sacrificing the intactness of the body for the survival of the spirit.

A composer published but didn't promote her works, secretly hoping she could continue to work in obscurity until she died, when she fantasized she would achieve a degree of the only kind of fame that she permitted herself—the posthumous kind.

Chopin's creating mostly in small forms was possibly a "phobic miniaturism" that said, "I stick my neck out, but not too far." Was this a phobic tithing by a form of avoidance? And did it carry over into and become manifest in his inability to play the piano in public because of stage fright? According to Schonberg (1981), Chopin, though he was "one of the greatest pianists in history . . . gave very few concerts" (p. 186). Were his difficulty in writing his improvisations down (according to a personal communication from Nancy Hager, Professor of Music at Brooklyn College) and what might have been his essentially platonic, that is, partially avoidant, relationship with George Sand manifestations of phobic tithing?

Was phobic tithing why the composer Anton von Webern wrote such short pieces, and the composer Erich Korngold, who wanted to write symphonies, instead wrote mostly movie music—background music meant to be hardly heard?

One patient, a pianist, instead of giving up the stage completely, felt less exposed and so less anxious conducting instead of playing the piano. Another pianist/patient was still able to play but only as a recording artist, not as a live performer. A third pianist/patient split himself in fantasy "down the middle" to become two people, one of whom, the good, right-handed one, was "given" a pianist's cramp, while the other, the "sinister" left-handed one, already "compromised" and so "not very threatening," was "permitted to live normally." Because the cramp affected only one "side" but not the other, he could still perform, but only a limited repertoire of works—those written for the left hand alone.

Leader (1991) notes that Freud, in his paper "Dostoevsky and Parricide," said that Dostoevsky's work "never went better than when . . . his sense of guilt was satisfied by the punishments he had inflicted on himself" (p. 51). He also mentions that Coleridge kept his inability to write great works "alive in order to produce . . . 'lesser' work" (p. 212) of inferior quality.

Did Tennessee Williams, the playwright, write later works that were not as poetic as his early ones, partly because his inspiration flagged, but partly because he needed to tithe in his art by continuing to write prolifically, but not as poetically, as before?

Second, the artist abandons creativity almost entirely, or entirely, progressing from partial to total block. One writer in her daily life went from not being able to attend cocktail parties, to not being able to shop in the supermarket, to not being able to leave the house at all. In her career, in a parallel regression, she went from writing prolifically, to writing works few and far between, to writing one work every few years and not publicizing that, to not writing at all. In the end she became both personally and professionally inactive, as she put it, "Seeing nobody, and doing hardly anything at all."

DYNAMICS

Phobic block often begins because of anxiety due to guilt and shame (which I will now simply call "guilt"), and guilt often begins when the inherently neutral act of creating is made into a *sexual* or a *hostile* event. For example, exposing oneself creatively becomes exposing one's genitals. As James Jones quoted in Leader (1991) suggests, you become "one of those guys who has a compulsion to take his thing out and show it on the street" (p. 237). Or doing one's work as an artist becomes not merely competing with others in the same field but bumping them off, that is, murdering them.

Guilt also originates in existential conflicts, such as the one between writing something popular for money and something academic for glory. Finally there is social guilt, discussed below and in chapter 16.

Sexual Guilt

As mentioned, sexual guilt might appear when creative exposure becomes the psychological equivalent of sexual exposure. As a result the artist feels ashamed in the eyes of the world. Is sexual guilt of this sort why Elgar, as quoted by Kennedy (1987, p. 55), said that "Great musicians are things to be ashamed of"? Sexual guilt can account for the seemingly paranoid fantasy often associated with performance anxiety—"All eyes are on me." Peter Gammons (1992) in *The Throes of Tossing a Baseball* reports how going "haywire" (a term used to describe stage fright in some ballplayers) makes ballplayers feel publicly humiliated. One practiced throwing with an inflatable doll instead of a batter, and when "that got reported . . . all it did was . . . humiliate the poor kid"(p. 145). In their own words, players report "A private hell becomes public" (p. 137) and "There were six thousand people in the stands, and I felt as if every one of them was watching me" (p. 141).

Freud's paper "Those Wrecked by Success" (1957) suggests that the incest taboo is an important source of sexual guilt. Freud suggested incest guilt originates in the forbidden wish to get close to the parent of the opposite sex. In the male (and to a lesser extent in the female) the fantasy that causes much of the anxiety associated with the guilt is the fantasy of punishment by castration. Castration fantasies rarely appear in their original form; mostly they take a derivative form in consciousness.

For example, according to Feder (1992), what Ives feared was not castration but hiding behind "silk skirts." Ives supposedly asked, "Is the Angle-Saxon going 'Pussy?' " And he proclaimed that his music was "greater, less emasculated than any of the so-called great masters! [like Wagner, and Mozart!]" (p. 337).

A male patient, a graphic artist, felt his block began in childhood when he made the decision to hold himself back based on something he read, on the sly, in one of his father's psychiatric texts. The chapter described koro, which is, according to Armando R. Favazza in his article "Anthropology and Psychiatry" (1985), the delusional "sensation that one's penis is shrinking and receding into one's belly, and a fear of death once the penis has sunk into the abdomen" (p. 256). Old enough to understand castration, but not old enough to understand delusion, he took the chapter literally, and swore on the spot, "This will never happen to me." Later in life, this complex was reactivated in the form of a compulsion to give up his graphic art because he viewed being an artist as being a sissy, and being a sissy as being homosexual, which he defined as "someone who was masculine, but who is made feminine."

Guilt Over Aggression

David W. Krueger (1984) writing about the fear of success in women (what he says is also applicable to men) emphasizes the oedipal *aggressive* over the oedipal *sexual* element as the main reason for guilty anxiety, and so the ultimate reason for defensive removal/block:

> Certain psychopathology manifesting as performance inhibition or "success phobia" has been causally linked with Oedipal conflict. . . . The desire in the small child to surpass a powerful rival generates both guilt and fear of equally violent retaliation, resulting in the inhibition or withholding of aggression. This inhibition of aggression is then extended in application to assertion in general. The phobic extension of this conflict is inhibition of assertion, which may apply to vocational or professional assertion. . . . Erikson discussed the polar positions of "initiative versus guilt" during this stage . . . with anxiety and guilt over self-assertion manifested in one's work and career. (pp. 65, 66)

The theory helps explain why, clinically, block often appears when an oedipally fixated artist becomes anxious due to confusing achievement and success with defiant aggression, really murder.

One artist believed that there was only so much to go around in the world and so what she got others (by definition) lost. This zero-sum belief that her successes meant others' failures for her turned healthy professional rivalry into unhealthy professional jealousy, a struggle to the death that revived more of the oedipal conflicts in which it began. Her guilt dictated her solution: to abdicate in favor of the rival—a form of block to the rescue, a way to reassure the world that she had not, and would never, desire her father or murder her mother.

Reading Schonberg (1981), it is difficult to avoid the suspicion that composers Arrigo Boito and Giuseppe Verdi were locked in a father-son oedipal rivalry, which resulted in Boito's abdication to the emotionally stronger rival Verdi—first by writing his libretti, and next by developing a block so severe that not only could he not write music, he couldn't even write a letter (pp. 266–267).

Some artists are not inappropriately guilty about aggression; they are in fact too aggressive for their own good, and, when the aggression spills over into their work, too aggressive for the good of their art. For them, getting over block may require becoming less aggressive.

Ravel was in his early years a surprisingly fertile culture dish of apparently oedipal comparisons that may have created inner conflict, which he later resolved by blocking during the last six years of his life. On the one hand he idolized Mozart, while on the other hand he seems to have been a kind of Salieri in competition with Mozart over who wrote more, that is, who was the better man.

Schonberg (1981) implies that Chopin was not the poor, suffering romantic history has painted him to have been. Chopin seems to have had an envious, green-eyed monster side. He was not only Liszt's rival, but Liszt's rival to the death, abusing the man. His less than genteel opinion of Liszt's music was probably an emotional, presented as an aesthetic, opinion: "As regards the themes from his compositions, well, they will be buried in the newspapers" (p. 194).

Artists afraid of their own aggression may deal with this fear by becoming paradoxically more, rather than less, aggressive. They have temper tantrums, but it is less a way to be aggressive than a defense against being aggressive, a way to drive others off early in the game to protect them from the artist—"Stop me before I kill." This behavior follows a basic rule of phobic avoidance: it matters little if one avoids by staying or avoids by driving away. As one artist put it, "The net effect is the same if I avoid you because I am afraid of you, or you avoid me because you are afraid of me."

Two patients drove others away partly because they were aggressive personalities, and partly to protect others from themselves. One author, when a movie mogul told him, "There is no hook in your story," flirted with destroying his career when he replied not with, "Sorry sir, I'll take that under advisement, and put one in so that you will buy my script and make my movie," but with, "Not, at least, compared to the one in your nose."

Another author, seriously injured in the Vietnam war when an American helicopter landed on him and took off both his legs, blocked whenever he tried to write because he thought that "exposing himself" was "exposing himself to danger." So, not surprisingly, he "clammed up protectively."

In his daily life he became highly aggressive whenever he felt threatened by "someone or something getting close." He operated according to the principle of getting there first, his golden rule being, "I will beat you up before you can even think of doing it to me." When driving he could hardly keep his hands on the wheel for giving everyone the finger. At a literary party that promised to provide him with contacts he needed for his work, he asked a book editor, "Where's the bathroom at?" and was told, mostly in jest by the editor trying to be friendly, "You should never end a sentence with a preposition." To this he replied not, "Thank you for correcting my flawed grammar," but "OK, how about ending my sentence with a noun: So, where's the bathroom at, idiot?"

Existential Conflicts

Fear of completion. Many artists can't finish because of the meaning of finishing. Finishing for example might mean committing oneself. In chapter 3 I suggest that fear of completion is related to birth anxiety, and not completing is a way to avoid that anxiety and the postpartum depression that so often follows.

Fear of autonomy. Leader (1991) suggests that fears of independence are one basis for a fear of successful self-expression, and notes that Coleridge's plagiarisms can be viewed as originating in a "fear of assertion of independent selfhood" (p. 215).

Fear of success (successophobia). There are many reasons for the fear of success, and the fear takes many forms. Perhaps the most common reasons for the fear of success are a guilty fear of one's own aggression, survivor guilt and a guilty wish to abdicate to discouraging parents as an act of love. Perhaps the most common form taken by the fear of success is not complete but partial withdrawal, and the most common form of partial withdrawal is the tithing described above.

Fear of success tends to appear (1) when a minor threatens to become a major work. Leader (1991), quoting Showalter, says that for the author Schreiner the "effect of . . . success was 'writer's block'. . . . Anything longer than half-a-dozen pages triggered her anxieties" (p. 248), and (2) when one's actions count—when the big moment arrives, and the artist has reached the point of no return.

Gammons (1992) describes Steve Blass's disease (a form of stage fright in ballplayers, named after Blass, a sufferer), by citing the following: "It got worse and worse. But you know what's weird? Warming up in the bullpen, he always had his same great stuff, right on the black. Put a batter up there, and he couldn't throw it close" (p. 142). A catcher couldn't understand why he was suffering a similar experience. After all, "this was my boyhood dream . . . and I was going to the park feeling sick to my stomach" (p. 138). Of course, the probability is that he was sick not *despite* but *because* he was realizing his boyhood dream.

A patient, a designer and manufacturer of teddy bears, complained for years of an inability to work. Typically, whenever he began to make bears for one of his shows, he got busy running classes teaching others how to make them, and he worked so slowly that he was not able to turn out enough bears to have a successful show—earn enough money to support himself and his family, and to provide himself with the samples he needed to further promote himself and his work.

Started on fluoxetine, his mood improved and he began working faster and more effectively. He even scheduled a major show of his works. But one week later he announced to his psychiatrist, "That stuff makes me feel great. Unfortunately, I feel too good to want to buckle down to work."

Two weeks before the show, while working in the shop, going the last mile toward completion, his saw slipped, and he almost cut off a thumb.

Successophobia partly explains why some artists need their critics and even actively and willfully court them, forming a close relationship with them. The artist begs for some external control. The critic obliges by in effect keeping the artist in check, by putting the artist down. One artist said it this way: "I feel most like Orpheus when someone is damning me back to hell for playing my lyre."

Social Guilt

An example of social guilt is self-blame because the artist cannot turn out one great work after another, as society expects him or her to do; realistically even great geniuses cannot maintain a consistently high level of work and produce masterpieces seamlessly.

Social guilt often starts with *artist abuse*. In artist abuse society mistreats its artists emotionally like some spouses mistreat their mates physically. Just as abused mates blame themselves for provoking their own abuse instead of blaming their mates for being abusive, artists, instead of blaming an unfriendly or openly hostile society, block, then blame themselves—citing their laziness, or lack of talent.

One reason society abuses artists is that it is full of individuals who have an unresolved oedipal relationship with their own children. They keep the strong artist down just like they keep their children down, and for essentially the same reason, to keep others from competing successfully with them. The result is that they see to it that the successful freshman artist becomes the sophomore failure, that is, they allow very few to repeat a first triumph. But few artists think, "This is society's oedipal problem." Most think, "It's my fault, because I don't have what it takes." Predictably they become depressed and relatively or absolutely unable to work.

Positive Features

Stage fright and other phobic blocks can have a focusing value. Phobias of conducting seemed to have encouraged Tchaikovsky and Sibelius to give up performing, clearing the decks for their composing.

Therapy

A cornerstone of treatment is helping the artist to distinguish what is inherent in creativity from what he or she has made of it. Viewing art and artistry in a more neutral light frees the artist from the frightening demons put there by him- or herself. Correcting cognitive errors is a good way to accomplish this. Most blocked artists can benefit from learning that just because art is spontaneous or out of control doesn't make it a madness, just because it is intense doesn't make it sexual, and just because it is forceful doesn't make it aggressive.

However, not only must the therapist deal with the artist's manufactured fears like fears of abandonment and castration, and inappropriate guilts like zero-sum and survivor guilt, he or she must also consider the artist's reality, that is, the real reasons all artists have to be afraid. All artists operate in a dangerous social milieu. For example, most artists have a real reason to fear most critics. Even those who are the most inwardly phobic are also under external stress which is itself enough to block all but the strongest souls.

Anthony Storr (1992) quotes Claude Debussy as having written that "the attraction of the virtuoso for the public is very like that of the circus for the crowd. There is always a hope that something dangerous may happen" (p. 32). Storr also relates that Jascha Heifetz, who may have had a performance block at the end of his life, claimed that "every critic was eagerly awaiting an occasion on which his impeccable technique would let him down" (p. 32).

That is why the therapist's job includes comforting in the presence of real stress. The therapist must not merely tell the blocked artist to work his or her neurosis through. He or she must also alert the blocked artist to how and when others are behaving badly to the artist, and need to be told to stop, and when, if they don't stop, the artist should sacrifice the relationship, for the art.

When stress is an extremely disruptive factor, threatening personal decompensation, the therapist might want to increase, not decrease, phobic defenses. An artist who couldn't perform live could perform for the tape as long as she didn't think of how eventually there would be an audience. She was told to warn everyone in the studio, "Don't even whisper that this tape is to be played at a future date, before all of America."

Sometimes patience or "the tincture of time" is the best treatment of all. Many phobias, and so many phobic blocks, tend to improve or remit spontaneously, sometimes completely. When the phobia is one symptom of a personality disorder, as when a successophobia is a manifestation of masochism, the phobia may disappear, seemingly on its own, simply because the personality disorder has improved over time and with increasing age. Some phobias change over into other, less blocking phobias. In favorable cases, a phobia in the professional life becomes a phobia in the personal life, so that today's performance phobia becomes tomorrow's bridge phobia; what the artist loses in the ability to get around comfortably he or she gains, or regains, in an ability to create unblocked.

Caveats in Treatment

In treating the fear of success in women, Krueger (1984) warns against cultural biases on the part of the therapist, like "the belief that women should marry and have children" (p. 157)—hardly supportive of creativity. He also warns against viewing internal problems as external, that is, pinning the blame on a world full of critical others when one's self-criticisms and successophobia are really to blame (p. 158). (As just mentioned, it is as, or more, important for the artist to avoid blaming him- or herself for provoking abuse, when the world is actually mistreating the artist.)

Most patients with oedipal successophobia feel more comfortable with a therapist who keeps his or her distance than with one who gets too friendly. Being competitive with the patient of course sounds the death knell for therapy when it inspires the patient to compete with the therapist and then to become guilty over it.

We suspect from what Ronald Hayman (1993) writes of Kubie's treatment of Tennessee Williams that Kubie (whose interest in the arts was well known and thoroughly documented in his writing) competed for attention and status with his patient. When Williams quite properly rebelled, Kubie seems to have made matters worse first by suggesting the problem belonged to Williams, second by analyzing Williams's behavior instead of correcting his own, and third by throwing Williams out of treatment (pp. 170–171).

One artist's therapist told his patient of his qualifications to treat artists: he had written on the subject, liked painting and music, had a fine arts degree, and so on. The patient, afraid of the competition, first responded counterphobically, by showing him pictures of his children, telling him how he got good grades on his school papers, priding himself on his college degree, flexing his muscles and showing his tattoos and his injuries received during the Vietnam war, and implying, "I can beat you up with one hand tied behind my back." Then he gave up his art because he didn't want to compete on the same ground as a man "as important to me as my therapist." The therapist, catching on just in time, responded not by analyzing oedipus (which really would have been a way to further put the patient down) but by silent admiration, by implication admitting his therapeutic error and undoing it—by giving the patient permission to be number one, at least in therapy.

Prognosis

Phobic blocks are difficult to treat both because they relieve anxiety (the primary gain of the symptom) and because they hold out the possibility of various real pleasures, like being cared for, really mothered (the secondary gain of the symptom).

Cure of block is more easily achieved when the artist is willing to suffer anxiety for art's sake. Cure is difficult or impossible when the artist is unwilling to accept some of the discomfort inherent in the creative act or process—when, for example, a performer with stage fright gives up too easily, and without a fight—and the motivation or even the talent of such an artist can be questioned.

5

CONVERSION DISORDER BLOCK

TECHNICAL CONSIDERATIONS

Conversion Disorder blockage consists of a group of physical blockages of emotional, or combined emotional and physical, origin, of which *writer's cramp* is perhaps the most familiar example. D. Wilfred Abse (1959) in the *American Handbook of Psychiatry* describes Conversion Disorder blockage as a "progressively severe disability due to spasm of the muscles employed in finely coordinated movements essential to the fundamental skills of the particular occupation of the patient" (p. 279). Ives Hendrick (1958) notes that the chief characteristics of Conversion Disorder blockage are "abnormal sensations, paralysis, or other [functional deficit] without demonstrable abnormality of the nervous system" (p. 374).

Since Conversion Disorder blockage is not due to neurological causes, the functional deficit conforms not to an end organ's neuromuscular innervation but to the concept (use) of that end organ. For example, the hand/arm paresis of writer's cramp conforms not to the neurological innervation of the hand/arm but to the concept of the hand/arm as "sexual organ" and/or "aggressive weapon."

As just mentioned, Conversion Disorder blockage may not be of purely emotional origin, but may be due to emotional and physical factors combined. This can happen as the result of what Fenichel (1945) calls "somatic compliance [where a physical complaint is] not produced . . . but . . . used by conversion" (p. 228).

The disorder may develop either (1) de novo, via the defense of *conversion*, or (2) by being borrowed from other individuals with similar symptoms, via the process of *identification*.

De Novo, by Conversion

Fixation. John Nemiah (1985b) discussing Conversion Disorder (Hysterical Neurosis, Conversion Type) notes that the classic psychoanalytic view of conversion is as "a fixation in early psychosexual development at the level of the Oedipus complex, with a failure to relinquish the incestuous tie to the loved parents" (p. 930).

Conflict. Nemiah (1985b) continues, "The fixation leads to a conflict in adult life over the sexual drive or libido because it retains its forbidden incestuous quality" (p. 930).

Fenichel (1945), discussing writer's and violinist's cramp, notes that the spasms are a "tonic substitute for action" that is, for an "intended" but "prohibited" activity (p. 224). Spasms also "have the function of an assurance of a specific inhibition [at the behest of] the superego. [A wish is inhibited] either because of its hidden sexual meaning or because, in the case of moral masochists, a forbidden success might be achieved by [the activity represented by the wish]" (p. 224).

Conflict resolution. Nemiah (1985b) notes that because of conflict a "drive is subjected to the defensive psychological maneuver of repression. The energy deriving from the drive is converted into the hysterical symptom, which not only protects the patient from a conscious awareness of the drive but also at the same time often provides a symbolic expression of the drive" (p. 930).

Fenichel (1945) notes that the motor paralysis of conversion hysteria is "the physical expression of repression. Hypertonus may be the representation of the general attitude 'I have something to suppress' " and a means of "securing suppression of action" (p. 224). The result is a symptom that is a compromise formation, an imperfectly balanced expression of both sides of what Fenichel (1945) calls "instinctual and anti-instinctual forces" where the "manifest clinical picture reveals the first aspect more in some cases, in others the second" (p. 269).

Gain. Hysterical symptoms such as writer's cramp relieve anxiety (the relief of anxiety is called the primary gain). Once in place, certain secondary advantages can be pulled from the fire. For example, the artist discovers he or she can stay home sick both to avoid the difficulties associated with going to work and to get care from mother or her substitute (this is called the secondary gain of the symptom).

The anxiety is, according to Fenichel (1945), an internal signal of the "danger from which the person tries to protect himself." These dangers include "external loss of love or castration . . . [or] a threat from within . . . a kind of loss of self-respect or even a feeling of 'annihilation' . . . [partly due to] guilt feelings" (p. 270).

The dangers differ somewhat in men and women. According to the analytic view, some men mainly fear castration—what Thomas Weiskel, as quoted by Leader (1991), calls "the threatening or inhibiting features of the father, either in the form of a giant literary predecessor or a natural phenomenon" (p. 136).

Hendrick (1958) describes a case of block in a male patient with hysterical personality disorder and suffering from marked castration anxiety as follows:

> A man who blamed the rigid Puritan philosophy of his New England family illustrated extensive inhibitions. . . . He suffered from defective capacity for self-assertion in his professional relations with his clients and in his social as well as erotic activities. He was only cured of the inhibition of normal social behavior, [a cure that was] accompanied by a general masculinization of features, voice, and gesture, when a series of primitive unconscious phantasies of *destroying* with his penis, [fantasies that] had led to the release of unconscious anxiety . . . that his penis would be bitten off by a woman . . . [was successfully analyzed]. (p. 173)

A male song writer and pianist who was later to develop a writer's block and a pianist's cramp combined, unconsciously wrote for his mother, and, also unconsciously, viewed his audience as the critical, observing, threatening father, watching, really spying on them, threatening to surprise them, in flagrante delicto. His critics too were watching, for, as he said, "they cut me down to size for writing seductive songs." He vaguely feared bodily harm as his punishment for being successful, because being successful meant displacing his father in his mother's affections. His block and cramp were an avoidance of danger and an atonement combined, the latter an autocastration, as punishment for his successful oedipal triumph over/castration of, the father.

Some women, like some men, fear defying the parent of the same sex, but the nature of the defiance is somewhat different. For some men it is more like murder; for some women it is more a being different from a devalued mother, growing up independent from, and so abandoning, her. As a result the feared punishments can also be somewhat different. Some men fear retaliative castration more than abandonment; for some women it is the other way around.

Not only can women have somewhat different anxiety-provoking conflicts than men, but they develop symptomatic cramp less often than men (all the cases of pianist's cramp I have heard of are in men). Women are more likely to develop a diffuse characterological block than a discrete symptom like cramp. For reasons that are not entirely clear, they tend not to cramp but to abdicate, reign in their talent, and perform below standards, including the "masculine standard." Instead of the encapsulated, factitious self-mutilation that is the cramped hand, we see a general cramping of the style and a mutilation of the career. They shrink into the shadows, play second fiddle, and abdicate to rivals, so that instead of deforming an appendage, they become one.

Gillian Gill (1990) in her biography of Agatha Christie calls this problem "the anxiety of authorship" (p. 209). Though "writing offered Christie a way to define her sense of self and a means to conquer the world . . . her attitude to her work was a mass of ambivalence, doubt, and uncertainty." Gill implies that Christie's pathological anxiety was over how difficult it is "for a woman of talent to have fame, fortune, and happiness, books and babies"—to be both a writer and "Mrs. Average Conservative Housewife" (p. xi), that is, to be like and unlike mother at one and the same time. Gill continues, in a quote taken from *The Madwoman in the Attic*:

> "Anxiety of authorship" is the key phrase for women writers that Gilbert and Gubar propose in opposition to Harold Bloom's theory of the "anxiety of influence" for men writers . . . [resulting from] the "male" tradition of strong, father-son combat. . . . This female anxiety of authorship is pro-foundly debilitating . . . it is in many ways a germ of disease, or, at any rate, a disaffection, a disturbance, a distrust, that spreads like a stain throughout the style and structure of much literature by women. (pp. 209–210)

Agatha Christie's Great Disappearance illustrates aspects of the dynamics of hysterical blockage. The disappearance was characterized both by a period of amnesia and an associated severe (and uncharacteristic) writer's block. Christie vanished after her husband had taken up with another woman, one younger and perhaps one she believed to be prettier. It is revealing that, during the disappear-ance, Christie checked into the Hydroponic Hotel, using the name Neele, the last name of her rival for her husband's affections. The use of this name reveals something of her fantasies at the time. Did she resent being displaced in her husband's affections, and want to be back in the number one spot? Did being left for another woman revive oedipal fantasies? Was her disappearance, and the block that followed, a guilty self-punishment for her own revived uncon-scious, unacceptable oedipal wishes?

Identification

In hysterical identification the artist in effect "catches" block from another blocked artist. Fenichel (1945) distinguishes among different kinds of identifi-cation based on motive. The first kind of identification is " 'with the fortunate rival,' that is, with a person whom the patient envies and whose place he had wished to occupy from the beginning." This kind causes artists to identify with a blocked mentor. This may have been the case for the pianists Byron Janis and Gary Graffman, both of whom seem to have developed problems with their hands, quite possibly in imitation of similar problems Horowitz is rumored to have developed with his hands. In the second kind, identification follows loss. An oedipal woman for example may not identify with her "rival, her mother, but with her beloved father . . . [for] whenever a person is forced to relinquish an object, he may develop a tendency to compensate for the loss by identifying himself with the object" (p. 221). This could account for Ives's block following the death of his father. The identification may have been a way to sustain the lost relationship with the father in fantasy, and the block may in part have been due to identifying with a father of lesser talent, an identification which in effect diminished the son's abilities. In the third kind, the identification is based in "identical etiological needs." Freud described an epidemic of fainting in a girls' school following one girl's reacting "with a fainting spell to a love letter." This form of identification says, "We should like to get love letters too" (p. 222). This variation is at the bottom of some epidemics of writer's block, like Beat Block, where the "beat" generation "dropped out."

Two personality characteristics facilitate and contribute to one or more of these subtypes of identification. These are competitiveness, which comes naturally to those fixated on triangular (oedipal) relationships, and passivity. As for competitiveness, it is a short step from working with one eye open to how successful others are, to becoming more and more like them to emulate their success (and sometimes their failures, that is, their block). As for passivity, it is easy to identify when one is already prone to yield to, and to follow (the blocked) leader.

DESCRIPTION

There are four broad categories of hysterical blockage: motor/autonomic, sensory, psychosomatic/factitious, and dissociative. These four subtypes of block parallel four subtypes of Conversion Disorder, as follows.

Motor/Autonomic Block

The most familiar form of motor block is writer's cramp not only in writers but in pianists, violinists, and others. An example of autonomic block is intention tremors that interfere with the smooth operation of a pianist's hands or the hands of a baseball pitcher.

Sensory Block

Paresthesias constitute one form of sensory block. An example: disabling sensations of pins and needles described in Gammons (1992) where a pitcher had "problems with feeling at the tips of my fingers. Was it psychosomatic?" (pp. 140–141). Another form is the fear of fainting. The fear that one might faint, associated with palpitations and dizziness, actual faintness, and occasionally (a pox of grooms and best men at weddings) actual fainting, is an hysterical feature commonly found as part of the syndrome of performance anxiety/stage fright.

According to Fenichel (1945), sensory block *is* a kind of "localized fainting; certain sensations that would be painful are not accepted. . . . [While hysterical] disturbances of sensation . . . impress one more as a defense rather than as a return of the repressed . . . [because] the elimination of sensation facilitates the suppression of memories that appertain to the body areas affected . . . [hysterical disturbances of sensation] also serve the repressed impulses" (p. 227). In effect, a fear of fainting involves a fear that the repressed would surface and be overwhelming.

The afferent stages of creativity, like motivation and inspiration ("feeling creative") can be affected by a kind of sensory block in much the same way that the motor stages of performance can be affected by motor block. In these cases, anxiety and guilt over artistic self-expression are often responsible. In a typical scenario, anxiety and guilt appear because sexual and/or aggressive fantasies become connected with creativity, causing conflict, and block is the resolution of that conflict.

Psychosomatic/Factitious Block

Familiar examples of psychosomatic block are emotionally caused ill-nesses that keep the artist from working, like nervous headaches, nervous bowel disease (Horowitz's colitis and Britten's diverticulitis may be in this category), and stress ulcer. Revealingly, artists often describe their creative block figuratively in psychosomatic terms, particularly in terms of intestinal blockage. For example, according to Heyman (1992), Wanda Toscanini (the wife of Vladimir Horowitz) suggested that Barber was "stitico," or "consti-pated" (p. 301).

The patient who made teddy bears, previously mentioned in chapter 4, suffered from a psychosomatic as well as a phobic block. He was unable to work due to severe, chronic, and painful constipation, a "colonic stasis" (as he put it), and one that he believed nicely expressed his mental torpor in physical terms.

In factitious block, we see a discrete self-mutilation that is a concrete, encapsulated physical expression of a generally self-punitive, self-destructive attitude toward oneself and one's art. (This attitude, commonly found in artists, also accounts for their general readiness to block.) A possible example is Schumann's unconscious destruction of his fourth finger using a practice device meant consciously to strengthen it. Did Schumann really continue to use this device until it caused irreparable harm to his hand? Or is another possibility here that Schumann seized upon supposed complications from using the practice device to explain what was in effect a pianist's cramp?

Dissociative Block

Christie's Great Disappearance provides us with a possible example of block due to multiple personality disorder and fugue, while Maurice Ravel's "amnesia block" (each time he tried to write down something that existed in his head he in essence forgot what he was going to say) provides us with a possible example of block due to psychogenic amnesia.

Block is the essence of the symptom picture of many cases of fugue, multiple personality disorder, amnesia, and other dissociative disorders. In particular, fugue and amnesia patients who leave their jobs, and patients with a multiple personality disorder who have a nonworking personality in their repertoire of identities, may be said to be blocked as well as dissociated.

Characteristics of dissociative block are: (1) It sometimes starts with a head injury. Christie's car may have crashed and Ravel was in a taxi accident. This can lend the dissociative episode an organic aura, and leave the patient's doctors uncertain as to whether the patient is suffering from either a physical or a mental disorder, or both; (2) It is often ushered in by a loss. Christie, for example, lost her husband and her mother; and (3) It has a kind of feigned, willful, quality, so that we are tempted to tell the patient to "cut it out." Christie for example was actually accused of perpetrating a hoax. Many patients in a fugue are accused of faking it to get out of trouble, particularly of the financial kind.

Some blocks result not from dissociation but from the *inability* to dissociate. Block of this sort is due to personal rigidity, one manifestation of which is a fear of letting go and being flooded in the altered trance-like state of "deep thought," or "being lost in thought," for some a precondition for creativity. The creative process is often like automatic writing, with the creator assuming the role of "medium." For example, according to Kennedy (1987), Elgar believed in "inspiration ('Music is written on the skies') and saw himself as the vessel into which music was poured from he knew not where. More prosaically, he called himself an 'incubator.' . . . He had musical day-dreams in the same way that other people had day-dreams of heroism and adventure, and that he could express almost any thought that came into his head in terms of music" (p. 333). That creativity proceeds in an altered state helps explain why creativity can be seriously impaired when the state can't be altered, as when the artist is constantly interrupted when he or she sits down to work.

THERAPEUTIC IMPLICATIONS

Treatment of Conversion Disorder blocks begins with an adequate diagnosis. In each case, physical disorder must not only be ruled *out*, but Conversion Disorder must be ruled *in*. Differentiate between emotional and physical blockage not merely for theoretical reasons but to avoid treating medical disorder psychiatrically and psychiatric disorder medically, and either doing no good or actually doing harm by delaying needed treatment or by offering treatment that is too radical and actually destructive. Cases where a surgeon does irreparable damage to a pianist's hand with unnecessary and harmful surgery to release tendons are an example of destructive treatment—all too common, and often all too disastrous in the extreme.

Treatment of Conversion Disorder blockage, which requires insight into and resolution of conflicts, is a possible exception to our general rule that uncovering techniques should be soft-pedaled or withheld at the beginning of therapy in favor of more supportive approaches.

Treatment of Conversion Disorder blockage is made difficult (1) by the silence characteristic of those who develop physical conversions, where mind disappears into body (as distinct from ideational symptoms, like obsessions, where "body disappears into mind"), and (2) by the tendency of those with physical symptoms to expect the doctor to provide the cure, really, to do all the work.

The above-mentioned patient who made teddy bears and suffered from crippling colitis presented little useful material for the grist of the psychotherapy mill. He was as unable to associate meaningfully to his emotional as he was to his physical block, describing each without explaining either. Not unexpectedly he also demanded his doctor treat him, that is, take over and do all the work. As far as he was concerned, if he had a medical symptom, he didn't have to work out his problems over time in psychotherapy. Instead he could demand, and get, a pill to fix him up—physically, emotionally, and professionally.

Another difficulty arises from the masochistic character structure so often found in patients who abuse their body the way conversion hysterics do. These patients often have considerable secondary gain, causing them to resist getting well because of the advantages they believe to be associated with getting, and staying, sick.

On the positive side the suggestibility and passivity of some hysterical blockers can make them *easier* to treat than their more rigid, more controlled, more obsessional counterparts. Some are so tractable that they respond well merely to suggestion/the placebo effect of treatment. Some of these patients appear to do well with almost any form of therapy offered—ranging from amytal interview to guidance counseling.

6
OBSESSIVE-COMPULSIVE DISORDER BLOCK

Obsessive-Compulsive Disorder block is the result of recurrent obsessions (intrusive, inappropriate thoughts) and/or recurrent compulsions (driven repetitive behaviors) that, according to John Nemiah (1985a) in "Obsessive-Compulsive Disorder (Obsessive-Compulsive Neurosis)," can be "manifested psychically or behaviorally . . . as ideas . . . or as impulses . . . ritualized patterns of thinking" (p. 911) or doing that preoccupy individuals and make them relatively or absolutely unable to "work and function socially" (p. 914).

Hayman (1993) writes that Tennessee Williams "walking toward the Hotel . . . suddenly started thinking about the thinking process—which struck him as both complex and mysterious. . . . 'At least a month of the tour was enveloped for me by this phobia about the process of thought, and the phobia grew and grew till I think I was within a hairs-breadth of going quite mad from it' " (p. 20).

Toye (1987) says that Rossini "could listen to no sound without hearing at the same time the major third. This caused him so much distress that Olympe [his mistress] had to provide the porter with a special fund to keep away barrel organs and other street musicians" (pp. 205–206). Toye also notes that Rossini suffered from an "obsession, which . . . tortured him . . . of being forgotten and despised by the world" (p. 206). Rossini's hearing the major third may have not been an obsession but a hallucination, and his obsession of being forgotten, a depressive delusion.

DYNAMICS

Obsessions are symbolic expressions of underlying fears. For example, in the analytic view, a patient who ruminated about why chairs have four legs, not three, was in fact ruminating not about chairs but about the possibility of his own castration. The compulsions that usually accompany obsessions are equally symbolic attempts to deal with those fears. Again, the same patient's compulsion to return home more than once after leaving the house to make certain the gas had been turned off was an attempt to reassure himself that his possessions were still intact, therefore he himself was intact. Why was he so concerned for his intactness? An artist, he was tortured with the possibility that doing art made him, as he said, "like a woman," and he needed constant reassurance that the weeping, passive aspect of creativity did not, as he feared, mean that he was actually in danger of becoming less of a man, that is, of becoming a homosexual, which he defined as a "castrated man."

An author constantly obsessed that she would lose months or years of work because her manuscript and computer disks would be stolen or consumed in a fire. Before she left the house she put her hard copy of the manuscript in the home safe to protect it. But she was compelled to return home to take it out because "the safe is the first thing they go after." Next she left the hard copy amongst a miscellaneous collection of papers so that it "would look like nothing special to the crooks." But now she began to think, usually after she was well away from home, "It's not protected lying out there where any one can nab it." So she returned home to put the hard copy back in the safe, and so on.

She made backups of her computer disks, and backups of backups, and stored them in different places around town. At first she was comforted and felt protected. But soon she began to worry that because they were all in the same town, a general disaster, like a big fire or a tornado, could consume them all. So she put copies in the houses of friends who lived out of town. However, she doubted they were any good because to get them there she had to pass sources of magnetism, like stereos and television sets, so had probably, she worried, demagnetized her diskettes on their way to safe-keeping.

So she took to carrying hard copy and diskettes in a protective case in her purse wherever she went. She thought, reassuringly, "To get them they'll have to get me." But then she worried that they *would* get her—a thief would knock her over, steal her purse and her manuscript, and publish her manuscript as his or her own.

Consumed by worry and doubt, she became a virtual cripple who, instead of writing the novel she intended, put down a few lines then spent hours, even days, protecting them from oblivion.

An aspect of many obsessions is the underlying fear of not having what it takes—of being worthless and defective. Hayman says that Tennessee Williams "calculated that he was using three-quarters of his energy and creativity on fighting his fears of failure with his writing" (p. 150). As Fenichel (1945) says (see also chapter 5), "what is mainly feared is a kind of loss of self-respect or even a feeling of 'annihilation' " (p. 270).

In the case of the writer afraid for her writing, analysis of the symptom revealed she was excessively protective of her writing because, believing that she was personally unattractive, she felt her work was the only good thing about her, the only thing others would love her for. And she felt its destruction "would wipe me out as a person" and "leave me with nobody to love me."

CLASSIFICATION

We divide the obsessions and compulsions into three classes that reflect Freud's (1957) division of anal character traits into orderliness/perfectionism, parsimoniousness/frugality, and obstinacy.

Orderly/Perfectionistic Obsessions and Compulsions

Orderliness and perfectionism can take the form of first doing then apologizing by overchecking, overcorrecting, and overrevising.

A writer compulsively put quotes around each use of the word "all." When asked why he did this, he replied, in essence, "because I don't think I'm smart enough to know about all of anything." Then he offered exhaustive, "all"-inclusive, but unnecessary, tiresome and unreadable lists, making what he wrote into an exercise in completeness rather than a heart-felt communication.

Leader (1991) confesses that he himself had a "neurotic compulsion to revise every other word I produced" (p. ix)—like Gray who blocked because of a "tendency to revise too much, an inability to finish things" (p. 120), so that "perfection . . . [became] a source of creative inhibition" (p. 231).

Checking compulsions are often found in patients who are basically depressed. Such individuals use perfectionism in art to undo the feeling that they are imperfect in life. We infer from the following that feeling defective/no good/worthless seems a likely explanation for Sibelius's ultimately self-destructive perfectionism.

According to David Blum (1994), Sibelius's wife "Aino attributed her husband's failure to complete the Eighth Symphony to . . . 'rigorous self-criticism.' " On one occasion Aino angered him. When he found a mistake in one of his published works, she tried to reassure him by saying, "nobody would notice it." But instead of being reassured he replied, "How can you say something like that?" She reports that "he was so hurt that he left the room." And, "One day . . . [he] had collected manuscripts . . . and was burning them . . . in the open fireplace" (p. 34).

Perfectionism in these cases is too little a means to an end, the sanding that makes a fine object even finer, and too much an end in itself, so that it fails to work as planned, either artistically or emotionally (defensively). Artistically, it almost never creates the magnificent accomplishment anticipated. It is rarely the stuff that makes Shakespeare's *Hamlet* or Beethoven's Fifth Symphony. More likely it compromises the work by imparting to it triviality of purpose and effect, which the audience often notices. The work takes on a rigid, repetitive, driven quality—art without soul, wearisome to all except those who like perfectionism itself.

Emotionally, perfectionism is often called upon to deal with low self-esteem, yet it is relatively ineffective. Usually the self-esteem enhancement itself becomes the victim of the insatiable perfectionism, that is, no enhancement is ever complete, really perfect, enough. Greater and greater efforts are required until eventually the art disappears into the perfectionistic compulsion.

How would fussy perfectionism improve self-esteem? Often, it allows artists to be in complete control of the process, which enables them to repress ideas and feelings believed shameful or amoral. In one version, an artist writes mathematical twelve-tone music to avoid writing tunes, which he believes predictably display sexual or hostile feelings. For other artists, fussing fools them into thinking they are more perfect, that is, better than the next guy—who for them is the imperfect, devalued other.

It may be that Harry S. Anchan (1994) wrote the following letter to the editor of *Stereo Review* with devaluation of the imperfect other and so self-enhancement in mind. The author is clearly tearing others down as a way to prop himself up:

> I'm glad Steve Schwartz ("How to Make Good Tapes" in March) thinks the term "total wuss" applies to those who put entire CD's or LP's on tape. Every tape I make on my three-head, three-motor cassette deck is pains-takingly, lovingly created from varied sources, such as my *Billboard* "Hot 100" compilations. (p. 8)

Here are two other examples of being defeated by grandiose standards maintained for purposes of self-esteem enhancement:

An artist was stalled because his self-image depended on his need for complete and unquestionable originality. He himself declared, "The only book I want to write is the only book on a subject. So I can't write because there are essentially no subjects on which there aren't already books." Then he added, only half in jest, that "no topic is worth my time and effort unless it matches in intensity and importance the fight to the death between the Boat Captain and the White Whale."

Sibelius, who was later to block completely in part because of his excessive perfectionism, according to Blum (1994), said of himself, "It's as if God the Father had thrown down the tiles of a mosaic from heaven's floor and asked me to determine what kind of picture it was" (p. 34).

In conclusion, what happens in so many cases of excessive perfectionism is that an artist who starts out to produce the perfect work produces instead the perfect block.

Frugal Obsessions and Compulsions

Scrooge-like frugality, often due to withholding, impoverishes everything it touches. The composer Anton von Webern wrote little more than a few hours of music in his whole life. Each of his later pieces is but a few seconds to a few minutes long. Charitably, this is the ultimate in concision. Uncharitably, it is the ultimate in anal retention, and, as one musicologist put it, it comes uncomfortably close to the grating behavior of people who recycle the bottoms of plastic bottles as containers for growing seeds, less to save money than to harangue their friends about how thrifty and clever they are.

Obstinate Obsessions and Compulsions

An obstinate artist senses what others want just so he or she can stubbornly avoid giving it to them.

The composer Ernst Krenek seems to have undone his great success with *Jonny Spielt Auf,* a jazz opera, with works meant to assure failure. It is as if as soon as he sensed his audiences wanted more operas with jazz he deliberately preoccupied himself with writing atonal works that were of limited interest and appeal to avoid giving others what they wanted.

A composer, withholding for moralistic reasons, was willing to give her audiences the requiem they wanted but not to put singable tunes in it. Secretly she believed, "Requiems are ok because they are devotional. But not tunes. Tunes give pleasure; all pleasure is erotic pleasure; and all erotic pleasure is amoral." As a result she became a rigid and remote artist whose disapproving attitude showed. Her audiences, without quite knowing why, sensed the horror she felt when anyone in her vicinity was in danger of having fun.

One critic suspected the composer Samuel Barber did something of this sort in *Anthony and Cleopatra,* an opera commissioned for the opening of the new Metropolitan Opera House in Lincoln Center. In his theory Barber refused to rise to the occasion, deliberately interrupting his arias in midstream to disappoint, to avoid giving the audience the good tunes they wanted, to withhold from them as a way to be free from the tormenting demands of the philistine first nighters, whom he unconsciously thought of as a bunch of jerks wanting not art, but frivolity.

Unswayed by the argument that Shakespeare wrote plots, Beethoven tunes, and Kafka jokes, another composer, refusing to cater to fools, did art only for the cognoscenti. Her audience sensed they were being condescended to, and got back at her by coughing throughout her performances or by actually walking out on them. This only angered her and inspired her to entrench even further to show them who is boss. To protect her pride by protecting her independence, she avoided any semblance of yielding by becoming even more rigid and stubborn, writing, "what I want to, the way I want to write it," not "what they want to hear." To deprive her audiences further, she expunged all tender and angry feelings from her works and deliberately withheld tunes or gave them grudgingly, in fragmentary form, not to please, but to tease—to frustrate and deprive people of what they wanted, precisely because they wanted it.

Soon, because meeting deadlines meant being told what to do, she couldn't finish her commissions on time even when she herself would have liked to do so. Pushing her to meet deadlines only made matters worse because she saw this as being pushed around. Yet leaving her to her own devices meant rejecting her, whereupon she slowed down even more. Furthermore, because she saw every suggestion as a command, and every command as an attempt to seize control, she wouldn't allow what she squeezed out to be edited, or if she did, she responded to each blue pencil mark with an argument and self-defense combined, to challenge the editor and maintain the interpersonal status quo.

As bad as things were, they got worse when excessive submission surfaced as the flip side of her obstinacy. Already depressed, she tended to get even more so when brought up short by audiences, critics, and editors for her remoteness and lateness. She got more depressed because she knew, deep down, that she stood guilty as charged, and that their criticism of her work was deserved. So, out of guilt, she retreated, tail between the legs, to become excessively passive and surprisingly cooperative. Like Barber constantly rewriting *Anthony and Cleopatra*, she wrote and rewrote to give the audience, critics, and her editors what they wanted; what she now regretted not having given them in the first place. Her writing and rewriting amounted to compulsive confessing and retracting "the evil she had done." She was trying to win back the love of those whom she felt she injured. But her works *sounded* revised. And besides, by now it was too late. Because, while she was working away to please her various critics, her critics, less emotionally involved in the interaction than she was, had long since not merely gotten over her artistic transgressions, but had completely forgotten about her.

A rather miserly chef and businessman also withheld when he sensed something was wanted from him, until he failed in the restaurant business because he served only small portions—not, like a psychopath, to see how much he could get away with, but because he resisted feeding people precisely because they wanted to be fed. As he put it, "I hate looking at all those open mouths, making demands on me. What do they think, I'm their mother?" Not unexpectedly he dealt with his guilt over his business failure by blaming the failure not on himself but on the problems inherent in running a restaurant business, which he humorously, but revealingly, called the "catering business."

POSITIVE FACTORS

There are so many positive factors in obsessionalism that sometimes it seems that being an obsessional is a prerequisite for being an artist; one reason for blockage is not being obsessive-compulsive enough.

For example, a perfectionistic artist is an artist motivated to get down to work, to organize, revise, clean up, and finish. Pride in work well done makes for work that meets high personal, and so high professional standards. Many audiences want and like the perfect work, all i's dotted and all t's crossed. This is one reason many readers love Agatha Christie. They love her precision and cloture. It is why, according to some, her *Ten Little Indians* is the supreme mystery masterpiece of all time.

The grandiosity that so often accompanies perfectionism, even when the grandiosity is somewhat misguided, is often enough by itself to give the artist a smug sense of achievement, which puts the artist in a good, productive mood.

The perversity of obstinacy works for, not against, the artist when it leads the artist to work hard and well to revenge him- or herself against unappreciative audiences or hostile critics. Oppositional obsessives have been known to be not resolutely elitist, to crush le bourgeoisie, but to write in an appealing popular style to crush, not the bourgeoisie, but the academics.

Obsessive tics can serve a useful purpose as self-starters, a way to rub the sand out of the eyes, to shake off the dust. Pinsker and Kantor (1973) described a repetitive, tic-like opening motif in the music of Antonin Dvorak, whose themes often begin with a statement of a variant of the same tune. (One form of the recurrent motif is the first five notes of the familiar "Humoresque.") I feel this motif, and related mannerisms in the works of Edward Grieg, Francis Poulenc, and others, are *useful* obsessions. They are like throat-clearing tics used to mark time while a speaker thinks of something to say or waits for stage fright to go away on its own. They are not fillers but bridges, used to step over the rapids of a temporarily flagging inspiration.

Finally, some artists who obsessively fear that death will come before they complete their life's work are motivated to obsessively complete their life's work before death can come.

TREATMENT

The following techniques seem to be safe and effective and, for good measure, to bypass the basic dilemma in treating obsessives: permissive approaches overwhelm the patient with too many possibilities, while directive approaches stifle the patient and provoke even more stubbornness.

Escape Hatches

One effective technique is suggesting escape hatches, a "what the hell" way out, of the sort that, when they occur spontaneously, distinguish the functional from the nonfunctional obsessional.

An obsessional, after spending hours checking the house to see if he left the gas on, was able to leave, that is, to call a halt to obsessing, by invoking the escapist "who cares," saying to himself, "I really hate this place anyway, and would like to see it burn down because I wanted a new one all along."

A cook developed the following "spaghetti obsession." When the cooked spaghetti was done, he put the pot—the spaghetti in its boiling water—in the sink, then poured the water out through a colander. But he began to brood that the sink was dirty, the bottom of the pot sat in the dirt, and as he poured the spaghetti and the water out from the big pot the dirt from the bottom of the pot was carried into the colander, and onto the spaghetti. After months of recooking spaghetti or at best spending minutes washing and rewashing it, he developed the following technique: he put the pot in the sink, and removed the spaghetti piece by piece with a slotted spoon. This way water and dirt on the bottom of the pot could not get on the spaghetti. It took more time, but not as much as rerinsing or recooking, and it increased his comfort level, that is, it reduced his anxiety about contaminating the spaghetti.

Artist patients have found two escapist thoughts, really reality checks, to be particularly helpful when they are stuck in place in their work: the permissive, "Stop already, you have to stop somewhere"; and the dismissive, "That's good enough for those jerks."

Reverse Psychology

Just as some individuals with insomnia can only fall asleep when trying to stay awake, some artists find that the motivation and capacity to function can exist in inverse proportion to demands made to function, whether these demands come from oneself or from others. Some therapists find they can relieve block in negativistic patients by recommending it, by making it, "just what the doctor ordered." A patient of Jay Haley, unable to go to work because he slept through the alarm clock, was told to sleep through it (personal communication). In part because this eliminated all the advantages of defeating his therapist, he jumped up to get ready for work before the clock even sounded. Reverse psychology undercuts stubbornness and takes the pressure off the patient. Some blocked patients feel so comfortable in the presence of a therapist not making the expected demands on them that they are able to resume working just for that reason.

Taking Responsibility

The therapist frees the artist to act by promising to be responsible for any negative outcome, saying in effect, "Do it, and if it doesn't work, then I'll take the blame."

Giving Permission

The therapist can give permission in a general way. He or she can say, "I give you permission to be an artist. Even though your father didn't want you to be one, I think it's a good idea." Or he or she can say, "Say what you want to say; let the chips fall where they may. You are who you are. Let them bind and torture you. You are entitled to your opinion. Besides, life is too short to worry about what others, like the experts, think."

Giving permission works because it relieves guilt when the advice given is good advice on its own and because so often the artist eases up after identifying with a more relaxed, less guilty therapist.

Softening the Superego

A therapist who disagrees vocally with the harsh dictates of an artist's superego puts his benign little voice in the artist's head to counter or replace the artist's malignant, destructive, guilt-provoking little voices. This is one reason cognitive treatment works so well: it counters the patient's irrational reasons to be guilty with a vocal list of rational reasons to be guilt-free.

Pharmacotherapy

A drug like fluoxetine can relieve obsessive-compulsive blockage by relieving the depressed mood that spins off the obsessions. As one patient said, "For me it acts like a tonic, so that even though I continue obsessing, the obsessions are not nearly so troublesome, or disruptive, as they once were."

7

POSTTRAUMATIC STRESS DISORDER BLOCK

CLINICAL MANIFESTATIONS

In blockage due to Posttraumatic Stress Disorder creativity slows or stops because the *act* of creating or the personal or professional *consequences* of creating are in themselves newly traumatic, or they revive one or more old traumas.

Both new and old traumas stop creativity because they are painful; they make the creator feel helpless and afraid. Freud, as quoted by Ernest Jones (1953) in his *Life and Works of Sigmund Freud*, defined the feeling of helplessness as being "without assistance to master some excessive excitation . . . [because] all the protective barriers are overrun" (vol. 3, p. 255–256). Harvey Dorfman, as Gammons (1992) says, described feeling afraid as a "life-threatening situation . . . like walking on a board three feet wide . . . across the Grand Canyon, and you feel [you are falling in]" (p. 138).

The resulting syndrome, Posttraumatic Stress Disorder and the block that accompanies it, is characterized by impaired function that results (1) from the feelings of helplessness and fear, (2) from the withdrawal that is a defense against feeling helpless and afraid, and (3) from a preoccupation with the original traumatic event and later events that relight the original trauma.

In creative people block is put into place as a way to avoid the pain of the creative process and its consequences. An association between being creative and being traumatized develops, which makes creativity itself a traumatic trigger.

In a typical case, exhaustion and demoralization result from the recurrent nightmares and flashbacks that are part of the disorder as well as from the general preoccupation with and need to avoid triggers, to the point where the individual has little or no life. It is not much of a *personal* life to be unable to turn on the television set because they are always showing war pictures and violence; to have to sit with your back to the wall and your eyes glued to the door every time you go to a restaurant because you fear a surprise attack from the rear; to have to cower in the corner every Fourth of July because the fireworks remind you of the battlefield; or to fear the snow because it reminds you of winters in France, where you fought and bivouacked during World War II. And it's not much of a *professional* life to be unable to concentrate due to painfully intense, distracting anxiety associated with autonomic symptoms like shaking, tremulousness, and sweating,

When block is due to a revival of an old (original) trauma, the block itself tends to resemble and reveal something about the original trauma and/or the original reaction to that trauma, that is, block is a prolonged flashback.

Most authors attributed the composer Maurice Ravel's final aphasic block (described below) to organic causes, such as the postconcussional effects of his taxi accident, or some other brain disease. As mentioned in chapter 1, the official version of the last five to six infertile years of Ravel's life suggests Ravel blocked from a neurological disorder. According to Thompson (1964), Ravel stopped writing in 1933 after being "stricken with a brain ailment which eventually caused his death . . . following an operation [on his brain] on Dec. 26, 1937, at the age of 62" (p. 1744). Orenstein (1991) says, "Because of medical ethics, the exact nature of Ravel's malady has remained obscure" (p. 108).

Another possibility, however speculative, is that Ravel's block was not of neurological origin but looked postconcussional because (1) the final block was directly connected to the earlier block, that is, a recurrent episode of an earlier Posttraumatic Stress Disorder, and so (2) it reproduced the pseudoneurological symptoms of the original "shell shock" Ravel experienced when he was an ambulance driver at the front during World War I: irritability, inability to concentrate, insomnia, and mental clouding and confusion.

Orenstein's (1991) account of the earlier block keeps the episode resolutely separate from the later block. Ravel, driving a truck and caring for wounded soldiers during the war, was nearly killed several times. "Amid the war's hardships, tragedies, and galvanizing experiences, Ravel was obsessed by his mother's failing health. . . . His own health had deteriorated sharply; in addition to frequent insomnia and poor appetite, he finally underwent an operation for dysentery in September 1916" (p. 74–75). In January 1917 his mother died. "Its immediate effect was some three years of virtual silence" (p. 75).

Though he felt "an 'intense need' to work . . . [he] was 'absolutely incapable' of obeying his impulse. . . . Unable to compose and haunted by his mother's memory, he was bitter and disillusioned. [After a] generous and timely invitation . . . [to a] colleague's country home . . . [he] painstakingly began to recapture his former creative enthusiasm" (p. 75–76). The positivity shown him— which I believe to be the most important factor in getting over creative block—allowed him to recover.

However, while his creativity returned, both his personal and his professional life continued to suffer somewhat. As for the personal, according to Thompson (1964), "Since the war . . . [Ravel both] lived and worked in seclusion at his villa in Monfort l'Amaury . . . avoiding public activity of any kind" (p. 1744). As for the professional, he seems to have suffered an ongoing partial block, for, as Orenstein puts it, for the rest of his life "only about one composition a year would be completed" (p. 75).

The differential diagnosis of Ravel's final "mysterious brain ailment" should include delayed posttraumatic block that bore a connection to, that is, was a recurrence of, his early posttraumatic block. It is possible that the first combat fatigue or Posttraumatic Stress Disorder block was revived as Ravel was writing his Left Hand Piano Concerto for Paul Wittgenstein, the pianist who lost his right arm in the same war and under the same circumstances that traumatized Ravel.

DYNAMIC CONSIDERATIONS

Successophobia

Successophobia due to survivor guilt is a significant factor in Posttraumatic Stress Disorder and in the block that is part of that disorder.

A number of combat veterans suffering from Posttraumatic Stress Disorder block, artists and nonartists alike, blame trauma recurrence for their block, but they overlook the reason for the trauma recurrence. One of the main reasons is guilt. Revealingly, though they complain of not being able to forget the traumatic period, they simultaneously recreate the combat atmosphere in their daily lives, say, with Vietnam badges like hats and T-shirts. It is as if they want to move on but their self-destructive guilt forces them back in time, summoned there in part because they *want* to suffer in the here and now; they believe that they, not their buddies, should have been the ones to take the bullet. In good measure that is why they develop the life constrictions they do. They need them, for they represent a guilty wish fulfillment and punishment rolled into one, a kind of longed-for symbolic death. This is why their symptoms are so often set in motion when accomplishment "threatens."

Anger and Depression

Angry resentment at the world viewed as unfair seems especially common in veterans, artists and nonartists alike, who did not enlist but were drafted. This anger at the world is expressed in a block that is effectively both a way to self-defeat and a way to beat others over their heads with one's bloody body. The guiding principle of block of this sort is, "I am willing to fail, but only as long as I can, or so that I can, drag you down with me."

POSITIVE ASPECTS

Traumatization, like any supposedly negative experience, can be inspiring. Early traumas seem to have inspired such works as the plays of Tennessee Williams and the many creative works on the holocaust. This is partly because traumas, as David DelTredici says, quoted by K. Robert Schwarz (1994), are "the grain of sand [that] gets lodged inside and ends up producing a wonderful work of art." And partly it is because individuals who have been traumatized find they can use creativity as a way to deal with their trauma and its effects. David DelTredici suggests that there are positive creative effects of being gay and hypothesizes that these are due to the effects of trauma: "Being gay can be an enormous childhood trauma, and that trauma can be a spur to creativity" (p. 24).

One artist said, in essence, "I will create something beautiful to undo the feeling that my life has been one ugly traumatic incident after another, and to leave something behind to deal with the sense of meaninglessness that as a consequence I feel about myself, and my existence."

THERAPEUTIC IMPLICATIONS

All concerned in treating creators with Posttraumatic Stress Disorder block should recognize that many of the usual rules don't apply in these cases. Uncovering treatments have to balance the positive effects of getting it all out of the system with the negative effects of trauma revival due to the therapy itself. In particular, the advice to write about what you know is often just the wrong thing for creators with Posttraumatic Stress Disorder. For when they create from what they know they often re-create the fearful images they know all too well. They scare themselves and have to stop. It might be better to give such creators the opposite advice: write only about what you *don't* know.

Practically speaking, the creator blocked from Posttraumatic Stress Disorder risks losing either way—getting "it" out (as above) or keeping "it" in (when the creativity suffers). So *artistically* speaking he or she might as well accept the anxiety involved in getting it out to avoid the creative loss associated with keeping it in: "If I have to feel anxious, experience flashbacks, and have nightmares, at least it is because I am doing something worthwhile, something creative."

CAVEAT

Recently there has been a tendency to see trauma as the basis of all, or almost all, emotional disorder. Real life is more complicated than that. Carol Tavris stated in her *New York Times* book review, "Beware the Incest-Survivor Machine" (1993), that we should be "wary of believing every case of 'me too!' [traumatic neurosis] that makes the news," leading to "an uncritical acceptance of certain premises about the nature of . . . trauma" (p. 16). Wariness is in order because, first, most people have been at least modestly traumatized either physically or emotionally, or both, in childhood. Most of us have had imperfect parents, who have to some extent been either purposefully or unwittingly abusive, if not physically, then emotionally.

Second, our individual sensitivity to/tolerance for trauma varies. This sensitivity/tolerance, which can be inherited or acquired, can allow events that many of us would discount or not notice to become traumas because relatively trivial occurrences are allowed to be more decisive in molding our lives than they otherwise might be. These so-called traumatic events are more of symbolic than of real importance; what is "traumatic" is internal truth, not external reality.

Third, people distort retrospectively, or even remember nonexistent traumas, because distortion is a quality of normal memory. This is gist of Tavris's (1993) article. In the absence of parents who have traumatized us severely, most of us, if we are so inclined, can, from nothing, or from slim stuff, conjure up severe trauma by mistaking tough love, or the controversial disciplinary spanking, for emotional or physical abuse.

Fourth, the tendency to distort retrospectively, and remember nonexistent traumas, is a common manifestation of emotional disorder. The schizophrenic can imagine traumas for the same "psychotic" reasons he or she imagines persecutors or hears voices. The patient with pseudologia fantastica can confabulate traumas as he or she confabulates any other event. The patient with a paranoid disorder can imagine or exaggerate traumas to avoid self-blame and to have an excuse for his or her paranoid anger: "Because it's not me, it's my trauma, I am not a bad person, I am merely reacting to, and appropriately angry with, an abusive world." Trauma provides the paranoid with a rationale that enables the individual to ignore a more frightening and more revealing truth—he or she has contributed in some significant way to his or her own problem. The patient with a Borderline Personality Disorder can imagine or exaggerate traumas as a reason to break up a relationship deemed threatening because too close. The patient with a Multiple Personality Disorder can have "the traumatized self" as one of his or her personalities. The patient with an Histrionic Personality Disorder, already suggestible and prone to develop strong "me too" identifications with others, can develop a traumatized identity by reading about being traumatized and can be motivated to belong, in some cases, to a group of people who have likewise suffered traumas. The patient with a Psychopathic-Antisocial Personality Disorder can exaggerate or make up traumas for purposes of gain. Finally patients with a confabulatory organic disorder such as Korsakoff's Syndrome can concoct tall tales of trauma to fill in memory gaps.

Fifth, later in life people tend to blame the circumstances in which a symptom first occurs for the creation of that symptom when the symptom is already in place, so that what looks like trauma occurrence is really trauma recurrence or, more specifically, block ascendant is really block recurrent. Fosse who supposedly developed stage fright "as a consequence of being booed" may in fact have been booed because of a bad performance due to a stage fright he already had.

Dorfman, (as quoted in Gammons, 1992) after talking to thousands of players concluded that stage fright "almost always can be traced to some trauma. . . . Traumatic memory forces one to replicate the experience" (p. 138). Fosse's stage fright can be traced "right to the field . . . [to a traumatic experience that] cost us the game" (p. 146).

Writing about impotence, Freud (1957) cautions that there is a "familiar erroneous line of argument" that when a failure, or by implication an emotional problem of any sort, is repeated several times we tend to conclude, by this faulty reasoning, "that . . . the first occasion acted as a disturbance by causing anxiety and brought about the subsequent failures; the first occasion itself . . . [we tend to call an] 'accidental' occurrence" (vol. 4, pp. 203–204).

Of course, some individuals do the reverse: they underestimate the significance of, or completely deny, actual early trauma. This often happens with minimal early traumas short of outright abuse, like humiliations. Yet revival of these early minimal traumas by equally minimal later traumas is so often responsible for causing creative block. The demoralizing things that most artists experience in the course of their daily work are really minimal traumas, and the reactions to those events—like insomnia, depression, and block itself—are, more often than appreciated, symptoms of subclinical Posttraumatic Stress Disorder. You might say that rejections from impersonal, uncaring publishers, disdain from fickle audiences, and attacks by hostile critics are not only the artist's life, but are also the artist's trauma and traumatic block in a nutshell.

8

PARAPHILIAC BLOCK

Creativity per se primarily arises and proceeds independent of such familiar aspects of psychic life as instinct and conscience. As Giovacchini (1984) says, creativity is one of Freud's "Higher Ego Functions" (p. 429). Ned Rorem, the composer, quoted by K. Robert Schwarz (1994) can rightly say, "A composer doesn't know anything about himself, and what he says about his own music is of no interest at all" (p. 24). Michael Kennedy, quoted in Carpenter's (1992) biography of Britten, can describe a similar and equally valid sentiment of Peter Pears, Britten's lover. Pears, replying to a question about the relationship between Britten's (paraphiliac) homosexuality and his music, says, "I do not believe that Ben's private life plays any role in the assessment of his artistry and personality. He was a musical genius. Is one really interested in the sex life of the great musicians or the less great? . . . I don't think so" (p. 178).

However, while creativity per se arises in mysterious, unfamiliar, and unfathomable regions of the mind, it regularly becomes secondarily contaminated by the not so mysterious, unfamiliar, or unfathomable—by conflict. It is this conflict that causes block. One source of conflict, paraphilia, can secondarily contaminate creativity and cause creative block.

Paraphilia causes creative block (1) by appearing in and adversely affecting the quality of the art produced, or (2) by adversely affecting the artist's ability to produce his or her art.

APPEARING IN AND SPOILING THE ART

Art can be spoiled when it becomes too much the expression of paraphiliac psychopathology. Just as a paraphiliac relationship is superficial, incomplete, and thwarted in goal, paraphiliac art is incomplete, undeveloped, and lacking in wholeness. Like paraphiliac sexuality, paraphiliac art goes only so far and no further; paraphiliac art expresses a limited spectrum of emotions, just as paraphiliac sex is more foreplay than consummation. Paraphiliac art falls short of achieving true glory just as paraphiliac sex falls short of achieving true love.

Exhibitionism

Exhibitionistic art, of the kind found in some dadaistic works, can be the symbolic exposure of the artist's ego, often genitals. It is show-off art. It intends not to express but to impress. It is meant less to move or edify than to startle, shock, or horrify.

Fetishism

Fetishistic art focuses on the part rather than on the whole, the symbol over that which is symbolized. It reduces art to one of its components in the same way the fetishistic paraphiliac reduces his or her love object to the perfect shoe on the perfect foot, or a woman to her undergarments. Some atonalists seem fetishistically limited by their preoccupation with the mechanical aspects of music—form and structure—at the expense of feeling and melody, while others, for example some of the romantics, are limited by a preoccupation with feeling and melody at the expense of form and structure. Again, Dada is a fertile source of examples. Marcel Duchamp's *Nude Descending a Staircase* is less the whole nude than she is a collage of body parts, and Meret Oppenheim's fur-lined cup, which some see as a reference to the female genitalia, is a classic example of emphasis on the part over the whole, that is, the symbol over that which is symbolized.

The elitism that is an integral part of fetishism can make for self-consciously elitist art. Just as the fetishistic paraphiliac believes the fetishistic preference to be superior to "base animal sexuality," that is, "your animal urges," the fetishistic artist sometimes does art deliberately not for "commoners" but for "superior people," the "cognoscenti." This can give the art a smug self-consciousness well-expressed by the term, "piss-elegance." It can make the art as snobbishly inclined and superficial as the artist. The artist is not composing opera or writing novels. Instead, he or she is putting on an elitist show, often for audiences that are just as fetishistically elitist, like the ones that come not to enjoy themselves but to impress themselves and each other with their sensitivity and good taste, for example with how they refrain from applauding between movements until the last strains of the entire work have completely died down.

Frotteurism

Frotteuristic art merely scratches the surface like frotteurists merely rub without penetrating. The frotteuristic artist hits and runs in art to maintain the same distance from his feelings (most are men) and from his audience as the subway frotteurist maintains from his love objects by encountering them in public places, making certain that all concerned are part of the anonymous crowd.

Pedophilia

Carpenter's (1992) biography of Britten suggests over and over that a relationship exists between Britten's homosexual pedophiliac urges, his art, and a recurrent artist's block appearing in his music. W. H. Auden notes an "attraction to thin-as-a-board juveniles, i.e. to the sexless and innocent" (p. 164) that could conceivably parallel what others have noted in his music: a certain sexless, closed fisted, cold, and numb quality in an art that is "restrain[ed] . . . from full emotional commitment" (p. 79).

Of course part of the negative effect of pedophiliac art can be attributed not to the art but to the audience's response to the art, based on individual and group dynamics. Often, the audience knows of the paraphilia in the artist and fails to distinguish the art from the artist. Next, it evaluates the art not on its own but according to ad hominem criteria. The audience as a result responds excessively, and negatively, based on its own guilty conflicts. For example, some audiences do not like Britten's music because they consider it to have an intrusive fey quality. Others see Britten's preoccupation with boys in his frequent use of boys' voices. They sneer and turn away from Britten, and his music suffers the same fate, as one psychiatrist put it, "As dolphins when they swim with tuna."

Transvestic Fetishism

For one psychiatrist, one artist's pop art paintings were what she called "flimsy transvestite" art suggestive of the artist himself; for example, how he came to parties not to socialize but to show off his "snappy little outfit," preening and posing, impressing everyone he could find, then going home alone. For her, this artist's self-conscious, display-piece paintings and his "nudie movies full of cross-dressers" were "cut from the same ribbon" as his exhibitionistic appearance and dress (in particular, she emphasized what she considered to be his outlandish wig).

AFFECTING THE ARTIST'S CAPACITY TO WORK

We can all think of cases where paraphilias cause a work inhibition. For one thing, creative people, like everyone else, have limited energy, and expending energy in one area (the sexual) means it will be unavailable for another (the artistic). The ultimately unsatisfying nature of any one paraphiliac act means that promiscuity is part of the picture of many paraphilias, and there is nothing as preoccupying and energy draining as promiscuity. It seems to have fatigued even the indefatigable. The annals of composing and writing are filled with paraphiliacs who perhaps should have acted out less sexually and written more, but didn't in part because they were releasing tension and pressure that could have gone into the art, in sexual, instead of creative, escapades.

Another factor is guilt. Carpenter (1992) suggests that Britten was suffering from his homosexuality/possible homosexual pedophilia due to an acute sense of guilt about his sexual preferences. And the sense of guilt, as Ronald Duncan put it, "the sin he felt he'd committed" (p. 186), seems to have been one factor in Britten's ongoing partial, and intermittently complete, creative block. For example, Carpenter says, "He hoped that by committing himself to Pears he would be able to eliminate his powerful feelings for boys" (p. 161). Yet the relationship with Peter Pears itself was limiting creatively. Michael Tippett, the composer, "felt that Britten was now making too much musical use of Pears. . . . 'I didn't really feel that it was a very good way to go' " (p. 378).

We see evidence that guilt was a factor from how Britten's block lifted when he was able to overthrow sexual guilt. As Auden in essence puts it, when Britten understood the message in, "O bless the freedom that you never chose" he went on at once to create sparkling musical settings of poetry (p. 168).

9

PERSONALITY DISORDER BLOCK

Personality Disorder block arises when an artist's creative disorder mirrors his or her pathological character traits, like Meissner's (1985) inability to "tolerate delay" (p. 138), and "impulsiveness" (p. 396).

Condrau's (1988) case illustrates how a schizoid writer's remoteness and personal disenfranchisement in his life was reflected in his block, in a writer's cramp that expressed a fear of communicating openly, and being "*un*free" (pp. 215–216).

A patient, a paranoid writer, hesitated to write and publish because she felt both she and her works were not up to standard. Her "little voices" told her that if she expressed herself others would put her down personally, saying, "You don't have what it takes to make it in the big city," and professionally, saying "That's been done before," or "That's too quirky to be appealing." Consequently when she wrote, she wrote bland, ordinary, washed-out impersonal works to avoid revealing herself and provoking criticism from others. For the same reasons she sorted and sifted her writings, editing them down to virtually nothing. Predictably, her tight, desiccated works displeased and provoked her critics, who condemned her writing as "cold and unwelcoming," full of what one called "unemotional outbursts." Becoming angry at her critics (her anger suddenly released her from all constraint), she wrote her critics blistering letters that antagonized them and ultimately hurt her subsequent chances with them. The next time she wrote something, the negative reviews poured in, her mood was adversely affected, she retreated from expressing herself in her work, and so on.

SPECIFIC BLOCKS DUE TO PERSONALITY DISORDER

Paranoid

An important feature of Paranoid Personality Disorder block is a negative feeling about others that stains the creator's interpersonal relationships and causes him or her to withdraw from the world and sometimes to regress into protective creative inactivity. This element seems present in the blocks of Sir Edward Elgar, Samuel Barber, and Mili Balakirev, among others.

For Elgar, block seems to have arisen because he expected his intentions would be misunderstood, he would be slighted, and his music disliked. Barber seems to have blocked when criticized negatively, yet he was also suspicious of compliments. According to his biographer, Heyman (1992), he reacted to compliments in the paradoxical way typical of those with a Paranoid Personality Disorder: as if they were criticisms. "When Ramey pointed out to the composer that [his] *Third Essay* had more themes than either of the earlier two, Barber seemed irritated, remarking: 'I haven't analyzed it myself, but if you say so, then it must be true. There are indeed, several lyric themes in this piece. After all, it's not a federal offense' " (p. 503). Schonberg (1981) quotes from Alexander Borodin's description of what seems to have been a paranoid streak in the severely blocked composer, Mili Balakirev:

> [Balakirev] is so despotic by nature that he demands complete subordination to his wishes, even in the more trifling matters. He cannot endure the slightest opposition to his tastes or even to his whims. He wants to impose his yoke on everyone and everything. . . . More than once he has said. . . . "Why should I hear their things; they are all so mature now that I've become unnecessary to them, they can do without me," etc. His nature is such that it positively requires minors around whom he can fuss like a nurse around a child. . . . Meanwhile the alienation of Mili, his obvious turning away from the circle, his sharp remarks about many, especially about Modest [Mussorgsky], have considerably cooled those sympathetic to him. If he goes on like this he may easily isolate himself and, this, in his situation, would amount to spiritual death.
>
> Borodin was an accurate prophet. Balakirev soon broke entirely from the circle. In 1872 he left music completely to take a job with a railroad company. He felt rejected and useless, and he became a religious fanatic. (p. 366)

Paranoid block is discussed in greater detail in chapter 2.

Schizoid

Schizoid Personality Disorder block can be due to a carryover of personal remoteness into the art. The art develops the same "cold fish" restricted range of emotions that characterizes the artist's life and relationships.

One writer became a children's writer less because she empathized with children and more to distance herself from the adults in her life and to keep from being an adult herself. Excessive, "blushing modesty" about adult things was her stock in trade with people and her works for children, with their limited vocabulary and range of emotions and experience, were just the thing for her project of self-effacement.

Block can be the secondary result of the absence of those inspiring interactions with the world that many artists need, both to catalyze the creative act and (in this society) to provide the contacts required for promotion of the artist and his or her finished works.

Schizoids may suffer from false block, that is, they may look as if they are blocked when they are not. They paint, or compose, but, being shy, they hold their finished works back from us, and it looks like they are doing little or nothing at all.

On the positive side, schizoid artists can please similarly remote audiences who define greatness in art by the extent to which the art spares, rather than involves, them. Such artists (Was Salinger one?) are especially beloved by audiences who like their instinct bowdlerized into allegory. Steven R. Cerf (1994), in the program guide for Britten's opera, *Death in Venice* puts it, in essence, as liking their Dionysus transformed into Apollo (p. 18).

Schizotypal

Artists with Schizotypal Personality Disorder block are among the eccentric types who inspire others to write essays on the origin of creativity in the unconscious, or, what amounts to essentially the same thing, on the relationship between creativity and madness. While in some schizotypals the disorder creates the opus, mostly schizotypals do the same conflict-free art as everyone else, because their creativity, like the creativity of many others, comes not from their unconscious but from their supraconscious (the composer Roger Sessions's word for the fount of creativity, as quoted by the composer Andrew Imbrie in a personal communication). In many cases, if there is an effect of the bizarreness it is not a primary one, on the art, but a secondary one, on the business of making art. Schizotypals may block because of an existential "depression" that leads them to believe that "because nothing really matters in the infinite scheme of things, there is as little reason to go on creating as there is to go on existing." Or they block because they are so difficult to live with that they drive away those on whom they could or should depend, those who want, and are in a position to, help them in their career or support and tide them over during the rough times all creators experience in their lives and in doing their daily work.

Psychopathic-Antisocial

The term "Psychopathic-Antisocial" Personality Disorder describes both the *mechanism* of the disordered behavior, that is, the self-serving manipulative illogic and its personal and social *consequences*—its ultimately destructive effect on everything and everyone concerned.

Psychopathic-Antisocial Personality Disorder block consists of 10 percent inspiration, 10 percent perspiration, and 80 percent manipulation. The creator with such a block is all too willing to be artistically dishonest if deemed for a good reason, say, to produce appealing and trendy works that serve an immediate purpose, such as getting love and acquiring money. Instead of creating, the artist is impressing, manipulating, condescending, and pandering, all for effect, and all without caring if the results are empty and fated to fail the test of time, even in their own time. In sum, while the masochist wants to work without accolades, the psychopathic-antisocial artist wants to get accolades without work. And it is often all too obvious, for the artist is all show and little substance; all art studio and no art; all effect, and no affect. Does Giacomo Meyerbeer qualify? According to Schonberg (1981):

> Meyerbeer was not a fast worker. . . . *Les Huguenots* in 1836 . . . [was followed by] *Le Prophete* in 1849 [with one opera in between]. . . . Meyerbeer knew what the public wanted, and he [was] determined to satisfy them. . . . Naturally Meyerbeer became rich and famous. . . . [He] would try to mold critical opinion . . . anxious to keep the press on his side, [he] always would invite the critics, before everyone of his premieres, to a splendid dinner. . . . They staggered away from those meals with grand feelings of fellowship. "How can a chap of decent feeling," Spiridion [a critic] wanted to know, "write harshly of a man who has been pouring the choicest vintages of France and the most delicate tidbits of sea, air, forest, orchard and garden down one's throat? . . . There were few music critics in Paris who were not in receipt of annual pensions of several hundred dollars, and in one or two instances they exceeded $1,000 annually. . . . Meyerbeer used to defend this by saying that he did not put these gentlemen under obligations. He was the person obliged, and he could not see anything wrong in giving evidence of his gratitude to them." (pp. 244–249)

Meyerbeer's smooth pseudological paranoid justification of the payoffs illustrates what is meant by self-serving manipulative illogic, and his focus on popularity rather than art for art's sake what is meant by show over substance. It also illustrates how showy works may not live long—leading to what might be called delayed, posthumous block. As Schonberg says, "Today [Meyerbeer's] music sounds synthetic, flabby, and overcalculated, and the melodic ideas are second-rate" (p. 249).

While Meyerbeer seems to have worked hard, Cage's aleatory works and some of Warhol's paintings may fall in the category of too much inspiration and too little perspiration—as one artist put it, "all novel concept, but no novel"— with the inevitable comeuppance when the newness wears off, and audiences and critics suddenly recognize that the Emperor has few, if any, clothes. Caught, the artist disappears from view, leaving behind only what might be his or her epitaph: "I wonder what we ever saw in that!"

Some forms of plagiarism are symptomatic of an underlying psychopathic-antisocial disorder. Psychopathic-antisocial plagiarism is the (mostly) conscious fulfillment of a (mostly) conscious wish to appropriate another's material for gain, and to get away with it.

However, not all plagiarism is psychopathic-antisocial, that is, there is a differential diagnosis of plagiarism. Plagiarism is *masochistic* when the artist plagiarizes to get caught; *dissociative* when it is an automatic, trance-like, "not me but another one of my personalities" behavior; *narcissistic* when the artist feels entitled to appropriate from others because of "who and what I am"; *grandiose* when the artist believes he or she can get away with it and/or if he or she gets caught others will "wink" at it; or *impulsive* when the artist is so driven by the need for immediate personal gratification that he or she is guided by the pleasure, not by the reality, principle, his or her judgment so clouded that the artist denies either the reality or the consequences of the act, or both.

Plagiarism is *not* personality-disordered when it is (mostly) unconscious, for example, when a composer reproduces a tune without knowing that he or she did it, nor is it personality-disordered when it is inevitable. Given the finiteness of artistic possibility, there probably are a limited number of effective permutations and combinations in any one field of endeavor. Both the unconscious and the inevitable kind of plagiarism are nicely illustrated by how such tunes as the "Skaters Waltz," and "You Are My Sunshine" bear an uncanny resemblance to such other tunes as "The Daring Young Man on the Flying Trapeze." (Plagiarism is discussed further in chapter 13.)

Borderline/Hysterical (Histrionic)

Individuals with Borderline Personality Disorder alternate rapidly between merging and emerging, that is, first they overvalue others then they quickly devalue them. They also shift between liking and hating themselves, often from the grandiose to the depressive self-view, with an associated affective instability that can make them look as if they are suffering from a bipolar disorder.

At times Britten seems to have related in a borderline fashion. According to Carpenter (1992), Britten and W. H. Auden were friends for many years until "Auden sent Britten a letter [about Britten's opera *Billy Budd*] including praise but also criticisms . . . Britten sent it back, torn to pieces . . . [and] would have nothing further to do with Auden" (p. 325). Britten often dropped friends so suddenly that his "Victims would . . . complain that Britten had given them no warning, nor any explanation why"(p. 319).

Artists' borderline start-and-stop relationships with significant people in their lives are often reflected in an intermittent block due to a similar relationship with their work, and for essentially the same reasons. The artist blocks when he or she shifts from all loving to all hating *occupationally* in a way that parallels the tendency to shift from all loving to all hating *interpersonally*. In such cases, the artist often treats his or her work like an object, suddenly and unpredictably shifting between liking it and casting it aside or destroying it in the same way he or she alternates between merging with, and emerging from, people—first, swallowing them up to get close, and then spitting them out to maintain distance.

Feder (1992), in his biography of Ives, implies Ives merged or identified with his father. "Identification with George [Ives, Ives's father] spawned creative activity"(p. 288). Then he appears to have emerged, or, as Feder puts it, "the same dutiful impulse that generated the collaboration between Ives and his father [meant that Ives] had to call a halt to it" (p. 289). Was this a reason why Ives essentially abandoned music, a gradual process which Feder dates to 1918? (p. 286).

Ives's turning from music (and to business) brings to mind a musician/writer who developed and maintained a writer's block as a way to relate to a father who believed that Wall Street was the one and only road to happiness. It was a way to submit to and merge with his father and to avoid being punished for defying him. In essence, his block was a metaphor for dependence upon, and a defense against independence from, the father. It was a way to reassure himself, his father, and the world at large that, "I do not function as a mature adult," which for him was the equivalent of saying, "I am not a hateful, murderous rebel."

This man's father used a polio epidemic raging in the boy's youth to impress the son with the dangers of defiant independence. He kept his son in the house for months on end so that he wouldn't catch the virus, citing in particular the respiratory paralysis that resulted from polio as the wages of not heeding the warnings. Not surprisingly, given this background, the son listened well when the father also warned him of other dangers associated with going out into the world, particularly the humiliation, failure and abject poverty that are a "part of every artist's life."

Consequently, instead of doing art himself, he became a rabid aficionado of the arts, sophisticatedly admiring the work of others, and fooling himself into thinking he deserved to be admired as well for his good, perceptive taste about others' productions. Throughout much of his life he dreamed not of being himself creative but of making a great deal of money to leave upon his death, in trust, to commission works by others.

Like a fever crisis which peaks before it breaks, in his middle years the identification actually intensified just before it was to be abandoned, as he came to side completely not with the artist as rebel, but with his controlling, discouraging, philistine father. He became Samuel Johnson's "pettifogging critic." His pronouncements, which came to be dreaded by the artistic community, were in fact little more than "neurotic aesthetics" recreated almost entirely from the stuff of his father's prohibitions and warnings combined. Just as his father warned against going out of the house into a viral world, he railed against artists for being original, speaking up, stepping out of line, and trying to be themselves—all because they reminded him of his forbidden wish to be his own man, free from his father's influence, and control.

This merging stage with his father ended with his father's chronic illness and death. As he said, in essence, it was as if "spontaneously, late in my 40s, it rained in the desert, and there followed a sudden artistic blooming. I now emerged, breaking through the crust of earth like a spring flower, to blossom into the artist I always wanted to be, but my father would never let me become while he was still alive."

Narcissistic

Narcissistic Personality Disorder block is the result of what Paul Federn (1952) calls an excessive investment in "fore-pleasure which actually does not constitute full satisfaction" (p. 354). The disastrous consequences appear both in the art and in the artist's relationships. Some of Berlioz's works can be viewed as a kind of artistic autoerotism, programmatic art with the artist as the subject of the program, at the center of things. Some would agree that Mahler's art descends from the universal to the too personal and from there to the too neurotic. Preening, bluster, longueurs, and heart-on-the-sleeve are words sometimes used to describe Mahler's narcissism and narcissistic block. Schonberg (1981) says that "down deep . . . he *enjoyed* his misery; he reveled in it; he wallowed in it, wanting the whole world to see how he was suffering. . . . for Mahler never transformed the self in terms of the object. He transformed the object in terms of his self" (p. 456). Narcissism (and narcissistic block) is also present in the endless climaxing of the more pretentious music of Alexander Scriabin, where the net effect, on some listeners at least, is to drive them away, just like some post-surgical patients drive their listeners away by dwelling on their operations, and like some ex-soldiers with Posttraumatic Stress Disorder drive their families away by repeating their wartime experiences, seemingly unconcerned that a captive audience, having heard it all before, doesn't want to hear any of it again.

Interpersonally, narcissistically entitled artists expect love even when their works don't merit it. Then when they don't get it, they complain of rejection, make no constructive changes, and write no more, even though the criticism was warranted and improvement possible. Other narcissistic artists stop work deliberately to let their past glories carry them as a test of love, because they want their audiences to love them even in the adversity of inactivity—to be fans faithful through thin as well as through thick. Others put their audiences to a test of love by writing incomprehensible works. They place so many difficulties in the path of appreciation that they can be certain that any appreciation they get is motivated and strong simply by virtue of its having surmounted obstacles. (Block solidifies when the audience decides the obstacles are not worth it and loses interest completely.)

Still others avoid a test of love because they are afraid of failing the test. They avoid the test by writing for an in-group instead of for a wide cadre of listeners, controlling negative criticism by preselecting their critics.

Finally, some artists have to stop writing because they destroyed their careers with their narcissistic behavior either because they were too brash, snobbish, and superior to be long-suffered, or because an overconcern with their own needs was matched by an underconcern for the needs of the significant others in their lives.

While most narcissistic artists look self-centered on the surface, many are in fact very thin-skinned and have difficulty surviving the narcissistic injuries they inflict on themselves for not being up to both self-imposed standards and the standards others (who sometimes criticize them to maintain their own narcissism) inflict on them. Without the sustaining narcissism they need in order to be able to work effectively, they begin a process of withdrawal intended to avoid feeling, and being, rejected. This closes off some possibilities for expression and inspiring and growth-enhancing input. Their creative urge diminishes, possibly to the point that they slow down or even stop creating entirely.

Much of this could have been avoided if from the start they hadn't taken themselves too seriously and loved themselves too much.

Avoidant

Artists with an Avoidant Personality Disorder block because, afraid of rejection, they divert themselves from their work by keeping an eye on the world, an eye that should instead be on the page. As they write they ask themselves, "What will they think of that?"—really, "What will they think of me?" Too soon they convince themselves that they are, or will be, unloved, and, feeling, "What's the use?" they stop working entirely. They withdraw in, and from, their work because of, and to handle, the same fear of rejection that causes them to withdraw in, and from, their lives. Once established, they use their block as a distancing maneuver to protect them from further involvement and so from further rejection.

Dependent

Dependents personally subordinate themselves to others hoping to be loved. They often agree with their critics to avoid making trouble. And they write with the same subordination and resulting lack of self-assurance that they show in life. An excessive, almost pathetic, desire to please, associated with an overcaring about what others think, can take the form of a self-sacrificial willingness to revise when there is nothing especially wrong. We might also see a certain temerity in the art itself. Here the art becomes as thin-skinned and defensive as the artist. We see works that are too "short and sweet," held back, cut off, always apologizing for themselves.

According to Schonberg (1981), Bruckner was so eager to get his symphonies performed that he allowed anyone who wanted to edit them. As a result the first editions of his scores were written as much by others as by the composer (p. 455).

Alex Ross writing in the *New York Times* in the article, "Worlds Lost in Seas of Sorrow" (1994) describes what happened to the composer Ervin Schulhoff's original talent. The article perhaps illustrates the block that can appear when a passive-dependent desire to belong replaces an active desire to be great. Ross feels that "what happened to this brilliant, original talent . . . was that he threw his own career off course by seeking a universally accessible symphonic style . . . more neutral, more anonymous than before [and put] himself in league with the most trivial Soviet bureaucrat-composers . . . [when] the seductive ambiguity of the earlier style gave way to plain-spoken bombast. A quintessential musical victim, Schulhoff suffered at the hands of history but also fell into traps of his own devising" (section 2, pp. 26, 36).

Though at times a tyrant, Britten seems to have had a soft dependent side. According to Carpenter (1992) he said, "When I have ideas which may seem very new or bold, I'm nervous sometimes of telling Peter [Pears, his lover] about them. He's such a strong personality that if he says 'no' or takes a negative view, I'm discouraged, and can't go on with them" (p. 429).

Obsessive-Compulsive

Nemiah (1985a) describes those with an Obsessive-Compulsive Personality Disorder as preoccupied with control and so "lack[ing] flexibility, imagination, and inventiveness" (pp. 913–914). Block appears when character traits that are not themselves an indication of abnormality become excessive. For example, neatness and orderliness become crippling perfectionism, brooding uncertainty, and ritualistic doing and undoing. These can merely delay the artist, or, in an effect that is more final, the artist not only stalls but simply cannot go on—and gives up completely.

When the disorder appears in the art itself, the art becomes simultaneously indecisive and inflexible, weak and stiff. As previously mentioned in chapter 1, some of the works of the composer Max Reger have a "complicated . . . [and] cumbersome" (p. 1761) quality, according to Thompson (1964). Or the art can become impersonal—as when composers write twelve-tone rows to leave little or no room for themselves as individuals. In the field of psychology, personologists, from whom we would expect the most human of revelations, can often instead do no better than write works notably free of humanity—turgid, cool scientific studies that view the individual not as a person but as a compilation of traits determined by answers to questionnaires. They view their patients as specimens, and that not in virtual reality but either too up close, through the microscope, so that they see the parts but not the whole, or too far away, through the wrong end of the telescope, so that they see the whole, but not the parts, and at that a whole so diminished that it no longer has either meaning or impact.

Passive Aggressive

In passive aggressive block, the artist uses art to play the role of the defiant and rebellious adolescent, deliberately turning out provocative nose-thumbing works calculated to shock and annoy, often at the expense of being moving and inspiring.

Reading various accounts of the early student days of Ravel, we are led to suspect that Ravel, as a student, sullied his works with academia's bete noire—parallel fifths and octaves, the worst "crime" any student could commit—precisely to express his independence from his elders, and sass them. Ravel did get the sympathy vote from a world that supported him against those who were treating him badly by not giving him the official prizes everyone agreed he merited. But ultimately Ravel may also have created problems for himself and his art. First, an immediate one: these were not his best works, and instead of student masterpieces we have student sit-ins. Second, Ravel had blocks with depressive components later in life. Two in particular plagued him, one in the middle of his career, and his final block, which consumed five or so of his last years. Both of these blocks might have been at least partly a self-punitive recanting and atonement combined for his early so-called sins, the sins "of defying the father."

Sadomasochistic

Sadomasochism can have a direct or indirect destructive effect on creativity. In the corporate world, a once good worker became partly crippled and unable to do her job properly after accidentally wounding her arm on the job. Then she mutilated her wound by manipulating it to keep it from healing. She did this to simultaneously revenge herself for the on-the-job injury by getting a large insurance settlement, and to get the sympathy vote, first for having to stay home sick, and then, for returning to work debilitated and in "more agony than most could bear."

In the artistic world, masochistically prone artists commonly and even deliberately (though often unconsciously) bring real trouble down on their heads. Perhaps the artists who were blacklisted in the 1940s and 1950s became communists in part to deliberately destroy themselves and their art. Without discussing the propriety of the blacklist, and considering only the matter of the fate of the art, wouldn't the serious artist have been better off bypassing political aspirations, putting aside political beliefs? Perhaps David Diamond should have pushed his musical, not his political, interests in the same way and for the same reasons that Mahler and Bernstein should have put aside conducting for composing. Perhaps Mark Blitzstein's political preoccupations were part of a self-destructive style manifest not only in his art—in a rather limited output— but also in his flirting with danger by picking up lowlifes in homosexual bars, behavior by which he ultimately got himself killed.

As for the indirect effect on creativity, sadomasochism can undermine or destroy catalytic relationships with others. A case in point is Britten's sado-masochistic abuse of his friends. According to Carpenter (1992), quoting Duncan: "No man had more charm, could be more generous or kind [than Britten]—as I should know; but behind that mask was another person, a sadist, psychologically crippled and bent. Perhaps that's what we all are, but with less power, and with less charm to attract others to us, we do less harm and cause less pain than he" (p. 499).

This contrasts to what is "written" in a page from what we might call Stravinsky's "book of unblockage." He sensibly and practically dedicated his *Symphony of Psalms* both to God and the Boston Symphony Orchestra, possibly to assure himself both entry into heaven and a first performance.

The following are some of the mechanisms sadomasochistic artists use to accomplish their destructive ends:

Provoking interpersonal-critical abuse. Gerald Alper (1992), in *Portrait of the Artist as a Young Patient*, says creative blocking is a "suicide of the self" (p. 7). Masochistic artists unable to commit creative suicide on their own often encourage others to provoke them to it. This allows them to be innocent victims, viewing the hand they have in their fate as tied behind their backs. For example, Capote's provocative *Answered Prayers*, telling his best friends' secrets, must have been at least unconsciously meant to bite the hands that fed him, and provoke them to strangle him.

Block often begins when the artist, instead of accepting and walking away from something believed "bigger than I am," rails against his critics. He or she, unconsciously denying they will attack back, relies, in typical masochistic fashion, on the fairness and good sportsmanship of people the artist has recently condemned for being just the opposite. For example, Edwin Diamond (1994) describes how the author Gloria Emerson mocked the critic Christopher Lehmann-Haupt in the preface to her book, *Winners and Losers* (p. 30). She must have unconsciously, and self-destructively, wanted to abuse, and provoke, a powerful critic in a high place. Is there another explanation for such suicidal rashness?

Generally, critic baiting/bashing is impractical, even when warranted, not only because any self-respecting critic will defend attack, but also because he or she will be in a better position than the victim to do so publicly. They have a ready-made audience, appreciative of their skills, eager and prepared to take what they say seriously, and desirous of participating vicariously in the fun of the general melee, what Freud (1950) might call (referring to ganging up on and killing the father) having a seat at the head of the table of a totem feast.

Besides being impractical and dangerous for one's career, critic baiting/bashing is as unwarranted as artist abuse to the extent that it overlooks how criticism is itself a creative field. A legitimate source of pride to its practitioners, like any other creativity, it is difficult, if not impossible, to do well, let alone perfectly, on a regular basis.

Spending money unnecessarily. Masochistic artists often put themselves into debt deliberately so that they have to take a job to pay back the money spent. They know they will have to work a bread and butter job that, as Alper (1992) points out, will be predictably depressing and "humiliating" (p. 22)—depressing because it is boring, and humiliating because so many bosses, personally threatened in the presence of someone so special, put artists down just to enhance their own self-esteem.

Abusing one's body. The *DSM-III-R* suggests that masochists do things to inflict pain on themselves, like "having an accident" (p. 372). According to what we read in the lay press, the violinist, Michael Rabin, slipped on a rug, hit his head, and died from the injury.

Because music is more intimately associated with performance than the other arts, accidental, or accidentally-on-purpose, physical disasters seem to "have happened to" musicians more often than to other artists and certainly more than would be expected to have occurred by chance alone. It is sometimes hard to avoid concluding that musicians like the composer Schumann or the pianist Murray Periah mutilated the part of the body that they needed the most as an autocastration and minisuicide combined.

Abusing one's manuscripts. Stories of accidents with manuscripts abound in the annals of art. Artists seem to lose manuscripts either on their own or by sending them to someone unreliable to lose them for them. Does a masochistic set-up of the self explain why George Chadwick (n.d.), according to the album notes for his Fourth String Quartet, sitting in a beach chair on Martha's

Vineyard, allowed the wind to take away all the pages of a just completed movement of his Fourth String Quartet? "Walking on the W[est] C[hop] wharf one windy day with my portfolio, a gust of wind blew the whole scherzo off into Vineyard Sound!"

Abusing one's audiences. Writing about Sir Michael Tippett's opera, *The Midsummer Marriage,* Cori Ellison (1993) refers to the opera as a "heartening antidote" to "dodecaphonic academicism." Others, more forthrightly, call some dodecaphonic music music written for agony soprano and chamber orchestra. One composer felt much of it contained an unconscious, sadomasochistic streak, and the composer's goal was not to please the audience but to abrade on its feelings, and to grate on its nerves.

Ignoring available accolades. One would think that accolades are welcome, whatever their source, and whatever their nature. But artists seem to demean, or ignore, available accolades, perhaps simply because they are available. Typical is how Rachmaninoff came to hate his Prelude in C-Sharp Minor because audiences continuously demanded he play it. This "I don't want to be known as the man who played Norman Bates in *Psycho*" attitude is an essentially self-destructive one, if only because the artist avoids trading on and up from an advantageous position.

Masochistic artists sometimes avoid available accolades because they think an accolade for one work automatically means criticism for all others, like the joke about the man given two ties by his mother: when he wore one in her presence, she complained because it was clear that he must not like the other one.

Masochistic artists also avoid available accolades because they want to look for love in all the wrong places. Instead of pleasing those ready to be pleased, and accepting love from those ready, able, and willing to give it, they turn away from their approval and rise only to the challenge of those who either specifically dislike their work and them, or are impossible to satisfy. Then they cannot do their work because: they are overconcerned with getting admiration and love; they have put themselves in the position of dealing with unpleasant, rejecting people and situations; they allow themselves to be shocked by rejections they should have expected, because they asked for them; and they come across as desperate, which increases their vulnerability; and those bent on taking them down a peg or two do not hear pleas and try to help, but smell blood and move in for the kill.

Deliberately setting out to be what they are not. Ezio Pinza, an opera singer, wants to be Mario Lanza, a popular tenor; while Mario Lanza, a popular tenor, wants to be Ezio Pinza, an opera singer. Intellectual artists try to appeal by charm and seduction. They write self-help books even when remote academic tracts are their speciality and strong point combined. Conversely, charming and seductive individuals try to win points for being intellectually bright and write academic tracts ill-suited to their background and possibly their personality. (The *Liverpool Oratorio* of Beatle Paul McCartney is an example.)

Becoming excessively modest and shy. The more passive masochists use the admirable traits of modesty and shyness in a way that, while still admirable, is not helpful. What happens is that they self-demean and discourage positive feedback. Often they consciously self-demean hoping others will disagree with them. But unconsciously they know all along that others will believe them, even readily agree with their own negative self-assessment.

Abdicating to rivals/critics. In "The Psychogenesis of a Case of Homosexuality in a Woman," Freud (1957) calls this "retiring in favor of someone else" (vol. 2, p. 216). Melville's letter to Nathaniel Hawthorne was a masochistic abdication to the more popular writer, and one that might have subsequently motivated Melville's later block (see chapter 17). Boito's musical block seems to have been at least in part an artistic abdication to his rival (and co-author) Verdi (see chapter 4). The more passive masochists, like Bruckner, and to a lesser extent Barber, write and rewrite the same thing to please their critics. When, like Barber, they continue to do so long after the critics have ceased thinking about them, their revising seems less a way to improve their creative work than to torture and punish themselves by doing obeisance to those who tortured and punished them.

If there is to be torture, it is perhaps healthier for the creator to torture others, following the models of such "healthy torture" of others as Shostakovich's hostile anti-Stalin humor and Wagner's satirization of the critic Hanslick in his opera *Die Meistersinger*.

The oedipal theories of guilt over murder of the parent of the same sex and of the related complex called "fear of success" only partly explain the behavior of artists who yield instead of standing up and pressing on. Two other factors are (1) a fear of social approbation for being pushy, a bad sport, and a sore loser, and (2) a masochist's morality of guilt, including guilt over good narcissism, so that the artist shies away from all "selfism" because it is thought to be completely "selfish."

Rescuing others. This form of block, often associated with abdicating to rivals/critics, can result from resolutely, masochistically placing another's well-being over one's own. After his mother died, Rossini gave up composing in part to stay with, and take care of, his father. Some peace corps volunteers we have known were in effect blocked artists or businessmen (or both). And this is true of some missionaries as well. While some in the know refer to the missionary, Albert Schweitzer, in terms suitable for a god, others comment wryly that as the result of his altruism he played the organ like a doctor and practiced medicine like an organist.

POSITIVE VIRTUES

Masochism, often anticreative when expressed in the behavior, can be protocreative when expressed in the art. The sensitivity that is so integral a part of masochism and can be such an interpersonal, self-destructive vice, can become a creative virtue when integrated into and expressed in the poetry of suffering.

In general, masochism is protocreative when the masochist suffers to do art, instead of doing art to suffer.

TREATMENT

The treatment of most, or all, blocked artists will have to take their masochism into consideration. For all artists either start out masochistic or become masochistic as a way to handle the abuse (like spousal abuse) that to some extent all artists suffer at the hands of friends, family, and society.

In treating masochism the therapist often has to deal with a negative therapeutic reaction—masochists have a tendency to get worse because they are getting better. Cognitive therapy is particularly helpful for patients with a negative therapeutic reaction. First, it is an intellectual approach, and intellectual approaches by their very nature bypass negative therapeutic reaction which is, by definition, an emotional (transference) response to treatment. Second, it helps restore sensible, nonmasochistic thinking directly by challenging the illogic of masochism. The artist who learns that one critic is not all critics maintains perspective and, possibly, his or her sense of humor when he or she avoids making "someone doesn't love me" into "I am completely unloved." The artist who recognizes that even the most omnipotent critical colossus strides the earth with feet of clay avoids feeling stomped on.

As one artist put it, "When I function logically I can function well. I avoid being like the rabbit in the middle of the road who, instead of running to avoid harm, freezes in place, cars bearing down, tightening up more and more the nearer they get, as I am every second coming closer and closer to being run over, and crushed completely."

10

ADDICTION BLOCK

Creators commonly block because, as Mel Gussow (1994) puts it in a review of Hayman's biography of Tennessee Williams, they "undermine . . . [themselves] with addictions" (p. 21). The undermining addictions cause block either directly or indirectly.

ADDICTION CAUSES BLOCK DIRECTLY

Inebriated art emerges as disorganized, random, and incohesive, resembling the webs that spiders spin when fed LSD, or the art that apes produce when given paper and finger paints, that is, the art is excessively primitive, "old brain" or "reptilian." It is disorganized because there is no cortical supervision, or it is too predictable/pedestrian because there is no cortical contribution.

The acutely inebriated artist cannot work because he or she is intoxicated. According to Layton (1992), Sibelius, before he was to give a concert, was instead "eating oysters and drinking champagne and . . . seemed uncertain whether it was a rehearsal or concert. After the concert . . . he appeared withdrawn and confused" (p. 55). The chronically inebriated artist cannot work because he or she is *constantly* intoxicated and deteriorates mentally and/or physically from the effects of the toxic substances used. (The physical causes of block are discussed further in chapter 11.)

Addiction competes for the artist's energy and attention by becoming a substitute release or pleasure. Hayman (1993) says "the prodigious energy that had once been channeled into [Tennessee Williams's] writing was being waste-fully and self-destructively diffused [in addictions]" (p. 211).

ADDICTION CAUSES BLOCK INDIRECTLY

Addictions can create block by negatively affecting an artist's interper-sonal relationships. Drinking, for example, is a lonely activity that produces more loneliness, and, as Rothenberg (1990) notes, the artist's "self-enforced loneliness . . . may enhance the proclivity to drink" (p. 117).

In a vicious cycle, not only does addiction cause block, but the block it causes creates further addiction. As possibly happened to Tennessee Williams, the cycle often starts when the artist discovers that taking addictive substances is, at least in the beginning, a way to relieve block. In fact, the idea that substance abuse facilitates rather than stifles creativity and releases from rather than causes block cannot be completely dismissed as a romantic fantasy. As Hayman (1993) writes:

> Looking back twenty-four years later . . . Williams remembered that within a week of starting to write he began to suffer from writer's block. Having so little self-confidence, he was leery of wanting anything badly. Would it be wiser not to place himself in such a vulnerable position? Almost certainly he would fail to get what he wanted, even if his only ambition was to finish a story or a poem. As he says, "Having, always, to contend with this adversary of fear, which was sometimes terror, gave me a certain tendency toward an atmosphere of hysteria and violence." (p. 17)

> [When] "strong coffee no longer sufficed to get the creative juices to flow," he moved from place to place even more restlessly than usual, drank more, and took more Seconal, washing it down with double martinis or with Scotch . . . from then on, as he says, he wrote "usually under artificial stimulants, aside from the true stimulant of my deep-rooted need to continue to write." (p. 155)

> [I was] "broken as much by repeated failures in the theater as by Frank's [his lover's] death. Everything went wrong. My life—private and profes-sional—and ultimately my mind broke." . . . He was already signaling awareness of having exhausted a vein in his writing . . . a long run of success that could not have continued indefinitely. . . . He could not write, he says, until he began taking shots of speed. (p. 198)

Some of my patients argue persuasively that they write best, or can only write, when using marijuana. I had one patient who, otherwise rather untalented musically, produced a beautiful song, a tribute to his granddaughter, when stoned, and brought in the tape to prove it. Another patient dealt with the breakup with a lover by smoking pot and writing a book. The book, produced almost entirely while she was under the influence of drugs, turned out to be one of the classics of the 1960s literature on assertiveness training.

Some patients say that they write better (at least until they wake up sober) because when they are intoxicated they *think* they write better than they *do*, and this improves their self-esteem to the point where they actually *do* write better. Others point to how drugs foster creativity directly and indirectly, directly by increasing fantasy, and indirectly by removing inhibitions and relieving the anxiety and depression that result from the creative life and the creative process, especially the sometimes terrifying, unresolved childhood conflicts this process can arouse.

As for the creative life, Rothenberg (1990) notes: for "male writers and other artists, there may be a particular need to [use addictive substances to] counter widespread cultural images of effeteness or effeminacy or . . . to deny actual latent homosexual tendencies" (pp. 118–119).

As for the creative process, Rothenberg (1990) suggests that the artist uses "alcohol to cope with the anxiety that is generated by the creative process itself. . . . [W]riters and other artists are highly irritable during intense periods of work or for some time afterward" (p. 129), because the "unearthing process is fraught with a good deal of anxiety as it unfolds [and because] anxiety and strain arise from carrying out very high-level performance and the especially demanding work of creative accomplishment. There is conscious cognitive strain in the use of unusual logic-defying . . . processes . . . leaps of thought . . . mentally difficult to employ" (p. 127) to the point that "writers become depressed" (p. 129).

An infinite source of original and recurring anxiety about being an artist, one that seems to so often lead to drinking or taking drugs in search of resolution and relief, is to be found in persisting multiple identifications and counteridentifications with the artist's parents. When the parent is creative, and the artist's creativity originates in an identification, the artist has to struggle with the "devil" of conflicts about incest and merging, that is, getting too close and losing one's identity. When the parent is noncreative or anticreative, the artist has to struggle with the "deep blue sea" of conflicts about abandoning the parent and being abandoned.

Clearly the study of the relationship between addiction and block is in its infancy. More work is needed to learn why an artist becomes a user or an addict and what determines the effect of his or her use/addiction on his or her career. For example, why do only some addicted artists go downhill from single or multiple addictions, while others seem to preserve themselves by a process akin (as one patient said) to pickling, and still others (perhaps this was the case for Beethoven's alcoholism) have a disorder that shortens life but has little or no effect on art? As a tentative beginning, in any one artist the following factors may determine the course and prognosis of a given addiction, and the presence or absence of block due to that addiction:

1. The nature of the artistic pursuit. The familiar story of Coleridge writing *Kubla Khan*, whether true or not, and experience with patients, suggest drugs interfere with composing poetry less than they interfere with, for example, painting or playing the piano.

2. The physical and emotional makeup of the individual artist including, but not limited to, his or her physical attractiveness, which partly determines the amount of money an artist earns and, what is related, what others will put up with.

3. Chance, which decides perhaps as often as any other factor whether the artist meets people who will support and coddle the artist, or abandon him or her at the first sign of trouble.

4. Sexual preference, which nowadays is much mentioned but hardly discussed and rarely, if ever, integrated into a theory of blockage. Is there a relationship between sexual preference, creative ability, emotional disorder, addiction, and addiction block?

Aspects of such a relationship seem to have existed for Tennessee Williams and Barber. The following excerpt from Heyman's (1992) biography of Barber illustrates and helps explain this relationship:

> Contributing significantly to Barber's low morale and compositional inactivity for five years between 1972 and 1977 was the forced sale of Capricorn, the home he and Menotti had shared for thirty years. The upheaval was to Barber equivalent to the dissolution of a marriage . . . by the middle 1960s their personal lives had become less and less interwoven, and Barber frequently found himself alone in their residence in Mount Kisco. . . . "I don't feel very musical," he wrote . . . in March 1972. . . . "I am not up to much. . . . [I] cannot get started on any musical work. Just tear up beginnings. Not the first time! . . . The continued unsale of Capricorn makes winter plans so difficult and depressing for us both . . . nothing inside of me!" (pp. 487–489)

Fischer-Dieskau noted about this time that he was "shy [and] considerably depressed. . . . Barber's depression, observable even to those who barely knew him, intensified as the sale of the Mount Kisco house became imminent and his health failed." He said, "I really feel as if I have no home." By 1973 Barber moved into an apartment which he "intensely disliked . . . and during this time often drank excessively, occasionally suffering memory blackouts" (p. 493–494).

5. Geographical factors, such as where the artist lives. In a number of cases, artists have gone to the suburbs or to a small rural town to compose or write only to become isolated because, of course with some exceptions, small towns don't suffer artists gladly. Instead they

tend to see them as a threat to the town's family and work orientation. The isolation, lack of acceptance, and general feeling of rejection can provide the artist with just the excuse he or she needs to develop an addiction tendency already in place, or actually lead directly to drinking or taking drugs.

PREVENTION AND TREATMENT

Are there any blanket words of advice about prevention and treatment of addiction in artists? Ideally, and speaking from the limited perspective of creativity itself, the cause of creativity is best served, and preserved, by avoiding substance use entirely, that is, by relative or complete abstinence. Whatever positive effects accrue from substance use, or abuse, they are temporary, rarely sustainable (for both emotional and physical reasons), and create more problems in the short and long run than they solve. Yes, it reduces tension, but this tension can advance art. Yes, it produces fantasies, but these come more from the unconscious, contaminating art, than from the supraconscious, producing art. Yes, it gets the brain working, but it also produces brain damage—the last thing a creative person needs. And yes, "everyone" is doing it. But everyone doesn't have a gift, so delicate, and so worth preserving. The artist who doesn't drink, smoke pot, use cocaine, or take LSD does the best of all.

11

PHYSICAL BLOCK

To date, the physical causes of block have been almost entirely neglected in the literature, perhaps because most writers on creative block are not physicians. In this chapter, some of these physical causes of blockage are discussed. The chapter is in two parts: The first part discusses block that is a symptom of medical or neurological disorder; the second part presents some nonpathological physical paradigms of creative block. These paradigms by themselves shed further light on creative block; additionally they suggest related areas where further research into the phenomenon of blockage is likely to prove fruitful.

This is but an introductory sampling of medical and neurological causes for block. The goal is not to present a complete differential diagnosis of medically and neurologically caused blockage, but to alert the clinician to the necessity of differentiating medical and neurological from emotionally caused blockage and treating accordingly.

Because of the enormous difficulties in clinical typing of some medical, and many neurological disorders, and the parallel enormous difficulties in relating medical and neurological clinical events to their underlying pathophysiological cause, medical, and especially neurological, diagnoses of creative block made here purely on clinical grounds must be viewed as somewhat to highly speculative, at least in all but the most straightforward cases.

CAL DISORDERS THAT CAN CAUSE BLOCK

ᴅɪꜱ.nhibition (Logorrheic or Hyperactive) Block

Disinhibition block is what Truman Capote, according to legend, and in another context, called "typing, not writing." There is material, but little organization, and so less art. Melville described disinhibition (not, however, the kind due to physical causes) so beautifully, but, alas, so prophetically, in a letter to Nathaniel Hawthorne: "I should have a paper-mill established at one end of the house, and so have an endless riband of foolscap rolling in upon my desk; and upon that endless riband I should write a thousand—a million—billion thoughts, all under the form of a letter to you" (Melville 1851 [1981], pp. 536–537).

While disinhibition block is mostly emotionally caused, it can also be a manifestation/symptom of medical disorder, such as hyperthyroidism or Cushing's disease/syndrome.

Inhibition (Retarded) Block

Inhibition block, the most familiar kind of blockage, can be a manifestation/symptom of diminished hormonal secretion such as that found in hypothyroidism (as in myxedema madness due to decreased thyroxin) or in Addison's disease (due to the decreased secretion of the hormone ACTH). It can also be, and often is, an effect of the treatment prescribed for medical disorders. In particular, block-like symptoms can result from the side-effects of medications ranging from antihistamines to antihypertensives. Older patients on a number of medications simultaneously (sometimes more than they need and can comfortably tolerate) often complain of retarded blockage-like symptoms, and too often the response to such a patient is more medication, which only adds new block-like side effects to the old blockage.

NEUROLOGICAL DISORDERS THAT CAN CAUSE BLOCK

An example of how blockage can be an unrecognized symptom of a neurological disorder is the case of Sibelius. Though Sibelius wrote little (or nothing) during the last thirty-one or so years of his life, drank heavily, and seems to have told untruths about the existence of an Eighth Symphony, I have not seen an official differential diagnosis of his blockage that includes the possibility that he suffered from Alcohol-Induced Persisting Amnestic Disorder (Korsakoff's Syndrome), though this could certainly have accounted for both his blockage and his tall tales (possibly confabulations) about having written what seems to be his nonexistent Eighth Symphony.

Along similar lines, there have been cases of pins-and-needles cramp of the legs in athletes (and others) due to alcohol-induced polyneuropathy misdiagnosed as conversion block; sensations of tightness, numbness and tingling of the hand due to a central neurological lesion misdiagnosed as pianist's cramp; and both Postconcussional Disorder and early Alzheimer's dementia dismissed as the result of depression due to emotional conflicts about creating.

Much of the following presentation is adapted from Seymour R. Solomon's (1985) "Application of Neurology to Psychiatry" in Kaplan and Sadock's *Comprehensive Textbook of Psychiatry* (vol. 4, pp. 146–156).

Disinhibition (Logorrheic or Hyperactive) Block

Frontal lobe lesions. These may cause a disinhibition, in part due to a loss of self-consciousness. Or they might result in fluent aphasias that look either like an inability to organize, or a conscious, purposeful refusal to organize, one's thoughts. For example, in the symptom of hypergraphia we have what Solomon (1985) calls an "obsessional phenomenon . . . [where the patient writes] extensive notes and diaries . . . [with] *verbosity* . . . the vocal correlate" (p. 153). This is in effect an organic version of what Nelson (1985) calls "note-taking disease" or "thesis block" (p. 99).

Gilles de la Tourette's Syndrome. This is in part a disinhibition disorder where the patient says things he or she otherwise wouldn't say, shouldn't say, then wishes he or she hadn't said, yet nevertheless keeps on saying them.

Inhibition (Retarded) Block

Frontal lobe lesions. These may also cause an inhibition, manifest as diminished motor activity associated with a lack of spontaneity and loss of initiative. This inhibitory block can be due to an interference with cognitive and emotional *elaboration* of thinking and feeling. The inhibition that occurs from spontaneously occurring disease is similar to the one that some clinicians deliberately induce by frontal lobotomy, viz. one done for chronic pain or mania. Here the intent *is* to inhibit, in the case of chronic pain, to interfere with the elaboration of objective pain into subjective sensation, and in the case of mania, to interfere with the elaboration of limited into generalized, and subjective into objective, euphoria.

Lesions in areas of the brain other than the frontal lobes. These can produce such inhibition-blockage-like symptoms/syndromes as psychomotor retardation, apathy, unconcern, agraphia (which Dorland defines as the "inability to express thoughts in writing, due to a central lesion" [1951, p. 51]), memory defects, disturbances of arousal, alerting, and awareness, expressive or motor aphasia (that can mimic conflicts over self-expression), Parkinson's disease (that can mimic emotional blunting, disinterest, withdrawal, or emptiness), and disorders of consciousness, including dreamy states.

Organic amnesia. This disorder can mimic amnesia of emotional origin and the blockage that is part of that amnesia. Ravel, for example, had tunes running through his head but forgot them when he tried to capture them. As previously mentioned, Orenstein (1991) notes that "Ravel's . . . mind was replete with ideas, but, when he wished to write them down, they vanished" (p. 107). The recent memory defect and confabulation of Korsakoff's Syndrome might have accounted for Sibelius's later symptoms of block.

Postconcussional Disorder. An impairment of concentration and memory can make it difficult or impossible for the artist to work effectively. Again, the example of Ravel, who had recently been in a taxi accident: "Professor Ala-jouanine, who examined Ravel during the last few years of his life, observed that the composer's ability to understand speech was far superior to his ability to speak or write. As the aphasia progressed, the reading of music became difficult and finally impossible" (p. 105).

Epilepsy. Epilepsy can be associated with an interictal personality (the personality disorder sometimes found in epileptics between seizures) that resembles some forms of blockage due to emotional factors. The interictal personality is, according to Solomon (1985), notable for a pseudo-obsessional viscosity characterized by the "tendency to adhere to each thought and action . . . preoccupation with excessive detail . . . thought processes [that] are circumstantial and perseverative . . . [and] a stern moralism and associated humorless sobriety [that] calls for strict attention to rules" (p. 153).

Dyslexia. Both input (such as the ability to read) and output (such as the ability to spell) are in effect blocked.

Attention Deficit Disorder (ADD). Some subtypes of ADD are of neurologi-cal causation and can cause/mimic inattention to, and an inability to concentrate on, one's work.

Stuttering. According to Charles W. Popper (1988) stuttering is characterized both by an inhibition of the ability to express what one wants to say—"blocks on sounds, syllables, or words"—and a tendency to perseverate in what is actually said—"prolongations, repetitions" (p. 693).

OTHER MEDICAL/NEUROLOGICAL ASPECTS

Biochemical Causes of Block

Synaptic depletion. Depletion of the level of intersynaptic brain serotonin may cause creative depletion/exhaustion directly, or it may cause it indirectly, as the biochemical lesion that causes depression.

Endorphin withdrawal. The endorphin rushes from the pleasurable fantasies of triumph and the reality of applause are very addicting. Endorphin withdrawal is one reason why failure is so devastating to the artist. For the artist deprived of the applause of success is deprived not only of love and money, but also of the pleasurable chemical effects of these substances.

Genetic Causes of Block

If the family lineage, amateur father to professional son, so often found in cases of creative *ability*, can indicate a certain genetic predisposition to being artistic, can there also be genetic predisposition to creative *disability*, that is, to being artistically blocked? Can constitutional factors contribute to diverse instances of blockage, ranging from specific blocks like stage fright, to diffuse blockage, such as a falling off of inspiration?

There has been much discussion about the role of hormonal difference between the sexes in causing creative blockage, along the lines of, "Why aren't there any great women composers?" Some answer, "testosterone levels." But how can they tell what is nurture (society) and what is nature (hormones)?

PARADIGMS OR MODELS (NONPATHOLOGICAL) OF BLOCKAGE

Paradigms of somatic blockage illustrate how common blockage is in every-day life and suggest areas of further research into the phenomenon of creative block.

Motor or Output Damping

Motor or output damping block occurs because two things cannot be done at once—the familiar difficulty of simultaneously patting the head and rubbing the stomach. Artists who have too many irons in the fire only to discover that being good at everything means not being great at one thing in particular may be suffering from motor or output damping block.

Sensory or Input Damping

In sensory or input damping block an external input, like noise, or an internal input, like anxiety, damps an external input, like reading, or an internal one, like inspiration. The most familiar example is constant interruptions interfering with the creative process.

This form of blockage can be for the good. For example, Dr. Stephen Hudis, a dentist, uses this blockage for good when he wiggles the lip as he gives a novocain shot, so that the former keeps the patient from feeling the latter. Artists use this blockage for good when they shut out the external world by playing music as they work to facilitate their descending into that state of deep thought that is often one prerequisite for working creatively. Some defense mechanisms, denial particularly, rely in part on damping external input (like negative feedback) to reduce internal anxiety.

Creativity usually is not the beneficiary but the victim of damping, which has the tendency to start small with good intentions, then spread and reduce the artist to complete silence.

Inertia

Nerve tissue at rest seems to want to stay at rest. This property of nerve tissue can account for certain aspects of artistic temperament like stubbornness and inflexibility, and can be one reason for that kind of laziness that yields only to persistent effort, what Joan Minninger (1980) calls the necessity to "keep on keeping on" (p. 157).

Paradoxicality

Asking our neurological mechanism to do something for us can have the reverse effect. Intermittent ("normal") insomniacs who want to fall asleep often cannot do so until they get up and work, at which time they become very tired and cannot keep their eyes open. Intermittently impotent men and women often find that the harder they try the more difficult it is to perform and have an orgasm. Absent-minded people who try to recall a name they have forgotten cannot do so until they give up trying, when the name obliges and returns as if on its own, when least expected. What and why this happens seems to be a mystery at the present time. But even though paradoxicality isn't understood, it can be used to lift block. Jay Haley got block to lift by suggesting it; he encouraged a worker to get up on time for work by telling him *not* to set the alarm clock (personal communication).

Insomnia

Intermittent insomnia of the spontaneous variety (distinct from chronic pathological insomnia and insomnia induced by drugs such as cocaine) is a nonpathological paradigm for block in that it is a blocked, natural physical function.

Low IQ

Low IQ, and the low intelligence it purportedly measures, can be a neurological paradigm, really a cause, for creative block. But in many cases it is uncertain if creative block results from or is a cause of low intelligence. At some point in the future, it may be possible to prove that IQ tests to an extent measure not only intelligence, but also the effects of creative block on intelligence.

Some view high as well as low intelligence as a combined model, correlate, and cause of creative block. For while on the positive side high intelligence helps us to think, on the negative side it also "helps" us to be depressed and paranoid. One characteristic of the truly intelligent is that their intelligence enables them to see too many possibilities in life: the negative as well as the positive. Nothing gets by them, and as a result they are often tense, angry, depressed, and paranoid—emotionally, intellectually, and interpersonally blocked.

Standard Dreams/Nightmares

The dreams/nightmares that all of us have, like examination dreams, dreams of running in place or being unable to move forward, and dreams of waiting for the bus or subway train that doesn't come, are often little more than throwback symbolic tales of blockage—dreams of, about, and from the universal Ur-tendency to block.

These dreams have a source in our current life, including our present-day conflicts and difficulties. But their main source is in our collective unconscious, which represents our collective heritage, genetically passed down from generation to generation.

Dreams that originate in the collective unconscious have an atavistic quality; they refer to behaviors that were useful in the past but are no longer so. For example, successophobic dreams of being unable to get somewhere may refer to ancestral, reasonable, and protective fears of going too far from home into unsafe territory. Of course, this becomes inapplicable when the unsafe territory is not the snake infested tundra but the stage on which the high-school valedictorian gives his or her speech. Everyone has these dreams because we all come from the same primordial stuff. They are difficult or impossible to associate to because they are not merely a product of what happened recently (the day's residue) but of what happened long ago, what might be called "ancestral" residue. Because of our inability to associate to them, these dreams seem to lack individual profile and meaning. As a result few patients, or therapists, attempt to interpret them even in a general way. Therapeutically speaking, they not only can, but sometimes should, be interpreted as dreams of blockage, to reveal the presence of hidden (missed) block (see chapter 13).

Reflexive Behaviors

Here, as in atavistic dreams/nightmares, block appears as itself, relatively undisguised. Reflexive behaviors—an animal rolling over and playing dead; an animal freezing when in danger of being attacked; denial of death hormonally mediated when suffering from a terminal illness or about to be hurt or executed; dissociating (fainting, seizing, or fuguing) to avoid an unpleasant inner reality like anxiety or an unpleasant outer reality like abuse; and hibernating to conserve energy (a possible biological prototype of seasonal affective disorder)—are all, from one perspective, a display of in-bred, primitive, prototypical blockage behaviors. As with dream images, these behaviors might be thought of as duplicating behavioral aspects of block that originated in evolutionary times, but have lost their original meaning and purpose and are no longer helpful, protective, defensive maneuvers, but counterproductive, harmful, reflexive flinching—a sudden, automatic stepping backward, but off the cliff. Agatha Christie's (1977) description of her stage fright is a good example of how primitive (as well as counterproductive) this reflexive behavior can actually be. Christie, one of our supreme intellects, puts it this appropriately "gutsy" way: "I could not control my *physical* reaction" (p. 152).

THERAPEUTIC IMPLICATIONS

Two therapeutic implications of the atavistic nature of blockage dreams and reflexive behaviors are (1) To the extent that blockage is primitive and nonverbal, that is, silent, "silent intervention" treatments like reassurance or kindness can help more than verbal therapies that rely overmuch on the development of insight. This is obvious to anyone who has said meaningless but soothing words to a dog paralyzed with fear because its path is strewn with large objects like garbage cans, and (2) Because of the old-brain (or "reptilian") character of some aspects of blockage, drugs like inderal and the benzodiazepines, which probably affect the old brain, can be as, or more, useful than psychotherapy, especially in the treatment of such primitive fear blocks as stage fright.

12

CHRONIC BLOCK

Chronic block results when an acute block has recurred once too often, or gone on for much too long. While many artists manage to experience full recovery after one or more episodes of block, others deteriorate and develop chronic, or end-stage block. The pattern traced on the way to end-stage block is one familiar from the development of other chronic disorders. As a disorder progresses to become first subacute then chronic, the profile of the acute disorder becomes less distinct and assumes a set of new and different characteristics, some of which are attributable to the chronicity itself. Eventually the characteristics attributable to the chronicity itself take over, until we can no longer tell what the problem looked like originally and no longer distinguish, within subsets of disorder, one end-stage disorder from another.

To take an example from the field of medicine, acute hepatitis can be of alcoholic, viral, toxic, other, or unknown origin. In the beginning we can often (but not always) distinguish one viral hepatitis from another and viral from toxic hepatitis due, for example, to chloroform poisoning. But over time those hepatitis patients who survive, and who survive with deficit and deteriorate, tend to develop, regardless of what initiated the problem, mostly similar signs and symptoms, such as: chronic weakness and fatigue, jaundice, loss of weight, and profound debilitation sometimes leading to death. Not only does it become progressively more and more difficult over time to identify the original cause of the hepatitis, but also the signs and symptoms of one chronic hepatitis (like chronic hepatitis B) are similar to those of another chronic hepatitis (like hepatitis due to chronic alcoholism). Furthermore, "new" symptoms, such as progressive wasting, develop due, partially, to the chronicity itself, so that we are seeing a different disorder, which we now call "chronic hepatitis" to distinguish it from the old disorder, "acute hepatitis."

Ruth Fox (1955) described a similar progression as acute becomes chronic alcoholism. She emphasized how alcoholism is a disorder that can begin as a symptom of many familiar emotional disorders, such as anxiety or depression, or physical disorders, such as headaches or back pain. As she says, "Excessive drinking [is] a symptom [that] may indicate that the person is . . . suffering from a specific disease entity, [such as] a psychoneurosis" (p. 147). The anxious patient drinks to face life, the depressed patient drinks to improve mood and get some sleep, and the patient with back pain drinks to relieve his or her physical suffering. But eventually alcoholism becomes a disorder in its own right, with its own social, personal, medical, and occupational stigmata. As Dr. Fox says, "The symptom is so gross that it must be treated all by itself, and stopped, before its roots can be explored and in turn treated" (p. 147). Anyone who has entered a restaurant for dinner and seen the look-alike people standing at the bar drinking since lunch can appreciate what Dr. Fox means—how end-stage alcoholism is an entity in its own right, how it presents a set of unique symptoms and problems, and how difficult it can be to learn what the early stages were like from the present clinical picture.

As for end-stage creative block, Samuel Barber and Tennessee Williams seem, when they were young and just starting out, to have been very different people with very different (intermittent) blocks. Barber seems to have been more organized (perhaps obsessional and depressive) than Williams, and seems to have blocked due to excessive perfectionism, while Williams seems to have been more fey (perhaps hysterical and borderline), and seems to have blocked due to affective dysphoria. Yet at the end, their blocks were depressingly alike: both wrote little; both had severe interpersonal problems; both drank heavily; both seemed to have signs and symptoms suggestive of organic deterioration; both were depressed; and, important for our purposes, both were considered to be, and treated medically as if they were, suffering not from creative block, but from substance abuse disorder.

In the clinical progression from early to end-stage creative block, recovery from one or several minor or major blocks is with deficit. The block is over but not its consequences. The artist is constantly anxious because he or she is fearful that block will return. He or she worries, "How am I doing?" and becomes hypersensitive and hyperalert to, and paranoid about, how others are evaluating him or her. Feeling isolated, and worried about the future, he or she tries too hard to please fans and critics and begins to create not to say something meaningful, but to be loved. This alerts the sadists out there that there is a wounded animal in the vicinity, and they move in for the kill. The artist retreats to lick wounds and heal. Others feel abandoned, and deprive the artist of the personal warmth needed for recovery. Substance abuse offers a ready source of immediate relief, but soon creates more problems than it solves. The artist seeks professional help, but treatment is difficult because of the complexity of the presenting picture; now there are too many real problems for the therapist to handle easily in psychotherapy (for reasons described below). An artist's wife or lover abandons him because after a few years of being unable to write he is not the rich and famous person she married. An artist's husband or lover abandons her because she is too preoccupied with her block to be sexually active. Finally, the artist drops out of sight, bitter, depressed, and paranoid. Everyone asks, "I wonder what happened to him?," or, "Where is she now?" but no one tries to find out because when the artist's production goes, so does his or her cachet. If we ever hear about the artist again, it is in the obituary pages.

THERAPEUTIC IMPLICATIONS

To date, most attempts to cure writer's block have been relatively unsuccessful, in part because the artist has waited too long to get help. It is much harder to cure chronic than acute block, and there are three reasons why. First, the therapist no longer can use the time-tested methods that have been developed for curing the familiar syndrome underlying the block. Treatment approaches to phobia, anxiety, depression, and so forth have been worked out, but treatment approaches for chronic block have not. The therapist, having entered the unknown seas of a field where little work has been done, and where even less of proven effectiveness has been discovered, is forced not to reinvent, but to invent the wheel. Second, psychotherapy is better at resolving emotional problems than it is at repairing broken lives. The longer a block lasts the more it affects the artist's life. Once the block has gone from the creative into the everyday life, as when it has disrupted needed relationships with others and caused financial problems, the therapist is forced to step out of the role of therapist and into the role of social worker. Social workers make effective therapists more often than therapists make effective social workers—a role essentially foreign to and sometimes incompatible with "pure" psychotherapy. And third, mostly applicable to conversion blocks such as pianist's cramp, to achieve complete recovery treatment must begin before secondary physical complications, such as disuse atrophy, have set in. It is difficult enough to be a concert pianist. It is usually impossible when the pianist has to overcome not only the competition and stage fright, but also wasted muscles or tendons beyond repair after having been surgically cut for no good medical reason.

13

MISSED BLOCK

Artists and those who study them tend to miss blockage either because they (1) overlook block that is overt, or because they (2) are unable to identify blockage because it is covert.

As therapists we overlook overt creative block because our threshold of suspicion is low or because we deny it when we see it. As a result when we speak of J. D. Salinger's unproductivity we emphasize his isolation; we say Herman Melville turned from writing novels to writing poetry; we call Truman Capote and Samuel Barber alcoholics; with Nelson (1985) in effect we excuse E. M. Forster's "uneven artistic output [as] . . . a natural condition of creativity for many" (p. 168); or with Rothenberg (1990) we err completely when we overlook block in Sibelius, though he wrote nothing much for the last thirty or so years of his life, and include him in a list of those artists who have "no demonstrable mental illness" (p. 158).

Block can be covert/hidden because it is in its early, formative stages (preblock); because it is transient; because it is embedded in the art as distinct from in the artist; because it affects what we consider to be a nonartistic skilled profession like law or business, or semiskilled profession like plumbing; because of poor insight on the part of the blocked artist, who might deliberately or unconsciously skew the history he or she gives the therapist away from block; because of poor insight on the part of the therapist trying to understand the artist; because it is acted-out interpersonally or professionally, say in derivativeness or plagiarism; and because it is not absolute, but relative.

EARLY BLOCK (PREBLOCK)

It is currently fashionable to blame block on parents who pushed us around when we were children, not on ourselves for allowing (and continuing to allow) ourselves to be pushed around. It may not be fashionable to think so, but the child who lets his or her parents talk him or her out of an artistic career can be less the innocent victim than we think. Even children, at least by the time they have entered the phase of anal-rebellion, can stonewall and plan their escape from discouraging parents. If they don't—if they yield because they identify with these parents—it is often not merely because all youth is helpless, but because a choice to block has been made actively and consciously or unconsciously, based on a hereditary, genetic timidity or an already apparent characterological passivity.

At the moment of decision, many children fail to capitalize on their native gifts by taking the nonartistic fork in the road. For example the individual histories of males with artistic block is replete with examples of how as children they abdicated to a father who wanted them to enter one of the safe professions; and they complied to avoid antagonizing the father, or identified with a passive, self-effacing petit bourgeois father as an expression of love. And the individual histories of females with artistic block is replete with examples of how they accomplished essentially the same thing by abdicating to or identifying with a self-effacing "stay at home and clean house" mother.

Psychologists who test such children to see what occupational field they should enter sometimes find them giving answers that reveal less about their preferences and talents than about their interaction with their parents, which reveals more about their personality than about their objectives and abilities. In one case a child who said, "I want to be a doctor," when he in fact wanted to be an artist, did so to express his compliance, while in another case a child who said, "I want to be an artist," when she really wanted to be a doctor, did so to express her defiance. In these cases the tests seem to have scored not the potential for professional success based on interest and ability but the potential for professional block based on interpersonal conflict.

TRANSIENT OR INTERMITTENT BLOCK

Blocks that are hidden because they are transient or intermittent sometimes precede major blocks much as small strokes sometimes precede massive cerebral hemorrhages. They tend to be unnoticed or if noticed called by such names as temporary lulls or much-needed rests. Many authors, such as Toye (1987) writing about Rossini, and Kennedy (1987) writing about Elgar, downplay how the artist blocked one or more times for a few months or so early in life before the final great block, and don't describe the block as such. Kennedy, though he states Elgar regularly got depressed and proclaimed that he was forever through with music, never uses the term block in connection with this composer's early and frequent creative stops and starts.

Block can start and stop due to *alternating* identification and counteridentification with a generally discouraging parent. Block can also start and stop due to persistent identification with a parent who alternately discourages and encourages creativity. (Transient/intermittent block due to either pattern of identification stands in contrast to persistent block, where the block lasts and lasts either due to a continuing identification with a parent whose main wish is to discourage a child artistically or to a continuing counteridentification with a parent whose main wish is to encourage the child artistically.)

A physician/writer would write a novel full time, then take a full-time job seeing patients and not write; then quit his job to write a novel full time, and so on. His behavior was the product of alternately identifying with (submitting to) and counteridentifying with (rebelling against) a father who disapproved of the artistic life but allowed the son nonartistic, that is, skilled, professional alternatives, so that, to paraphrase an old joke, he could be any kind of doctor he wanted to be. The dangers of not cooperating were conveyed in illustrative anecdotes that told of the terrible consequences of defying authority. One was the father's favorite "don't make trouble" story—a combined credo and warning that related the terrible fate of the medical school student who was thrown out of school merely for disagreeing with the professor.

Because of his childhood habit of alternating between rebellion and guilty abdication, he went, later in life, from a rebellious phase, where he did art full time but ate poorly, to an abdication phase, where he worked a bread-and-butter job, ate well, but wrote nothing at all, then back again. The obvious solution, but the one that was never taken, was a part-time job and part-time creativity. But this solution was unsatisfactory because it would have eliminated the element of neurotic gratification that he got from alternately defying and submitting to his father.

We see parallels to this patient in the composer Lukas Foss who, as another composer, Francis Thorne, tells the story (personal communication), alternately got himself thrown out of Paul Hindemith's composition class at Yale for disagreeing with the professor, and then went to Serge Koussevitsky, the conductor, to get reinstated; then he disagreed with the professor all over again, with the same results, and so on.

BLOCK IN THE WORK ITSELF

Fear of Positive Feelings

The fear of positive feelings may be why Barber could compromise some of his most lyrical melodies by giving them a sour, tight, "scruntchy" withholding cast in an overuse of the interval of the minor second; why

Shostakovitch sometimes contaminated the sublime with the ridiculous, say by making jokes at inappropriate times; why Cage overused improvisation, leaving it up to others to write his compositions for him; why Joyce used neologisms few could understand without considerable help; why Stravinsky embraced unemotionalism directly, according to legend, announcing that there was no place for feeling in music; why Debussy, in his opera *Pelléas et Mélisande*, seems to have preferred declamation over melody, at least in the vocal parts; why some poets discuss their relationship with "man and mankind" in the abstract to avoid confronting and dealing with any relationship with one "man" in the concrete; and why so much scientific literature is full of precision but empty of the open-armed humanity that would give the precision life and relevance. This kind of block appears even in works on block. For example, rarely in Leader's (1991) otherwise comprehensive list of reasons for blockage do we see the human dimension. Reading Leader leaves us with the impression that artists block because of oedipal conflicts, which is certainly true. But we fail to get the impression that artists also block because of low pay and an abusive society, which is certainly also true, and often as, or more, important.

Withholding

Did Sibelius have an Obsessive-Compulsive Disorder of the same kind manifest in artists who miss deadlines to torture their editors, and did this disorder figure early on in his manner of working in his Fourth Symphony? Here he presented a bit of the melody, then a bit more, keeping the whole back until the very end. Was this a musical expression of an orneriness/stubbornness that worked here artistically, but surfaced later in a nonproductive, neurotic withholding of his Eighth Symphony from the world?

Some artists who withhold in their masterpieces stay much more stuck in place than Sibelius did in his music. Were Victor Hugo's massive discursions at the expense of the story line unconsciously intended to divert? Did he know he had a good story, yet keep it back, to torture his readers? The answer is yes if we judge intent on the basis of readers' reactions. One psychologist I know, Dr. Fred Harris, an avid, sophisticated, and omnivorous reader, refuses to read *Les Misérables* because Hugo's (1862) diversions anger him. Others dislike Wagner because they sense something almost personal in his taking so long to come to the point. Rossini said, "fine moments but some bad quarters of an hour" (Toye 1987, p. 221). And the critics' remarks about Barber's *Anthony and Cleopatra*, on the order of, "more went on between than during the acts," seem at least in part to have been provoked by what one critic thought might have been Barber's hostility to opening night audiences, who some see as philistines wanting not to hear art but to be fed pap.

Fear of Commitment

Some artists express a fear of commitment in meandering and repetition. They never develop an idea or come to the point. They do this in order to avoid expressing themselves—which means showing their hand and having to take responsibility for what they say.

BLOCK IN A NONARTISTIC FIELD

Even the experts tend to overlook artist's block when it occurs in what are considered to be the skilled nonartistic fields, like law and business, or the semiskilled nonartistic fields like clerking. Who would suspect the owner of a local convenience food store of artist's or creative block just because he regularly parked his beat-up broken car in front of his store, hood up—an unappetizing sight indeed, really a gesture of defiance—unconsciously meant to turn his customers' stomachs and drive them away?

There are people/patients who looked like professional misfits though they were in fact creatively blocked:

- the train conductor who falls asleep at the switch because he is an insomniac when in fact his insomnia is part of a secret plan to stay awake all night so that he cannot do his job the next day
- the office worker who instead of doing her work spends the first part of the week looking forward to Wednesday afternoon, which she calls "hump day" ("thank God the week is half over"), the second part of the week looking forward to Friday afternoon ("thank God it's Friday," or "TGIF"), then all of the weekend, starting with Friday night, dreading Monday morning when she will have to return from a weekend of terrifying anticipation to a work week of terrifying actuality
- the boss who bankrupts the company because he demoralizes his workers by remaining silent when they do a good job, speaking up only to criticize them for doing a bad one (less a way to supervise workers than a way, as one wag said, to "make mice neurotic")
- the therapist who sleeps during therapy sessions, or with his patients
- the therapist who hides her humanity, and that of her patients, underneath the protective cloak of the controlled study
- the therapist whose objective is not to uncover the patient's problem but to find the perfect therapeutic drug combination to suppress it
- the worker who takes a second job she doesn't really need ostensibly to support herself in style, only to find the second job encroaches on, then completely cannibalizes, the first

- the school child who is afraid to go to school because of a fear of leaving his mother, then, forced to go, never arrives because he falls down and hurts himself or arrives only to be taken away again because on the way he vandalized a car, or a cemetery

- the student with a so-called learning disability whose dyslexia is a subtle sabotage of those who want her to read

- the doctor who has trouble with his relicensing because he answers the questions on the renewal form honestly, admitting he had psychiatric care (though it was over twenty years ago) for impotence, a problem more likely if anything to enhance than to interfere with his devotion to his medical work

- the fashion model who used to be the adolescent who got the tragic pimple on prom night and now is the adult who breaks out in acne the day of every important shooting

- the anorectic adolescent who refuses to eat, saying, "Let me take just one more roll of fat off to look good," but really meaning, "One more pound down and I'll be too weak to work"

- the single who cruises in the wee hours to meet "Mr. Right" but, instead of gaining a lover, merely loses a good night's sleep

BLOCK THAT IS OVERLOOKED DUE TO POOR INSIGHT

The Artist's Poor Insight

Throughout life many individuals rationalize their block as preferential, or sensible. They keep a pedestrian bread-and-butter job for the friendships they make at work, or because it makes sense to assure themselves that they can always make a living in case they fail at being an artist (when in fact they are assuring themselves that they will fail at being an artist so that they can always make a living).

Rabid aficionados rarely realize the extent to which their hobby is a way to be passive at the expense of being active. Many of them are talented people who dissipate their talent by becoming members of the audience instead of the performing troupe. A stereophile putting a great sound system together; a user of interactive television having input into the program; a jokester telling, really retelling, great jokes; and a computer buff using the most complex programs he or she can find and master think they are creating, when they are really being less creative than recreative. While there are exceptions, in so many of these cases not only is self-esteem elevated out of all proportion to actual accomplishment, but the false sense of well-being engendered keeps the individual from doing the original work of which he or she is capable.

The Therapist's Poor Insight

Jack-of-all-trades are often admired instead of treated as blocked. We admire Rachmaninoff because he conducts as well as composes instead of wondering if he was a slow composer because of his conducting. We admire Bernstein for being the eclectic Renaissance man, when we might pity him instead for what seems to be his frantic overactivity; perhaps he spent too much of his life not composing but searching for an approving father.

BLOCK THAT IS ACTED OUT

Some individuals act out self-destructively by changing careers, or simply quitting their jobs at the pinnacle of success, or to avoid that pinnacle. I have known homosexual creators who die young from AIDS because, threatened by too much success, they celebrate their first applause by getting drunk, having unsafe sex, and deliberately giving themselves a fatal illness. We merely bemoan the effect of AIDS on the artistic population, rather than bemoaning the tendency of a blocked artistic population to give itself AIDS.

Self-destruction is also accomplished indirectly by offending others who are, or might be, in a position to provide emotional support or advance a career.

One creator sacrificed her personal life to enhance her professional life. She went on long promotional tours and accepted teaching assignments far from home. Ultimately her husband complained and threatened divorce, and she became too depressed to do any work at all.

An advertising executive, a womanizer, tried to seduce women on the job, turning his workplace into a personal brothel. These on-the-job affairs, which sometimes came precariously close to sexual harassments, were meant as self-esteem enhancers. They were, of course, ineffective, first because he couldn't handle low professional self-esteem with personal solutions, like amorous conquests, and second because his personal conquests, instead of enhancing self-esteem, provoked unintended personal and professional criticism. As it turned out, the boss found out about what he was doing, complained about his poor judgment, and threatened to fire him. He got depressed because he was being criticized. Then his performance worsened, which provoked more criticism, which caused him to become more desperate to be liked, and this caused him to try to have more and more affairs, and harass more and more women, and so on.

Older people are often experts in this kind of self-destructiveness, especially when they act more over-the-hill than they actually are. An eighty-six-year-old man suffered from a sadomasochistic creative block consisting of an inability to play his clarinet blamed on physical causes and encroaching senility. In fact the real reason was that his false teeth didn't fit properly, and he hyperventilated, which made his fingers too tingly to move properly and close the instrument's holes. He could have easily gone to a dentist to have his teeth adjusted or remade so that the embouchure would form properly. But he claimed, falsely, that he lacked the time and money. And he could have consciously controlled his hyperventilating by willing himself to hold his breath. But he didn't, citing "an emotional disorder beyond my control." His psychiatrist finally understood the real nature and meaning of his behavior when it appeared in the transference to the psychiatrist: He asked the psychiatrist, "What kind of music do you like?" and when the psychiatrist replied, "Contemporary, odd-ball stuff," he promptly returned with a gift tape of the Gershwin Piano Concerto and the Bernstein Overture to *Candide*. Though neither even remotely qualified, he said, "These would be just perfect for you." When confronted with the apparent contradiction, he blamed his "misjudgment" on his poor memory due to encroaching Alzheimer's (a favorite way many elderly have of rationalizing their block). What was encroaching was not Alzheimer's but true intent: the wish to deprive the psychiatrist of pleasure in music in exactly the same way he deprived himself of exactly the same thing.

DERIVATIVENESS AND PLAGIARISM

Assessment of derivativeness/plagiarism (or, what amounts to the same thing, of originality) requires correction for:

1. Subjectivity, when it is acceptable for Haydn to sound like Mozart, Dvorak to sound like Brahms, and Ravel to sound like Debussy, but woe to Andrew Lloyd Webber for sounding like Puccini.
2. The field the artist is in. Derivativeness, though undesirable in one creative field, like music, can be desirable in another creative field, like physics, where a prominent fingerprint can be a manifestation not of genius, or originality, but of idiosyncrasy.
3. The time in which the artist works. For example, it appears that the baroque artists were not obsessed with originality. They were content to speak in the tongue of their era.
4. The artist's intent. William Schuman's derivativeness (in his popular songs) was, so the story goes, part of a deliberate plan to write his next song just like the last hit song, so as to make as much money as possible.

Complex issues surround plagiarism. How much do we have to copy before it is plagiarism? and How conscious does the copying have to be? Is Elgar right that it is "a composer's business to invent tunes, not to quote them or base them on the quaint sounds of the past" (Schonberg 1981, p. 510), that is, using folk tunes without telling is cheating? Because we can explain something should we excuse it? Is plagiarism excusable if it is a masochistic need to suffer by ultimately getting caught, an irresistible impulse or compulsion to appropriate, or even, developmentally speaking, a dependent fixation on a mother figure associated with a fear of being independent? Or do these formulations signify the use of analytic insight as a defense against guilt and the accusation of willfulness?

There are two types of plagiarism: the benign and the malignant.

Benign Plagiarism

One form of benign plagiarism is self-plagiarism where the artist borrows parts or wholes from his early work. Many authors "write" a book consisting entirely of old papers collected under a new roof; Rossini writes *Le Comte Ory* by appropriating much of his earlier *Journey to Reims*; Barber takes his old themes from *Vanessa* for his Piano Concerto and from his Second Symphony for *Anthony and Cleopatra*; or Dvorak or Poulenc merely repeat certain fragments, not as if suffering from a morbid fixation but as the artistic equivalent of the raconteur's pleasurable retelling of a beloved old joke, as a way to get started, as a bridge over temporary lack of inspiration, or because in reality they need something quick and easy to fulfill a commission.

Also benign is the unsuspecting kind. Meredith Wilson's "I'll Never Say No" from his musical *The Unsinkable Molly Brown* can be found in the Brahms Horn Trio in E-Flat Major; Bernstein's "Ohio" from his musical *Wonderful Town* in the Brahms Second Piano Concerto; Beethoven's Fourth Piano Concerto in Mozart's Eighteenth Piano Concerto; Edouard Lalo's Symphony in G Minor in Dvorak's Cello Concerto; and the first eight notes of a melody in Barber's Piano Concerto in the song, "Margie." Modeste Tchaikovsky asks us to imagine Tchaikovsky's surprise when he discovered that the opening theme to his *Pathétique* Symphony (p. 721) was almost the same theme as the opening theme to Beethoven's *Pathétique* Sonata. Is it heresy to mention Bach here? After all, he appropriated Vivaldi's concertos, if not as his own, than at least for his own purposes.

Indeed, benign plagiarism may even be a universal driving force behind all creativity. In one philosophy everything creative ultimately consists of little more than elegant and clever recycling of old material, so that Bach's Mass in B Minor has much in common, if not spiritually than at least technically, with Warhol's recycled Campbell's soup cans. Can it be that all genius is merely collage and parody, well done, as Oliver Knussen quoted by Humphrey Carpenter (1992) might put it, the "small components [of others deployed] within big masses" (p. 260) of one's own?

Malignant Plagiarism

Malignant plagiarism is, in contrast, to the right on one or both of two continuums: the first between a completely unconscious and a completely conscious act, and the second between a little, and a lot of, stealing. However, none of the discussions of plagiarism have convincingly drawn the line between benign and malignant plagiarism.

RELATIVE OR PARTIAL BLOCK

In cases of partial block it is often hard to know if an artist is working beneath potential, that is, how well he or she could have done compared to how well he or she actually did. A judgment call is difficult to make in part because all standards of excellence and effort are relative. We are hard put (except perhaps in extraordinary cases on the level of Bach or Shakespeare) to detect inherent goodness independent of fashion and individual preference. And it is difficult to answer such questions as, "Is partial block present in any composer who writes fewer works than George Phillip Telemann, or any writer who writes fewer novels than Georges Simenon?" Some cases where the artist possibly could have done better, or more are:

- Leonard Bernstein's block, characterized by keeping a finger in every pie.
- Anton von Webern's block, characterized by a total lifetime output of about three hours of music.
- Thomas Hardy's and Herman Melville's blocks, characterized by changing from novelist to poet, with (some think) lesser results.
- James Michener's and Grandma Moses's blocks, characterized by getting started late in life.
- Milton Babbitt's block, characterized by "not caring if they listen" (the quote misattributed, but applicable), that is, by a possible disdain for one's audience.
- Mili Balakirev's and Alexander Borodin's blocks, characterized by taking long breaks, instead of settling down, and working right through.

14

POSITIVE ASPECTS OF BLOCK

The therapist treating writer's block soon discovers that blocked artists however much they complain of their block also find it desirable and relinquish it reluctantly.

BLOCK AS A DEFENSE

William W. Meissner (1985) in his article, "Theories of Personality and Psychopathology: Classical Psychoanalysis," includes block in his list of the basic defenses, calling it an "inhibition, usually temporary in nature, of affects especially, but possibly also thinking and impulses . . . close to repression in its effects, but . . . [with] a component of tension" (p. 389).

For one artist block was defensive because it reduced the anxiety and the fear he associated with creating. First, there was anxiety over the exposure that went with creating. In describing this anxiety he said that stage fright was a metaphor for his life. Then there was the threatened punishment for that exposure. He said he felt pursued when creating, as if he were playing a game of hide and seek, and as if he were not merely "it," but an animal being chased, soon to be caught and punished for the naughty things he said, which he felt of course revealed the naughty things he did.

Block also had realistic advantages. It protected him from what he hated most about the artistic life, particularly, as he put it, "alpha, intercourse with the narcissists in the audience who feed on my talent, who feel they own me, and act on it by demanding I think of them at all times, though I don't even know they exist, and beta, having to put up with the critics who abuse me until I am tempted to follow the advice of President Calvin Coolidge—to not say anything at all so that I won't be called upon to repeat it."

Defensive block also provides many artists with a source of secondary gain. As a sick person the artist gets sympathy, not criticism, from others. They hold his or her hand, and mother him or her a little.

BLOCK AS A CONDITION OF ART

Blockage can be a pro- not an anticreative force when it provides grist for the artist's mill. An artist can write about his or her block, or use his or her own experience of overcoming block to help others to do the same thing. Block also fosters art in the manner we believe Jean Cocteau was suggesting when he said, "without resistance you can do nothing" (Nelson 1985, p. 4). For art kept underground can simmer there like a fine stew, ripening, and developing flavor. And art kept underground can gain strength from pressure undischarged, building up a head of steam, developing power.

BLOCK AS A USEFUL EXPEDIENT

Block Can Be a Prop for Self-esteem

Many artists reason: block is a disease, and a disease is something you can't help, and use the "disease of block" as a face-saving excuse and justification for anything from taking an undeserved vacation from work to suppressing what is on their mind because they are excessively guilty about what they have to say. One artist, ashamed of his inability to be as successful as he would have liked, said, "Block may not avoid failing, but it at least avoids the reputation of being a failure." Another artist liked the idea of being what he called a "creator emeritus"—a grand old man of art—because for him the status of has-been was an improvement on his former, alas well-deserved, reputation of being a "never-has-been."

Block as Cogitating

While for some artists obsessive brooding is tantamount to obsessive blocking, for others brooding and postponing action is useful as a delaying tactic that gives the artist time to study a situation carefully, and make difficult choices (like a career decision) leisurely and without pressure. For still others brooding is a way to relieve guilt by justifying action after the fact—to come up with good reasons for what was done impulsively, or even maliciously.

BLOCK AS A POSITIVE INTERPERSONAL FORCE

Block helps many artists maintain relationships at the expense of their art, instead of the other way around. For some, block is a way to control/avoid expressing anger in order to keep relationships intact. For others block is a way to keep peace within the family by creating or maintaining satisfying neurotic relationships at home, as when an artist takes a bread-and-butter second job to support a mate's financial irresponsibility, to appease one who is creatophobic, or to maintain a passive role. For still others block is a way to deliberately, or unconsciously, withdraw from art to find pleasure elsewhere, in friends and family.

A well-known opera star constantly worried about her voice going, who would take care of her financially and personally after she passed her prime, and how she could meet anyone marriageable if all she met were theater people who were either, as she said, "gay, or insincere and flighty straights." So she left the opera, married an "ordinary business man," had several children, and stayed home, "behind my picket fence." She told her therapist, in essence, "You may call this professional artistic block. I call it personal release, and fulfillment."

An artistic woman married a blue-collar man. He intrigued her because he was sexy and as unlike her father as any man she could find. But though life in the bedroom was at first close to perfect, outside of the sexual relationship problems arose because he was creatophobic, that is, he saw her artistic endeavors as a threat to his supremacy and as an embarrassment to his friends, "who don't care for that sort of stuff." In desperation, and at the expense of her self-satisfaction, she blocked "to keep my marriage going."

An artist's wife seems to have come alive when, and only when, her husband was depressed and blocked. She was so solicitous of him then, and only then, that one suspects that she needed him blocked because she liked, and needed, to take care of the sick.

This kind of block once formed becomes a part of the daily lives not only of the artist but of his or her friends and family, and is maintained in part because it is pleasurable, and in part because everyone is as threatened by potential unblock as is the artist him- or herself.

BLOCK AS A WEAPON

For some, blocking is an interpersonal weapon. Many editors suspect, and they are often right, that they are being tortured by artists who withhold when they request, and legitimately need, something from them.

Spouses, parents, and strangers who want the artist to create (some do) can also be tortured and defeated by artistic block. This may seem unusual, but I know of at least one case where a woman became a doctor to defy a parent who wanted her to be an orchestra conductor.

A musical comedy writer who started off writing "for his mother" found block useful first to express oedipal disappointment in her, that is, to gain revenge on her for loving his father more than she loved him, then, when she died, to get back at her memory for what he believed to be her abandoning him.

For one restauranteur creative block consisted of burning the food to revenge himself on customers who complained it was underdone. Along similar lines, a well-known men's only restaurant some years back deliberately either under-cooked or burned food served to women to discourage them from coming in and "liberating the men's bar."

A landlord's artist's block involved dumping valuable properties to be rid of impossible tenants who, as he described them, "rent a loft for the large rooms, high ceilings, and wall-to-wall windows, only to complain of the dwarfed furniture, echo, and drafts."

Artists like Rachmaninoff overkill the same way the landlord does when they block to be rid of their own "impossible tenants," like narcissistic audiences who make outlandish, inappropriate, or perseverative demands of the play "Melancholy Baby" kind, or judge the composer or writer not by the wonderful things he or she does, but by his or her dull moments, dead stretches, and misspellings. For many such artists block is a revenge: a defiant but self-sacrificial throwing out of the bath-water to maroon the baby. The reasoning often goes like this: "You had my flawed presence. You complained. Now let's see how you like my perfect absence."

15

FALSE BLOCK

Some artists think they are blocked when they are not, and they are not because either (1) they are talented, but lazy, or (2) they are perfectly normal, that is, they are not suffering from blockage at all.

LAZINESS

There are talented people who do some work but on the whole take the easy way out—individuals whose main creative contribution is in the concept, not in its realization. For example, John Cage argues convincingly that *4'33"*, about 5 minutes of silence, *is* music because it is the *inverse* of music.

Those who do what they like to do but not what they have to do will not write until the spirit moves them, or they write but try to avoid the difficult and unpleasant part of writing, such as editing what they wrote. Some in this category say they need naps after the slightest exertion because of a chronic fatigue that is really a too-easy fatiguability, and, finding anything at all stressful to be Stress with a capital *S*, they develop what one called "a low threshold for burnout because I have a low threshold for burn."

Those who wait for inspiration to avoid working and continue to wait though it does not appear, do this so that they can convince themselves they are actually involved in a project. Among the members of this group we find those who dissipate their talent in Bohemianism. They work hard, but mainly at maintaining an image. They focus on creating not art but a life-style. Specifically, they confuse being an artistic type with being an artist, and artistic temperament with artistic production, and in general they tend to blur the distinction between grandiose daydreams and grand accomplishment.

Therapeutic Implications

Artists who have talent but do not use it because they are lazy do need sympathy. But they need it *after* they get help, say in the form of a little push toward organizing their lives and realizing their potential.

NORMALITY

Normal pseudoblockers think they are blocked when they are not. They might think they are failures because their standards are impossibly high. A children's writer, going over her life, thought herself lazy though she wrote thirty-two books in as many years. In order to be able to call herself blocked, she had to selectively forget that this is, overall, an impressive lifetime outpouring.

For some, a second idle becomes idle forever, anything less than all becomes nothing, and anything short of exhaustion becomes laziness. How much work they did yesterday doesn't make up for how little they are doing today, even when they worked overtime yesterday to make up in advance for a holiday they planned to take today. For others, being slow and precise is the same thing as being blocked. Ruth Belov Gross (1991) thought herself blocked because she was considered, thoughtful and careful, because she "approaches her work with meticulous care." "It isn't easy," she says. "It can take me hours to write one paragraph." This may not be block. Schonberg (1981) tells us that it sometimes took Chausson days to write one measure, and he was a great, and productive, composer (p. 418).

Common Reasons for Normal Pseudoblock

Normal silence. Even the most dedicated, talented, and hard-working artists should not expect themselves to work effectively nonstop. Creating is in general a discontinuous process full of what Nelson (1985) calls "Random Silences" (p. 166). Diurnal variation is one reason for what appears to be the random discontinuity of creativity, though it is not random at all, but a natural, intraday variation whose rhythm is both expected and predictable. It is characterized by and results in having progressively less and less to say as the day wears on, so that, for reasons unknown, creativity declines in the afternoon, is revived overnight, reappears in the morning, then declines again later the next day. The reverse process is at work when creativity improves as the day wears on. This often happens because the artist has a depression and a depressive block, both of which (characteristic for depression) improve toward afternoon. When creative swings are unpredictable from day to day this suggests that not internal but external triggers are at work for creativity, or, what amounts to the same thing, are at work against it, and for creative block.

Normal preference. Some of us criticize ourselves for not wanting to be an artist, and view being an artisan or other so-called nonartistic professional as a sign that we are blocked creatively. But raising a roof can be as, or more meaningful than, raising the muse, although we must admit it is stretching a point to view the author Michael Crichton (as according to legend he sometimes viewed himself) as a blocked doctor. The cave man who hunts is not necessarily a blocked artist unable to paint the walls of caves. Thinking it is is a manifestation of what Giovacchini (1984) refers to as our overinterest in "artistic, cultural, and humanistic affairs" (p. 475) where we in effect come alive at the mere mention of creativity, and only then.

Preference is different from true block rationalized as preferential (and appropriate and justified) behavior. To illustrate, a decision to take an early retirement can be preferential (and appropriate and proper) for basketball players and ballet dancers who want to quit when they are still young, and ahead. But painters, composers, and writers should never retire for that reason. Theoretically, they could go on forever.

Competing interests provide an infinite source of material for rationalization of block in this way. For example, Chou Wen Chung, a composer and instructor, started a cello concerto in the 1970s and didn't finish it until the 1990s. His (all too patent) excuse: "I was too busy teaching" (personal communication).

Personality traits. Normal workaholism, discussed in chapter 3, is a common personality trait that accounts for pseudoblock. As discussed in chapter 2, shyness that is within normal limits is another.

A normally modest creator looked blocked because he refused to show others his work, though it was going well. He was not ashamed of his work, nor did he want it taken from him by guile or force so he could disavow responsibility for writing and publishing it, nor was he looking to gain points for modesty, nor was this a false modesty like that of the composer who, applauded at his premier, instead of proudly accepting the applause and bowing thankfully, applauded back because he couldn't handle the congratulations. It was because, "I am simply a private person, who hates people who brag, and show off, and so I refuse to do so myself. Being shy is not, after all, a federal offense."

Sociopathy. A sociopath who is blocked because he or she lives in and develops the ways of a blocked society is abnormal to those who focus on the block itself, but normal to those who focus on the degree of social adaptation. Blocked societies are the familiar ones that post bumper stickers that read, "The worst day fishing is better than the best day working." They discourage artistic thinking, behavior, and endeavor. They criticize the artist freely and often personally. They make him or her generally uncomfortable or an outcast. Some even specifically prohibit artistic activities like music and dancing, and often do so on moralistic grounds hidden beneath spurious financial ("we can no longer afford to fund this") or aesthetic ("this is not my idea of art" or "this is obscene") considerations.

PART II
CAUSE

EXTERNAL CAUSES

THE RELATIONSHIP BETWEEN EXTERNAL AND INTERNAL EVENTS

Though many artists have real problems that are upsetting enough to dampen even the most lively spirits, and block even the strongest souls, most discussions of creative block emphasize internal over external cause. In particular they let society, its audiences, and critics off the hook as potential sources for creative block. By ignoring society's contribution to blockage, they make things worse for the artist because, by blaming the artist entirely for block, they add the element of external criticism to the already heavy burden of internal guilt.

Society has tended to blame women composers for being lesser lights than men because they were women. It was not testosterone levels but the lack of positive feedback that created a relative dearth of "great" women composers before the mid-twentieth century. Few women composers "made it" in the eighteenth and nineteenth centuries because composing, more than, say, writing fiction, is performance dependent, and the prejudice of the times kept women from getting as many performances as they needed. Yet hearing one's works performed is necessary for intellectual, personal, and emotional growth. Without it artists become like Spitz's marasmic babies: in the absence of any, but especially positive, input (stroking), they fail to thrive.

Today things have changed, and although a case can still be made that there are no great women composers, the reasons are different. It seems as if there are hardly any Mozarts or Beethovens at all—women or men. Finally, women are treated equally, or nearly so, as men. Alas, and this is where block comes in, too often all that this means is that they are treated equally badly.

Of course, in the real world, most blocks are the result of the interaction between external and internal events, and the separation between the two is mainly an artificial one. In real life block commonly happens when the artist brings something of his or her own sensitivity to external events that are entirely or almost entirely not of his or her own making. For example, the artist contributes a psyche that has been previously traumatized, so that the artist is intolerant of rejection present because of rejection past. Fate is not tempted. Some pitchers block just because they lose a game, but most block because of what the loss means to them. Or, financial problems, bad enough in themselves, usually only cause block when they stir up moral conflicts like the one between writing pure, academic, abstract artistic works for glory, and so-called impure, popular, concrete ones for money. Bad reviews, never welcome, become insupportable for those who already feel guilty about their success because they feel they achieved success by defying their parents or by stepping over their colleagues' dead bodies on their way to the top, or for those who need unalloyed love from the world, either because they were deprived of or overindulged in love when they were children.

Grieving artists are particularly apt to react adversely to external events. The annals of biography and autobiography are full of artists who functioned free of block until they lost a parent or a spouse, when they collapsed, often because of a relatively minor incident. Grief can make artists blow things up out of proportion, creating major out of minor events. In particular, it causes them to view constructive criticism as destructive and to confuse every attack on a creation with an attack on the creator. Life becomes a love-me-love-my-music contract, one that the artist makes with the world unilaterally, and that the world breaks unilaterally.

Sometimes, of course, external reality is so harsh that it would affect anyone merely trying to do his or her work. At other times external reality is of one's own making. In this scenario an artist eager for a case of block may look for or provoke an event he or she can use as a convenient excuse to have a block he or she always wanted to have, but couldn't justify. Some artists, in other words, are a case of block longing for a reason to happen.

A writer of technical books said he was able to turn out a book a year until his brother died and his wife retired. Then he began having production problems and difficulties with publishers.

He blamed his block entirely on his wife, saying she destroyed him because now that she was retired she constantly wanted to go away on ski vacations when he needed to stay at home and go to the library, the only place he could write. The constant blaming so depressed her that she left him and filed for divorce. Now he claimed, "I can't work because I miss my wife so much."

But why was the library the only place he could write? Surely because writing is portable, there must have been other places. There must be something he could do on the ski slopes, say, in the morning, before his wife got up, or in the afternoon, when she was taking a nap.

One day he confessed that he saw to it that the library was the only place he could write so that he could hang over his wife's head how she was taking him away from his work. And he further confessed that he needed to be taken away from his work to handle his survivor guilt. He felt it was unfair for him to be above, while his brother was under, ground. The least he could do was to pay his brother back for this unfairness by burying a part of himself—his art—alongside his brother, in the grave.

EXTERNAL CAUSES

Reasons for Rossini's Great Renunciation

Each time Rossini was asked why he stopped writing (Great Renunciation) he gave different answers. Some interpret this as avoiding the topic. Perhaps it indicates facing it squarely and with a remarkable degree of insight into the multiple factors that caused what was clearly an overdetermined symptom. As Toye suggests, "No single reason . . . suffices to account for his 'great renunciation'; several causes . . . combined to bring it about" (p. 176).

Speculating on the story of Rossini's block, any or all of the external causes given might explain his block, but most or all are applicable, if not to him, than to others in similar situations.

Death of a parent. After Rossini's mother died in 1827, he actually gave up composing for some months. Toye (1987) says her death "marked the beginning of the ebb of his own lighthearted exuberance" (p. 133).

Failure of a major work. Following his mother's death, Rossini wrote two more operas, *Le Compte Ory* and, his last opera, *William Tell*. After the qualified success/failure of *William Tell*, he essentially gave up composing entirely.

Business reverses. Toye tells us that in 1829 Rossini lost a contract from Charles X for five operas to be composed for an annuity of six thousand francs a year for life (pp. 141, 154).

Exhaustion. As Thompson (1964) puts it, "The six months of intense labour that the composition of [*William*] *Tell* cost . . . [Rossini], the constant strain he was under, and [the] insomnia due to over-wrought nerves so preyed upon his health that ten days after *Tell* had been launched he departed with his wife for Bologna for an interval of repose before attacking new work" (p. 1836). Toye (1987) says, "He was exhausted to a . . . pathological extent after [*Tell*]" (p. 169).

Rational career decision making. According to Toye, Rossini supposedly said, of his "philosophical determination to give up my . . . career. . . . Such foresight is not vouchsafed to everybody; God granted it to me, and I have been grateful for it ever since" (p. 167). Toye, suggesting that retiring for Rossini was an act of good sense, adds: "It is even possible that he acted wisely . . . having already produced his best work" (pp. 173–174).

Social/political factors. According to Toye, Rossini said, "This art (of music) . . . cannot escape the influence of the times we live in, and the sentiment and ideals of the present day are wholly concerned with steam, rapine and barricades" (p. 167).

Generation shift. This seems to have affected Rossini as it affects most or all artists active for twenty or so years. For no self-respecting teenager (and even older audiences at times act like teenagers) embraces the last generation's heroes. According to Toye (1987) Rossini blamed "the fashionable craze for Meyerbeer's music," saying it discouraged him and made him feel that though "there should have been room for both of . . . [us] these people wanted nothing else but Meyerbeer" (p. 172).

Jingoism. Toye implies throughout his book that Rossini's reputation, and perhaps Rossini himself, suffered at the hands of powerful composers who were in effect xenophobics, composers like Carl Maria von Weber, who elaborated what was a natural loyalty to his motherland and fatherland into a misplaced, neurotic, rather exclusive, love for its art, accompanied by a dislike for everything written by foreigners, because it did not come, as Weber might have put it, from one of our own people.

OTHER EXTERNAL CAUSES

The Real Difficulties Inherent in Being an Artist

We can profitably view the internal difficulties associated with creating as external when the artist views creating as an irritant, a not-me event passively witnessed as happening to, as much as happening in, the ego. This is particularly true for those artists who if they feel they participate in the creative process at all, feel they do so like a medium participates in a seance—conjuring spirits up from another world, one not so much inside, but outside, the self.

While for some creativity is pleasurable, for others it is painful, emotionally fatiguing, physically depleting, or energy draining, that is, it is simply just too much work. Some days all creators feel depleted and exhausted. They have to force themselves to go to work. What could be more natural than to avoid their torture by blocking?

Leader (1991) says artists like E. M. Forster "simply give up . . . [because they have] a technical problem . . . [they cannot] solve" (p. 11). He notes that Wordsworth's sister referred to her brother's task as "so weighty that he shrinks from beginning it" (p. 184). Writing, Michener (1991) tells us in *The Novel*, is "drudgery" (p. 4), exhausting and tiring. And William Kelley, co-author of the movie *Witness*, used to say with a sigh, "You have no idea how much this takes out of me" (personal communication).

The Finite Pool

Leader (1991) suggests that some artists block because they feel that the world's artistic treasures have been spent. Citing the "rich and intimidating legacy of the past" they complain that "every great poet . . . every genuine, though lesser poet, fulfills once for all some possibility of the language, and so leaves one possibility less for his successors" (p. 116). The result is "influence anxiety" (p. 126), that is, the burden of "their sense of what has already been written" (p. 115).

Things got considerably more difficult for many artists after the great creative explosion of the twentieth century. Many artists came to believe that because everything had already been done, there can be nothing new under the sun. Some even resigned from doing their work, feeling that it was no longer possible to be original.

The Finality of the Printed Page

Leader (1991) points to a justified fear that "once you put something in writing, you run the risk of being misunderstood, and you cannot explain or defend yourself as you can in argument or conversation" (p. 222).

Distraction

Many but not all creators work in a self-preoccupied state, deep in thought, drawn into themselves. They find that when the doorbell or the phone rings it causes a painful resurfacing, the emotional equivalent of the bends. Resurface too often and not only is the pain cumulative but interruptions create further expectations of interruption, and an association is forged between working and having one's work disturbed. Anxiety about being interrupted breeds anxiety, and the artist blocks because he or she fears he or she will block. Finally, there is anger about the interruption, and guilt about the anger, with the depression that often ensues and makes things considerably worse.

However, the reaction to interruption, an individual matter, is often what counts. What interrupts some is soothing and solacing for others. Noise doesn't bother some artists. Some can work well, or better, on noisy, crowded trains, enjoying the company, while not minding, or blocking out, the noise. Others must have Proust's quiet room, lined with cork. Usually what counts is not the noise but the fantasies about it.

Suburbia was not the answer for the artist who left noisy New York for quiet only to find that for him the sounds of children-at-play and wailing sirens summoning help in the small town were even worse than the urban noises. The sounds themselves were not intolerable. What made them so bad was that the children at play aroused disturbing fantasies relative to the family he didn't have (but the others on the block did), and that the sirens reminded him of wartime, and hence his own guilty aggressive wishes.

Audience Ignorance

Leader (1991) mentions "American philistinism—the lack of recognition or acclaim accorded *Moby Dick* and the works that followed it" (p. 28) as a reason for Melville's block of thirty-five or so years duration.

This philistinism is still alive, not confined to America, and involves more than ignorance—particularly the sadism discussed next.

Sadism

One artist suggested that it was for the same reasons that some people like to hunt and shoot songbirds that a man as passionately devoted to music as James Irsay made jokes on his radio show about how the composer Ernest Chausson rode his bike into a wall and died, pathetically young, depriving himself of life, and the world of much beautiful music (November 19, 1993, New York radio station WQXR). In speaking of the incident he said not, "How sad," but something on the order of, "Take his music, but not his bicycle lessons." The why, or cause, of sadism to artists is beyond this text, but specific sadistic behaviors toward artists that are capable of causing block can be identified.

Double-binding artists. Society puts artists in no-win situations. For example, so often we both push them to be like someone we admire and complain of their lack of originality. John Simon (1994) discusses the dilemma Richard Chamberlain, the actor, has in following Rex Harrison in the lead of *My Fair Lady*: he is caught between being derivative on the one hand and idiosyncratic on the other. Society says its eclectic artists lack a point of view while its artists with a point of view lack flexibility. It calls an abstract style inaccessible and a popular style pandering. The composer Elliott Carter is not romantic enough, while the composer Samuel Barber is too romantic. Women who don't write prove the inferiority of women, while women who do write are at best too masculine for their own good, and at worst shameful whores.

Sibelius, who suffered from one of the severest of all the terminal blocks, was abused for trying to make a living. Society forced him to write third rate material for money then condemned him for being a third rate composer. As Schonberg (1981) says, "Professionals look for consistency in a composer. They distrust a creator who constantly turns out music that is not on a high level, and are apt to regard as freaks those few works that do cause a ripple. How could the composer of both *Valse Triste* and the *Romance* in D flat for piano be taken seriously (p.

411)?" Society in essence gave Sibelius the choice of eating or impressing, plus no satisfactory, face-saving way out—no reasonable thing to do to satisfy the conflicting demands the world made on him. Is this partly why he stopped composing for the last third or so of his life? Did he conclude, not unreasonably, that it was simply a matter of fighting a battle that he couldn't win?

Society double-binds by constantly changing the rules. Aestheticians/critics, instead of consulting with each other and speaking as one voice, agreeing on what is desirable or, recognizing that there are different, equally valid approaches, so stating in negative reviews, speak as individuals, each with different ideas and preferences, each presented as the final and absolute word and command. The artist, unable to please everybody, predictably makes enemies in high places. This is tolerable. But what is not tolerable is that the ones who are pleased, feeling sated and satisfied, move on and forget all about continuing to congratulate the artist. There is deadly silence. But the ones who are displeased, the enemies made, feeling angry and dissatisfied, too often become stalkers, and as such make the artist's life miserable, and they often will do so forever.

Giving artists too much freedom. Unlimited freedom can be bad for the artistic soul and so ultimately for the artistic reputation. In the eighteenth century classical period, standards were rigid, and though lateral expansion was encouraged, true in-depth experimentation was not. Perhaps the great classical composers of the seventeenth through the nineteenth centuries were prolific because they could do their work without being buffeted by too many permissive crosscurrents. But later, when bad-boy rebelliousness was permitted and in vogue, the Romantics like Berlioz and Liszt, the Impressionists like Debussy, and the Modernists like Stravinsky and beyond found life getting harder, not easier. Now they began to taste the negative effects of artistic freedom. Now they began to long for restraints and controls to keep confusion and cacophony at bay, and allow order and beauty to shine through. Now musical block began.

Abusing artists. Allan Kozinn (1994), after hearing an audience talking about vocal burnout at the New York debut of a "bass-baritone of the moment," remarks that "a new singer might be given a couple of seasons of grace before this kind of talk gets started" and notes that, "the line between art and blood sport is thinner than is commonly admitted" (p. C15). Another example of how audiences cannot wait for failure is the regularly appearing review of the movie, *Cleopatra,* in the *New York Times* which claims that it is "not as bad as was hoped."

Kozinn doesn't comment on the precise effect this has on the artist. But it realizes two of the artist's worst nightmares: being found wanting and being mutilated, that is, being abandoned by mother and castrated by father. Both male and female artists fear castration, with only the details differing between the sexes. Males are mostly afraid of being rendered impotent, while females are mostly afraid of being devalued.

The result of artist abuse is a vicious cycle of self-questioning, self-hatred, depression, failure, and more self-hatred, until the artist becomes desperate for a positive reaction (sometimes any reaction, even a negative one). In a panic the artist goes fishing for compliments, only to ply waters that are muddy, polluted, full of sharks and empty of fish.

TRANSFERENCE OF AUDIENCES AND CRITICS TO THE ARTIST

An artist's audiences and critics sometimes appear to be not a group but a gang. As individuals they seem bland, ordinary, even benign, but together they develop a group transference neurosis, or psychosis, to the artist. Their transference reactions are of two kinds: too positive (the rabid fan) and too negative (the abusive audience/critic). Both kinds are too excessive for the good of all concerned. The extremes run between a Constant Lambert, the critic/composer who praises Sibelius to the skies until even Sibelius has trouble fulfilling Lambert's expectations of him, and the homophobic critic who deals with his own forbidden homosexual desires by criticizing the homosexuality not just in Britten himself but in his words and music.

Alas, both exist side by side, or alternately, in what amounts to the dual personality of some fans. A case in point is one Metropolitan Opera fan who loved opera so much that he wore a personal stereo to a performance so that he could hear the Opera Quiz during the intermission. Yet, he listened to the opera itself only to devalue it and its singers for minor flaws and transgressions, like dull stretches in the opera itself, or a wobbly high note in a singer's performance of the same opera.

It is one thing for a psychoanalyst to be a blank screen on which the patient projects deep fantasies, and quite another for an artist to be a blank screen on which the audience and critics project deep irrational feelings. In fact, in this respect, the analyst has an easy job compared to the artist. The analyst is trained to deal with transference, only faces one transference at a time, and asked for this work in the first place. But the artist is untrained, is faced with many ambivalent or grossly hostile so-called "patients" simultaneously, and feels, and rightfully so, "Who needs this?" In particular, there is nothing about being an artist that suits him or her for being a transference figure, especially when the transference is of the narcissistic, irrational, ambivalent, and immature kind artists so often have to face.

Besides, artists, unlike analysts, can't defend themselves by analyzing negative transference, or telling the "patient" to cut it out. Instead all they can do is feel bad about it, and respond to it in human terms by withdrawing for self-protection. In analysis the analyst often stays one up vis-à-vis the patient. In art the artist is often one down vis-à-vis the world.

There are three kinds of transference to artists and their art: the narcissistic, paranoid, and the hysterical-oedipal.

As for the *narcissistic*, as mentioned in chapter 3 and above, John Simon's (1994) review of *My Fair Lady* told us not only about the play, but also about John Simon, how much the grammarian he is, and how disappointed he was when he was upstaged—an oedipal preening at odds with the purpose of this, or any other, review.

As for the *paranoid*, the tendency critics have to assess a work after a first hearing is too close for comfort to the tendency paranoids have to jump to conclusions based on projective identification. What they simply can't know on first acquaintance they supply from within. A work touches a sore point, there is a knee jerk reaction, and the artist gets kicked. In such cases apologies often are extended, but twenty years later, too late to be of much value.

As for the *hysterical-oedipal*, it seems these days that everyone in society is either an upstart oedipal child or a parent threatened by one. The papers are full of stories of the oedipal child expressing rivalry through art (some rap songs, for example) and oedipal parents responding, putting artists-children down through threats or punishments (censoring rap songs, depriving public broadcasting of funding), or by disinterest (giving up on the group and turning to another, hotter group). Oedipal parents often encourage and accept a rock group's freshman but not its sophomore endeavor because they are more apt, now that things are getting serious, to be threatened than pleased; more likely to criticize the group for doing a bad job just to destroy it than to praise a good job just to support it—and with predictable effect. People in power, ranging from what *The Wall Street Journal* calls the "career-blocker" (p. B1) boss who squashes his or her employees' chance to shine to the similarly inclined critic who becomes jealous about another's ability and success, give even artists who are not successophobic a real reason to be afraid of success. We do live in a world that conditions artists too soon and too well to believe that a good way to earn money, maintain one's relationships, and keep one's sanity is to compromise one's art or that a good way to do all of these things is to give up art to "work" for a living, and to create nothing at all.

Narcissistic, paranoid, and oedipal transference antagonism on the part of critics explains why so much of what we call aesthetics is little more than sugar-coated visceral, eroticized, transference. But the artist who doesn't know this reads these aesthetics at face value. The artist sees them as too intense to be insincere, and too sincere to be incorrect. The artist takes them personally. The artist finds it painful to write. He or she gets out of the kitchen because he or she can't stand the heat. And we have lost a good cook, and many good meals to come.

One composer's wife put it succinctly, however sadistically, saying in an unguarded moment, not thought to be for publication, that all of her husband's critics should have a frontal lobotomy. At first, her overgeneralizing was dismissed as overreacting. But when this otherwise entirely sensible person was asked what was she thinking, and why, she explained in a way that seems now perfectly rational that "Critics are prejudiced; they make fun of my husband's work out of envy and to advance their own cause, to make their reviews interesting, at his expense. And with no one to protect him he is like a beautiful bird left to the predators. He is a finch hunted to extinction, and just so they can sport its exquisite feathers."

Of course, the fan or critic, whether pro or con, cannot be entirely blamed for this generally regressive attitude toward art and the artist, for art itself promotes transference both to itself and to those who create it. First, by its very nature it puts the artist on a pedestal—a ready-made parental position that tempts fans and critics to parentalize—to alternately overvalue the artist as omnipotent, then devalue the artist as defective. Second, it bares the soul, which always unnerves, and often disorients and primitivizes onlookers; that is, it causes them to regress. Third, it gives permission to feel while simultaneously stirring up strong, forbidden feelings, also causing regression. Fourth, it has a certain enchanted impracticality about it that catches all concerned up in unreality, intensifying the first three. It is no surprise then when the fan, and critic, relate to the artist in a regressive, narcissistic, paranoid, hysterical fashion, making the artist into something besides an artist, such as a catalyst for the expression of present fantasy, and past memory recollected, whether fantasy or fact.

POSITIVE FACTORS OF THE ARTIST'S STRESSFUL LIFE

Some trauma is good for most art. Traumatized artists at least do not write "Switzerland art"—the cuckoo-clock kind that is produced in countries that remain neutral at times of crisis. Trauma is bracing; it makes life interesting; it motivates the artist to abreact the trauma, one basis for much that is creative; and in some, perhaps extreme, but favorable, cases it causes the artist to pull back from life, not into block, but into art. Even something as inherently traumatic and stressful as death can inspire. While Chopin and Berlioz blocked in the face of death, Schubert wrote right up to the very end, perhaps hoping to "beat the devil." And as Layton (1992) says of Sibelius, "Nothing concentrates the mind on essentials more than the thought that one's days may be numbered" (p. 42).

THERAPY

The consequences of society's mistreating its artists are tragic in the extreme, not only because mistreatment causes the individual artist to block, but also because a society full of blocked artists becomes not an age of gold but an age of iron.

What is the artist to do about it? First, an artist shouldn't overreact to positivity because to be consistent he or she should then overreact equally to negativity which is, after all, merely the flip side of the same coin. As Cole Porter might have warned, fans, like lovers, are always "too hot not to cool down."

Second, no artist should gratuitously expose him- or herself to a public eager to whipsaw and overwhelm. Even book signings, which seem so innocent, can become dangerous, from the passing criticisms, often made in jest, that can ruin anyone's day, especially the day of a sensitive artist.

Third, an artist must understand how audiences and critics work. They work irrationally. They are mostly fantasy and hardly reality. As one artist put it, "all music, for all audiences, is mood music." That is, while audiences speak of their reactions *to* the artist, the artist is merely a trigger and a catalyst *for* their reactions. The fan who compliments the artist is mostly talking not about the artist but about him- or herself. He or she may be bragging: "*I* have the good taste to appreciate you," "*I* survived five hours of your conducting Wagner," or "*I* got the hard ticket to the trendy event." Like cooks who say they are gourmets who "only use real lemon juice, not that bottled kind" to puff themselves up, audiences who toast artists are usually not interested in paying the artist a compliment, but are instead more interested in having an excuse to pour themselves a drink.

17

INTERNAL CAUSES

Creative block is a symptom that, like other symptoms, originates in and defends against anxiety, and so resolves conflict. First, classical principles of symptom formation are discussed: (1) the contributions of the id, ego, superego (conscience), and ego-ideal to block, (2) how block defends against anxiety, and (3) the transferential origin of some of the anxiety.

Second, more modern concepts of symptom formation are discussed, specifically how block can originate in disordered regulation of flow and deployment of creative (psychic) energy, specifically (1) depletion of creative energy, or (2) excessive creative energy, causing the ego to flood.

CONTRIBUTION OF THE ID

Creative block can result from id contamination of the ego when the process of creativity becomes eroticized, as when it becomes not creativity but exhibitionism, or when it becomes a vehicle for the expression of aggression, as when an author's pen is too much "mightier than the sword." Block results because the sexual or aggressive component of the creativity causes undue anxiety, which moreover is appropriate not to the creativity but to the (forbidden) sexuality or the aggression. Next the ego, attempting conflict resolution, intending only to suppress the sex and aggression, goes too far and as Leader (1991), quoting Ehrenzweig, puts it, "sweep[s] the whole mess into the waste-paper basket" (p. 106).

When Debussy wrote *Pélleas et Mélisande* he didn't just write an opera. He also wrote to express his hostility to Wagner; that is, he designed his opera to be as unlike the operas of Wagner as possible. While many think Debussy managed, in spite of it all, to create a masterpiece, others find *Pélleas* a bore, a musical expression of block unlistenable because (at least in the vocal parts) it self-consciously avoids melody, and what melody there is is fragmented and unelaborated.

Creative block can also result when id material affects the product—the art—directly and adversely, as when it spills over, making art too erotic or too hostile for its own good, and for the comfort of all concerned. Writing becomes exhibiting oneself, including cornering others, forcing them to look. The artist creates not art but pornography; and/or empty, contentious, carping, scolding, mean-spirited diatribes; or disdainfully elitist works, as one artist put it, "hostile to the unintelligentsia."

Leader (1991) suggests id contamination of the creative ego occurs and causes block when "genius is . . . associated with sexual transgression" (p. 130); when creativity becomes childbirth and the creator, a male, develops a "taint of feminine identification" (p. 237); when completion equals leaving, so that finishing becomes associated with abandoning and being abandoned with the result that "separation [is] a symbolic meaning in [the] act" (p. 72); when "writing words of one's own" becomes "transgression" (p. 198); when writing becomes assertion and this causes guilt or a fear of retaliation or the aggression is internalized and causes depression; or when creative "regression in the service of the ego" is equated with surrender and passivity (pp. 79–80).

The most common reasons for block include:

1. The ego equates professional excellence with hostile competing with, winning over, and ultimately castrating the rival father (particularly in the male) or with rejecting by counteridentifying with and so abandoning and destroying the devalued mother (particularly in the female). The artist blocks to avoid "committing oedipal murder" and to avoid the punishment for that murder.

2. The ego equates doing art with having sex, and the artist blocks because of sexual guilt.
   An artist discovered that being an artist had cachet, and did art to be invited to, and make out at, cocktail parties. Then he blocked first because of guilt over his sexuality and second when the inevitable rejections (deemed punishments) occurred—when he was not invited to an important event, or when he became frustrated by all the party types who were too competitive to acknowledge, and too self-preoccupied to care, how great he was.

3. The artist equates professional with personal relationships and blocks because he or she feels unloved or abandoned. Almost every artist

develops an inappropriate personal relationship with his or her audience, and feels personally unloved and abandoned, and blocks, when the too often inevitable rejection of his or her work finally occurs.

There are several other ways id contamination of the creative ego can cause block:

1. The ego equates creative production with the production of feces and the artist blocks because the art is deemed unacceptable because "fecal," and withholds the "feces" that others demand be produced ("anal struggling"). Some obtain direct, erotic pleasure from fecal retention itself.
2. The ego equates the weeping quality of creativity with urination, and the artist blocks to avoid the embarrassment of "wetting the bed."
3. The ego equates the weeping quality of creativity with passivity and femininity, and the male artist blocks to avoid "being homosexual" (one possible reason why Charles Ives gave up composing to go full time into the insurance business).

Positive Aspects of Id Contamination

Rossini hinted at the power of love to catalyze rather than to inhibit art when, according to Thompson (1964), he said, "If he had had children he would doubtless have continued to work" (p. 1838). Some see Ravel's "Bolero" as an example of how desirably sexy and seductive art can be. Anger often improves art directly, by giving it body and bite, or indirectly, by energizing a specific great cause, or generally motivating the artist to "give 'em hell," that is, to write well "as the best revenge."

Treatment Implications

It is hard to create effectively; using creativity to express personal conflicts makes it even harder. If blocked, the artist should clear his or her creativity as much as possible of these conflicts, making, to paraphrase Freud, "ego where once there was id."

However, impurities will remain. It is better for the artist to live with them, and be patient with him- or herself, than to do nothing at all as a self-punishment. No artist should do the radical thing Horowitz did: instead of merely scrapping the kind of music that had become offensive to him, the flashy kind his audiences wanted, he "simply quit altogether" (Schonberg 1992, p. 178).

CONTRIBUTION OF THE EGO

Block is inherent in the very ego functions that contribute to creativity. For example, creativity requires intelligence, intelligence makes for hypersensitivity, and hypersensitivity makes for block.

If, as Ernst Kris, as quoted in Giovacchini (1984) said, creativity is a kind of "regression in the service of the ego" (p. 439), we would expect a degree of creative block in those artists who are too rigid, moralistic, or guilty to regress comfortably, if at all (as happens in some cases of obsessive perfectionistic block) and in those artists where the regressive process, once started, goes too far (as happens in some cases of decompensating schizophrenia).

CONTRIBUTION OF THE SUPEREGO

Fenichel (1945) notes:

[T]he occupational inhibitions often represent the superego type of inhibition. . . . Under present-day conditions children often become acquainted with the conception of work under the aspect of "duty," demanded by authorities, as the opposite of "pleasure." All conflicts around authorities, all struggles between rebellion and obedience, therefore, may be expressed in the attitudes toward work. . . . [Fenichel (1945) also notes that] certain persons with a particularly intense sense of guilt dating back to their infantile sexual conflicts labor under the constant necessity of paying off a debt to their conscience. . . . The extreme representatives of this type are the personalities described by Freud under the headings "those wrecked by success," the "criminal from a sense of guilt," and the "moral masochists." These individuals seem to feel that they must not utilize the talents or the advantages that are theirs by natural endowment and character; they inhibit those of their functions that might lead to success. Their inhibitions gratify the demands made by the superego on the ego. (p. 183)

Superego guilt is the most commonly seen reason for block. Two of the more common manifestations are guilt over self-expression and guilt over accomplishment and success.

Guilt over self-expression can take the form of mechanistic writing, a general tentativeness of expression to avoid commitment, or constant revision that amounts to a kind of atonement. Zinsser (1985) notes that "Americans are suddenly uncertain of what they think and unwilling to go out on a limb—an odd turn of events for a nation famous for the 'rugged individualist.' A generation ago our leaders told us where they stood and what they believed. Today they perform the most strenuous verbal feats to escape this fate" (p. 24).

Could it be that shame due to guilt was a reason for Rossini's Great Renunciation? Rossini's last opera, *William Tell*, and the *Stabat Mater*, one of the few works that followed it, contain emotions not heretofore found in Rossini's work. Do we hear his grief showing? Did he know it did, and stop writing because he was ashamed of it? There is no proof of this theory, but his hesitation to complete the *Stabat Mater*, and his refusal to let it be published until after his death, are at least suggestive that something along these lines might have been occurring.

An artist feeling guilt over accomplishment and success (successophobia) is happiest when his reviews are bad, his purse is empty, and his hall is thin. Successophobia may be due to oedipal or survivor guilt. Oedipal guilt is guilt in fantasy about incest and murder. Survivor guilt, unlike oedipal guilt, is guilt over something that has happened or might happen. In reality, the guilt makes the artist an ineffective competitor because he or she thinks mainly, or only, of the plight of the loser, the one whose downfall the artist believes to be his or her fault and responsibility.

Of course, oedipal and survivor guilt often occur together. Perhaps what brought the pianist Van Cliburn down was combined oedipal and survivor guilt occurring after he won the Tchaikovsky competition, meshing with combined oedipal and survivor guilt after his father died, in part because his beloved mother became potentially available, at least in fantasy (Perlmutter 1994).

Positive Aspects of Guilt

Guilt has its bright side. A writer who, when she had a good day, felt she had to pay back with a bad day also felt that, when she had a bad day, she would be paid back with a good day. Guilt keeps us from misbehaving both personally and professionally—for example, when it forces us to go to, and keep at, our work. It creates high aspirations that have both a survival and a creative value. It also regulates psychic energy by stifling inner artistic freedom, preventing flooding when spurts of inspiration go beyond irrigating the creative field to drowning the crops, that is, guilt keeps the artist from getting so emotional that he or she becomes lost, panicky, and confused. As romantic impediments often create not lesser but greater romantic interest, artistic impediments, constitutional rights notwithstanding, give life to art, if only because sublimation into artistic expression is the only expression possible when guilt stifles the freedom to say anything that comes to mind. That is one reason why guilty artists, forced to find new, safer ways to think and feel—creative ways to leak what is internally prohibited—often produce art with two qualities that are the hallmark of the true masterpiece: (1) an understated subtle quality that reflects the suppressive forces, and (2) an overt triumphal quality that reflects the ultimate surmounting of these forces. In contrast, the artist free to say anything that comes to mind sometimes produces unsublimated art, flush with freedom but as primitive as art by dolphin or ape; as empty of magnificence as the behavior of an uncivilized, unmanageable child; or as random as the productions of an adult free associating without an analyst as a guide to give shape, meaning, and direction to what is said—rhapsodic and aleatoric, but unstructured.

Treatment Implications

Although Zinsser (1985) admits that no cure for writer's block has been found, he does list some helpful therapeutic suggestions, mostly directed to the artist's superego. Consoling the artist that he or she is not alone, he suggests that blocked artists try relaxing, building self-confidence, and writing in the first person. He suggests the author ask himself, "Who are you *not* to say what you think?" There is no need to feel conspicuous, cautions Zinsser. The artist can avoid boring people by telling them something interesting, and Zinsser reassures the artist that he or she is likely not to be boring since "there's only one you. Nobody else thinks or feels in exactly the same way" (pp. 22–23).

CONTRIBUTIONS OF THE EGO IDEAL

When we speak of an artist's ego we are often really speaking of the "ego ideal"—the "what I want to be" part of the superego.

Leader (1991) quoting Milner suggests the ego ideal of most artists presents " 'an extremely idealized notion of what their products ought to be' " (p. 95), and that block results because artists feel that their "actual work would fail to live up to . . . orgasmic expectations" (p. 96).

Many artists go way beyond having high standards for themselves to taking themselves much too seriously. Zinsser (1985) notes that writers block because they ask what their

> article must be . . . [to] seem important. He thinks how august it will look in print. He thinks of all the people who will read it. He thinks that it must have the solid weight of authority. He thinks that its style must dazzle. No wonder he tightens: he is so busy thinking of his awesome responsibility to the finished article that he can't even start . . . and, casting about for heavy phrases that would never occur to him if he weren't trying so hard to make an impression. (p. 21)

A common manifestation of excessively high standards in artists is that their britches never fit. Artists are always restless, rarely satisfied, always striving to do something they didn't do, or to be something that they are not. Even the greats, instead of sticking to what they are good at, strive to be different, bigger, or better. Rachmaninoff wants to be a conductor, and T. S. Eliot a playwright.

So often this is because the sources of self-esteem are fundamentally irrational—like the composer whose happiness depended on satisfying a self-image that didn't include revising. She needed to view herself as not only prolific, but as a composer who could write effortlessly forward like Mozart, in one continuous outpouring, without stopping to think or correcting errors.

Therapeutic Implications

Friends, family, and therapists can often help the excessively idealistic artist get over block simply by advice and example meant to reshape an overly demanding ego ideal into one that is more realistic, practical, and kind. An example from Barber's uncle, Sidney Homer, quoted by Heyman (1992), is his recommendation that Barber do what *he* does: "just go on doing . . . my thing" (p. 513).

BLOCK AS A DEFENSE

Anxiety originates in guilt over forbidden instincts and appears when instincts, forbidden or no, have gotten out of control, and threaten to create guilt or overwhelm and flood. (How instincts out of control threaten to overwhelm and flood is discussed further in the section, "Flooding.")

The primary gain of block is the defensive reduction of anxiety to tolerable levels. The secondary gain of block is the practical advantages to which a block once in place can be put. The blocked artist gets attention and love, regressive pleasure from staying home sick, and even (as was the case for one patient who deliberately overdid his Posttraumatic Stress Disorder for immediate gain) a handicapped sticker and the good parking spaces that go with it. And there is sadistic fun from refusing to work when your friends and family are agonizing over ways to get you, the blocked artist, over your blockage and back to your desk.

There is an exchange: block prevents the creator from doing his or her work. But it also protects, and some of the specific defenses responsible for creating block can, in favorable circumstances, help creativity to flourish.

Acting-Out

Artists often find acting-out relieves a general dysphoric feeling, particularly a feeling of being unloved, one that commonly plagues artists because of their constant and high-level exposure to the negative feedback. Many undo the feeling that no one wants them by becoming promiscuous, hoping to convince themselves that "No one rejects me." This works temporarily, but it dissipates energy needed for work and rarely, if ever, provides the artist with the hoped-for satisfying, nonrejecting, relationships.

Repression

Repression relieves the anxiety associated with conflict by suppressing one or more aspects of that conflict. It also relieves the anxiety due to flooding by limiting the rate of flow of instinctual material. It calms and protects, but when it stops the flow it also stifles.

Denial

Denial allows the artist to function in the face of real internal difficulties, like physical illness, and real external difficulties, like financial problems and the latest and greatest put-down from a critic. The artist can avoid depression by convincing him- or herself that the "bad things they say I write are not so bad after all." It also compromises judgment, so that the artist produces inferior works or doesn't edit out the inferior parts of superior ones. One typical result is the longueurs that have sunk so many familiar operas.

Projection

Projection, which amounts to putting oneself in the other person's shoes, can make the artist a better artist by increasing his or her capacity for empathy. It can also reduce tension by enabling artists to attribute things they don't like about themselves to the external world. "I am a bad guilty person" becomes "I am a good person, but misunderstood." This works until the world becomes a dangerous place, as such not a source of relief from, but a source of, and reason for, blockage.

Internalization

Internalization of external images enlivens the internal world but creates new internal threats. Internalization of anger reduces guilt about that anger and spares others the consequences of the anger. But taking anger out on the self causes depression and the low self-esteem that so often causes block.

Undoing

Undoing is a way to retract something the artist has said or done that on reflection seems to have been wrong, or gone too far for self-comfort or the comfort of others. But mostly it leads to unnecessary apologies, the art not of self-expression but of self-effacement. This was the case for a painter who apologized for her serious side by doing greeting cards instead of watercolors, and a writer who wrote obscure academic tracts to apologize for his all-too-palpable instincts. As suggested previously, Rossini's Great Renunciation was partly an apology for the new (filial) emotions that came through in *William Tell*, his final opera.

Reaction Formation

Via this defense the bad lazy person becomes a "good workaholic," for example he or she has the procreative conversion that François Rabelais referred to when he said that "a young Whore [is] an old Saint" (Bartlett 1992, p. 316). Fenichel (1945) describes such individuals as those who "repress instinctual demands . . . by becoming . . . hard workers," but, often they become "robots so to speak, without any pleasure in work . . . [which they are] compelled to do . . . uninterruptedly" (p. 183).

Regression

Regression to an early developmental stage is part of the creative process—"regression in the service of the ego" (Kris 1952). But it is part of block as well when it is mostly a way to avoid the anxiety that is an integral part of being a mature creator. There are three levels to which an artist can regress, each with its advantages and disadvantages: oral, anal, and phallic.

Good oral regression is associated with all the familiar advantages associated with romanticism, however self-indulgent. But bad oral regression can make the artist into a spoiled brat. We often see resentful sulking when things don't go the artist's way. Sometimes the artist only works when the mood strikes. He or she becomes an erratic amateur working when inspired, instead of the resolute professional who becomes inspired when working.

Good anal regression is a way to maintain independence and control, but bad anal regression causes the artist to view even the most neutral personal interactions in terms of who is doing what to whom, so that what can, and should, be a cooperative endeavor becomes an adversarial situation. Artists who view every interaction as a struggle often block to win using withholding as their trump card. They play this card even when others make reasonable requests of them and when they make reasonable requests of themselves; they usually see these not as requests but as demands, an unacceptable form of being controlled even if it is self-control.

To defeat parents who demanded he get all A's in school, a student developed an agoraphobic separation anxiety that made it difficult for him to leave home to go to school. On those increasingly rare occasions when he was able to get there, he developed a pseudodyslexia that made it difficult for him to spell and read, akathisia that made it difficult for him to sit still long enough to learn, and characterological stubbornness/rebelliousness that made it difficult for him to view cooperating with the teacher as anything short of abject, complete, and, for him, unacceptable submission.

Phallic regression imparts a personal sense of mastery which can spill over to become a helpfully assertive lifestyle or a powerful work of art, but it forges an association between art and rivalry. For the male, art becomes castrating the potent father, and for the female, art becomes devaluing the ineffectual (house-wife) mother. Block then results from guilt, or as Leader (1991) puts it, results in the male from the "internalized image of the father" (p. 37) who threatens to harm. In the female a parallel cause of block is internalization of the angry, hurt mother who insists her daughter follow in her (devalued) footsteps.

Did Ravel write in whole tones to destroy Wagner, and did he block in the last years of life to atone for a fantasied destruction of the father?

Though Thompson (1964), in discussing Rossini says that the "long prevalant idea that the success of Meyerbeer with *Robert le Diable* and *Les Huguenots* and of Halevy with *La Juive*, following so soon upon *Guillaume Tell* discour-aged . . . [Rossini] irremediably has been pretty well exploded" (p. 1839), perhaps Rossini (or if not Rossini others like him in comparable situations) envied Meyerbeer and Halevy, and desired to put them down, or "castrate" them (Toye says Rossini is said to have demeaned them as "Jews" [p. 169]). Feeling guilty about his hostility to them, perhaps he then dealt with both the envy and hostility by a self-destructive abdication, his Great Renunciation.

In writer's cramp (more common in the male than in the female) block results in part because the act of writing, holding the pen, etc. has developed specific, and forbidden, phallic implications. For artists on display, pianists and conduc-tors among them, pianist's cramp and other similar disorders like conductor's shoulder can be put into place to suppress forbidden phallic exhibitionistic impulses. Thesis block, found in scientists who study rather than perform, is sometimes a way to suppress a phallic desire to know, forbidden because of its hostile (competitive), or sexual (including intrusive voyeuristic) implications.

There are several variants of phallic block, each little more than a way to relieve phallic oedipal anxiety. Here, each is given the name of a legendary artist who either blocked in the way and for the reasons described, or who is the inspiration for this form of block in others.

In *Beethoven block* the artist postpones or avoids writing a symphony altogether to avoid competing with "the master." Elgar, Brahms, and Milhaud hesitated long before they judged themselves ready for the trial by fire that so many composers seem to feel a first symphony must always be. Benjamin Britten wrote symphonies, but seems to have felt constrained to minimize their stature by calling them something else (assigning them qualifiers such as "simple," "spring" or "da Requiem.")

In *Borodin block* the artist remains safely the dilettante, again to avoid competing. He or she writes *and* keeps a 9 to 5 job. Too busy or tired to finish much of anything, he or she gives the unfinished works to others to complete and edit. Borodin gave his works to the composers Nikolai Rimsky-Korsakov and Alexander Glazunov. Perhaps this way he defied the parents while maintaining the personal fiction that he defied them only so much, and no more. The result, as a number of writers have said wistfully, is that we can only imagine what the composer might have achieved had he not had a second job. (Of course, his devoting himself to this job was possibly as much the result as the cause of his writer's block.)

In *Shostakovitch block* the artist, instead of expressing and exposing deep feelings and beautiful ideas, spends, really wastes, some time and energy devoting himself to sassing parental authority, when his real talents are not political but musical.

In *Antheil block* a once "bad boy" who in his youth aggressively sassed authority recants by becoming a conservative, or even a plagiarist. George Antheil wrote very shocking music in the 1920s including a *Ballet Mécanique* that included air-raid sirens in the score. But the 1950s finds him pulling back and plagiarizing much of the first movement of his Fifth Symphony from the first movement of Prokofiev's Fifth Symphony (written the year before), possibly as a reassuring obeisance to those he feels he hurt with his defiance.

In *Ravel block* shame and guilt arise when the artist compares him- or herself to someone incomparable. Ravel seems to have felt throughout his life that he was defective in comparison to Mozart.

In *Melville block* an artist removes his genitals actively, before they can be removed passively. Freud (1957) calls this "retiring in favour of someone else" (vol. 2, p. 216), an abdication in favor of a rival. That Melville's block may have contained an element of abdicating to the rival, Hawthorne, is suggested in the following passage from one of Melville's letters to Hawthorne (Melville 1851 [1981]), where Melville first compares himself (unfavorably) to, then deliberately, protectively, accepts being cast in an unfavorable light as compared with, Hawthorne:

> I was in New York for four-and-twenty hours the other day, and saw a portrait of N. H. And I have seen and heard many flattering . . . allusions to the "Seven Gables." . . . So upon the whole, I say to myself, this N. H. is in the ascendant. My dear Sir, they begin to patronize. All Fame is patronage. Let me be infamous; there is no patronage in *that*. What "reputation" H. M. has is horrible. Think of it! To go down to posterity is bad enough, any way; but to go down as a "man who lived among the cannibals!" . . . I feel that I am now come to the inmost leaf of the bulb, and that shortly the flower must fall to the mould. (p. 534)

Another comparison Melville (1981) uses is with Goethe. Here he seems to be both putting himself down and reassuring himself that he is not lowly by devaluing Goethe: "As with all great genius, there is an immense deal of flummery in Goethe, and in proportion to my own contact with him, a monstrous deal of it in me" (p. 534).

Rationalization

Rationalization is a secondary more than a primary defense, that is, it is a self-comforting justification for other defenses already in place. An artist who is really in repression prefers to think, "I stop writing not because I have repressed forbidden sexual thoughts but because I live in an unappreciative world, or because I don't need the money."

Sublimation

Sublimation is usually considered to be an inherently protocreative defense, one that enhances rather than interferes with creativity. In sublimation an instinct is converted into a work of art, as when hostility writes an artist's battle scenes or murder plots. In such cases block can appear when the defense *cannot* form. Sublimations tend to form imperfectly, or not at all, in societies that are too permissive, that encourage the artist to get it all out, often with satisfactory personal, but disastrous artistic, results.

Therapeutic Implications

There are two ways out from phallic/oedipal block. One involves competing guilt free, as in the case of a medical student who went far in life by becoming openly competitive, guilt-free. He threw the competition off his trail by announcing to his dormitory mates that he had no intention of studying hard, like a grind. Then he turned out the lights and worked by flashlight, and got the best grades in his class. He was not ashamed because his motto was not "do unto others" but "to the victor go the spoils." He called his competitiveness "professional rivalry"—the innocent sounding name some people with malignant intentions use to justify what is in effect assassination of another.

The second way involves tithing—avoiding a generally guilty self-sacrificial life by making a few token, partial, self-sacrificial guilty gestures—ranging from the sublime, like writing something less than the masterpiece one always intended, to the commonplace, such as taking a part-time job to never get enough sleep, or to never have enough time to do creative work, or to do it properly.

BLOCK RESULTING FROM THE ARTIST'S TRANSFERENCE TO AUDIENCES AND CRITICS

Two of the most common and most destructive transferences artists have to their audiences and critics are the exhibitionistic and the depressive. The exhibitionistic artist is in effect showing off, and, like many show-offs, entirely too dependent on applause. The depressed artist uses audiences and critics as substitute parents, giving them absolute power of conferring and withholding approval and love. Now the artist is at risk because his or her self-esteem depends almost entirely on what others think, so that no positive self-evaluation is final and complete until transferentially validated, that is, until "the parents" have spoken.

Therapeutic Implications

Clearly, if excessive transference promotes, then interpersonal neutrality and inner orientation protects from, block.

Though no artist writes entirely without an audience and critics in mind most should try to give up their more unrealistic expectations of love and admiration from strangers and settle for inner rewards. According to Toye (1987), Heinrich Heine (quoted in a somewhat different context) might have put it this way in referring to how Rossini's Great Renunciation was not a bad solution to Rossini's problems: "A genius . . . is satisfied; despising the world and its petty ambitions, he . . . strolls down the Boulevard des Italiens with a smiling face and a caustic tongue" (pp. 173–174).

DISORDERS OF REGULATION OF FLOW AND DEPLOYMENT OF CREATIVE ENERGY

Depletion

The term energy depletion seems interchangeable with what Leader (1991) calls creative exhaustion due to "run[ning] out of steam" (p. 28).

In one form of depletion the artist seems only able to work with early experiences. In effect, the "fire can only burn in fossil fuel," and there seems to be a limited supply of that. Later experiences cannot be used to refuel. After the early experiences are used up, the artist begins to repeat him- or herself, or falls completely silent. In another, energy is simply dissipated. Hayman (1993) notes that "possibly Tennessee acted out so much with his lovers that he was left with little need to complain in his plays about the lack of paternal love and the bullying" (p. 173).

But most cases of depletion are really cases of inhibition. Rossini describing what he considered to be his own depletion, according to Toye (1987) said: "Music needs freshness of ideas; I am conscious of nothing but lassitude and crabbedness. . . . I wrote operas when melodies came in search of me, but, when I realised that the time had come for me to set out and look for them, I . . . renounced the journey and ceased to write" (pp. 167–168).

Rossini's incapacity to write much music after *Tell* appears suspiciously to be an inhibition. Otherwise, (short of head injury or other sudden onset of medical or psychiatric disorder) how is it possible that the man who wrote the *William Tell Overture* on day one had little or nothing at all to say on day two?

The same is true of Melville. Leader (1991), quoting Updike, suggests Melville blocked because he "spent the treasure of experiences laid up in his youth" (p. 28), that is, that Melville was depleted, to quote Melville's own metaphor, come to the "innermost leaf" (p. 29). He blocked not because he was depleted but because he was inhibited, and one reason for his inhibition, as described above, lay in his nefarious comparisons with others and the consequences of those comparisons.

Flooding

Was Tennessee Williams talking about his anxiety about being flooded when, according to Hayman (1993) he described a writer who "crawled back" because of anxiety about being "let out of the small but apparently rather light and comfortable room of his known self into a space that lacked the comfort of limits . . . a space of bewildering dark and immensity . . . [that] gave him unbearable fright" (p. 69)?

Gedo (1989) sees the cause of block in flooding due to the "unearthing of unconscious material intrinsic to the creative process," what he calls "traumatic episodes of overstimulation" (p. 57). Rothenberg refers to the "anxiety and strain" associated with the creative process "as it unfolds . . . from carrying out very high level performance" (p. 127). And many authors speak of anarchy so that the artist falls silent to deal with a fear of losing control. Block may occur because unconscious thinking appears in awareness, or only when it appears in awareness *and* floods, instead of being accepted and integrated, or allowed right through to be inscribed verbatim, as in some poetry.

Perhaps Rossini's *Tell* expresses heretofore suppressed emotions (Toye suggests this was "filial devotion" [1987, p. 251]). In one theory, that we think can neither be proved nor disproved, after Rossini's mother's death he was too much the griever to be able to have enough ego to continue denying certain deep feelings with "bel canto" trills and arpeggios, leaving block as his only alternative. (A few religious works got through; and later he was able to take up his pen writing humorous, satirical trifles.)

A familiar though controlled form of flooding is the destructive Freudian slip. In an ultimate form of blockage, slips can, and have, destroyed careers. There is a sudden masochistic moment of truth, really an impulsive renunciation of good sense, that dynamically is a secret wish to test the waters, hoping to be forgiven and loved in spite of, and so in a sense for, oneself. But of course block is ordained because this is hardly likely when the soul-bearing is, as it usually is, reserved for the most uncompassionate people and in the most important and unforgiving professional circumstances.

PART III
THERAPY

PART III
THERAPY

18

TOWARD A NEW
THERAPEUTIC APPROACH

THE PROBLEM WITH EXISTING TREATMENT

To date the methods employed for treating creative block have left much to be desired. When they have worked it has sometimes been because of the placebo effect, with remission, or cure, the result of the positive relationship with the treating physician, which contrasts to the abusive relationship the artist has with everyone else. But often they have failed and the therapist has become just another person who either did not extend a helping hand or having extended one used it to do harm, bruising and battering an artist already down, acting like another Eugene Ormandy, the conductor, who, according to Heyman (1992) tells the composer Samuel Barber that an hour of his music is "too much of a good thing" (p. 499); another Saint-Saëns, the composer, who, according to Orenstein (1991), tells the composer Maurice Ravel that his music is "cacophonous" (p. 124); or another Virgil Thomson, the composer and critic who, as Schonberg (1981) relates, in his first season as music critic of the *New York Herald Tribune*, tells Sibelius that his Second Symphony is "vulgar, self-indulgent and provincial beyond all description" (p. 410).

A common culprit where therapy fails or does harm is the misuse of the classic analytic approach so that therapy begins and ends with the attainment of insight. Insight is always partly humiliating and critical, and more criticism, this time from the therapist, is just what the artist doesn't need, especially at times of blockage.

By way of illustration, according to Hayman (1993), when Tennessee Williams blocked in the late 1950s, he consulted Lawrence Kubie, a psychoanalyst who has written on the topic of creativity and madness and "was familiar with his work, and recognized 'the psychic wounds expressed in it,' " only to have one of his doctor's first utterances be "Why are you so full of hate, anger, and envy?" (p. xvi).

The question mark didn't fool Williams. Charitably, Kubie's comments may have been strictly intended to impart insight, but it is likely that they were meant uncharitably: consciously or unconsciously intended to be hurtful. At any rate, what he said, regardless of intent, must have come out little different from and have had the same effect as what Ormandy told Barber, Saint-Saëns told Ravel, and Virgil Thomson told Sibelius.

Kubie was doing what many analysts do: rejecting, disapproving, and criticizing in the guise of analyzing. They do a great deal of harm directly, and they do more indirectly by acting like an artist's rejecting mother, and/or bloodying father.

Yet most approaches to treating creative block emphasize the need to develop insight. And on paper the rationale for doing insight therapy seems reasonable enough. Fenichel (1945), for example, persuasively recommends uncovering, saying:

> Freud has repeatedly called attention to the fact that one of the most difficult tasks in psychoanalysis is that of conquering a severe unconscious sense of guilt. There are, however, cases most amenable to treatment where the patient does not bow so completely to his superego that he fills his whole life with ruinous inhibitions, but instead inhibits one or two specific functions. To this group belong a considerable number of the so-called occupational neuroses, like writer's cramp or violinist's cramp. . . . Many patients upon completion of analysis, state that they have acquired a new sense of the fullness of life; this new feeling probably appears not only because they are relieved of the necessity of spending a great deal of energy on repressions and symptom formation but also because those experiential capacities that were inhibited have become accessible anew. However, the removal of an inhibition of this sort is by no means an easy task; the older and the more ingrained a given inhibition, the more difficult it is to remove. Psychoanalysis of children, in this respect, is in a better position than psychoanalysis of adults. It may succeed in preventing inhibitions from becoming deeply rooted in the personality, and thus may act as a prophylactic agent. (pp. 183–184)

Many authors essentially follow Fenichel in suggesting insight as the way to cure block. They stress how psychotherapy is a creative, growth-enhancing process, and suggest that the way to get over writer's block and become great is to face and overcome inhibitions to creating by understanding them.

But real life is not so simple. The classic approaches in emphasizing insight overlook how, especially in the beginning of treatment, the artist needs something besides insight, and certainly not the kind that Kubie gave Williams, and not in the abrasive way he gave it.

Many blocked artists need, especially in the beginning of treatment, a supportive positive relationship to tide them over and help out. In the early stage of treatment artists are often too sore and too needy to embark on a program of self-research taking place in a cold, remote, laboratory-like atmosphere. They need a hot meal, but what they get is a cold shower from a remote psychoanalyst who confuses explaining and uncovering with curing and digs deep only to give the blocked artist, already suffering from a combination of shell shock and stage fright, more suffering.

Blocked artists are really demoralized. They need to hear something good about themselves, not something bad. Though artists seem full of self-love (narcissistic) they are usually as masochistic as narcissistic. Their narcissism is often a pathetic, and ultimately failed, attempt to defend themselves against the complete dissolution of their self-esteem that their masochism dictates. Besides, sensitive souls that they are, they seem to have picked just the wrong field in which to get the attention and love they crave. Now, at least in the beginning of therapy, identifying problems is invariably perceived as identifying weaknesses, which is in turn uncomfortably close to being personally criticized.

Dr. Richard Wagman (personal communication, 1994) said that blocked artists are in need of a little love. Agatha Christie (1977) put it this way: "Writers are diffident creatures—they need encouragement" (p. 506). Henry Pinsker said (personal communication, 1995) that "I know no one who is functioning so well that I wouldn't offer praise when I could."

Elizabeth Zetzel said (personal communication, 1960) "You have to shore up the ego before dipping down into the id." In effect she was saying that you have to attend both to the blocked artist and to the artist who is blocked. Schuman (1981), discussing the treatment of persons who, for characterological reasons, experience writer's block, says: "Modern analysts . . . advocate that the employment of interpretations, which may prove narcissistically injurious, be postponed until the patient has been helped to evolve an object transference from the initial narcissistic transference. . . . The modern analyst has a special interest in communications which elaborate the patient's resistances" (pp. 116–118).

Condrau (1988), speaking of daseinsanalysis for a patient with writer's cramp notes in passing that there was a "symptomological reprieve" when Otmar, his patient, though he "himself never acknowledged this overtly . . . engaged in an important . . . *corrective emotional experience* (emphasis added). Probably for the first time in his life Otmar had revealed himself to another person who had not reprimanded him, who had consistently respected him as a person, and who had regularly sought to understand and accept him as the particular individual he was" (p. 218).

Finally, Gedo (1989) says:

Psychoanalytic treatment may restore or establish creative possibilities by overcoming specific obstacles. . . . At the same time, it may also help to overcome creative paralysis in a more nonspecific manner by providing (sometimes for the first time) a secret sharer of the kind Joseph Conrad apparently required to realize his artistic potential. It is by no means unusual to witness the flowering of a creative career in the context of a treatment that can only be rated a failure in terms of the usual criteria used to assess psychoanalytic process. Although such an analysand may gain little or no insight into his inner psychological world, the therapeutic relationship may enable him to consolidate certain successful working methods that can later be maintained without external psychological assistance. (p. 59)

In sum, technical pyrotechnics meant to uncover, correct cognitive error, recondition behavior, or improve interpersonal relationships, if employed too soon, too extensively, and too exclusively in treatment before a positive relationship is established with the therapist, will either fall on deaf ears or drive the patient away.

DEVELOPING A NEW APPROACH TO TREATMENT

The Process

Developing a new treatment approach begins with suspension of the idea that writer's block is curable only with insight (or cognitive, or interpersonal therapy), and, if that doesn't work, it is the artist's fault for not fitting into that Procrustean bed. Instead, sift through what *has* worked, gleaned from (1) the folkloric cures of the past, including the little tricks that blocked artists develop on their own to get around their block, (2) cases of artists who have gotten over their block as if by spontaneous remission, and (3) examples of actual successful psychotherapeutic cure, planned or unanticipated.

As for the tricks, artists often develop disarmingly simple, but effective, self-help methods on their own, methods that could teach their therapists a thing or two. Therapists, after learning these tricks from one patient, can suggest the same tricks for another, and the tricks get even better because they gain the imprimatur of authority. Examples of little tricks include: setting aside a room just for one's work; for a public speaker with stage fright, talking not to the audience but to a benign friend in the audience or, imagining a friend there; and, as Condrau (1988) describes, for a writer with writer's cramp, releasing the capacity to write by using a pen that makes no marks, which has the effect of "fooling" the patient into thinking, "It's okay, I'm not really writing" (p. 215).

As for spontaneous remissions, on close inspection they often turn out to be not spontaneous, but carefully, although not necessarily consciously, crafted, often by a friend, a family member, or therapist, who has come to the rescue. As Orenstein (1991) mentions, it was a timely and welcome invitation from A. Ferdinand Herold to Ravel to spend time with him in the country that helped Ravel get over his block (p. 76). Kennedy (1987), quoting Rosa Burley, says of Sir Edward Elgar:

[Jaeger dealt with Elgar when he was] in black despair over the intracta-bility of the material and the utter impossibility of ever getting it into a satisfactory shape [with an] immense amount of encouragement, accom-panied by assurances that he was the only person able to do it, and reminders that it must at all costs be done. . . . [This shifted] him into the next phase—which was one of increasing hope and enthusiasm. Tunes, contrapuntal patterns, and sequences . . . [began] to suggest themselves for various sections of the work, and would start to build up almost without his conscious control into something like the completed whole. (p. 104)

Hayman (1993) notes how Tennessee Williams after a period of block, felt reborn after staying with his grandparents and had his first play produced (p. 36).

These vignettes illustrate Gardner's (1993) point. Examining the period during which a creator made his or her most important breakthrough Gardner notes:

[N]ot only did the creators all have some kind of significant support system at that time, but this support system appeared to have a number of defining components.

First, the creator required both affective support from someone with whom he or she felt comfortable and cognitive support from someone who could understand. . . . The relationship between the creator and "the other" can be usefully compared with two other kinds of relationship: the rela-tionship between the caretaker and the child, in early life, and the relation-ship between a youngster and his or her peers. . . . I was surprised by this discovery of the intensive social and affective forces that surround creative breakthroughs. (pp. 43–44)

Finally, there is the cure that works. Perhaps Zinsser's (1985) belief that no cure for writer's block has been found is not totally accurate. The case of Otmar, presented earlier, is an example of at least temporary symptom relief. The annals of word of mouth are full of examples of blocked writers and composers who after supportive therapy started writing again with little or no fanfare, and sometimes with little recognition of how it happened, why it happened, or even what had happened.

What has been learned from the process of trick formation, "spontaneous" remission, and documented (planned or unintended) cure of block is used to develop a new approach to treating creative block. Ask what in the main characterized the real-life cures just noted, and the answers are first, they avoided tackling, and so undermining, the defensive, anxiety-relieving aspects of block, and second, they addressed what is probably the most overlooked factor in blockage—the negativity that the artist experiences in his or her world, that translates into a negative mind set and causes the defective functioning that blockage represents.

The New Approach

Use an eclectic approach. Its (mainly supportive) methods are drawn from all schools of thought, ranging from the psychoanalytic and cognitive to the manipulative strategic techniques of Jay Haley.

Use insight judiciously. As noted, too many observers overlook the dark side of insight, whether of the psychoanalytic, cognitive, or interpersonal variety. The dark side is invariably somewhat humiliating and critical, causes narcissistic injury, and makes the artist feel bad about him- or herself. The use of insight should be restrained at least until block has begun to lift. There is time for insight once the immediate crisis is resolved, for usually when block has lifted the artist is less desperate, less depressed, and more comfortable indulging his or her curiosity, perhaps to try to prevent another episode of block.

Supplement insight therapy with other methods. In both the acute stages of block, which are in themselves traumatic, and the chronic stages, where the artist is demoralized by the cumulative effects of block on his or her professional and personal life, it is likely that insight, however helpful, will be an incomplete antidote. It will be found wanting and go unappreciated, not only because of what it does do (increase anxiety) but because of what it does not do. Insight does not meet a blocked artist's immediate needs for positivity and loss replacement. Insight therapy overlooks how the blocked artist is a starving person who requires not merely a dietitian but also a cafeteria.

Treat the cause as well as the symptom. When the artist is ready, and only then, therapists should treat for the underlying problem that produces the block. The artist who can't get started may have a different disorder from the one who can't finish, and both may have a different disorder from the one who finishes then loses or tears up the manuscript. If Barber can't start because he is in effect a constipated obsessional (according to Heyman, Wanda Horowitz described Barber this way [1992, p. 301], and Barber agreed) he should be treated for his obsessionalism. The same holds true for a Schubert who can start but can't finish his Unfinished Symphony, because he is in effect a successophobic; a Paul Dukas or a Johannes Brahms who finish then tear up their works because they are acting in a masochistic fashion; a Rossini whose Great Renunciation is possibly in part a prolonged, and potentially reversible, grief reaction following the death of his mother (hinting at the depth of his grief, Toye (1987) reports that Rossini said, bursting into tears gazing at his mother's picture, he was "reminded . . . of the pleasure she would have taken in his triumph" [p. 188]); and a Ravel who could think of what he wanted to say but not actually say it, possibly not for emotional reasons, but due to a postconcussional syndrome/organic aphasia. In particular, avoid treating schizophrenics who are blocked as if they are neurotics, because the patient with voices telling him or her not to write predictably gets worse with uncovering. While a depressive may need total push therapy, the obsessive totally pushed merely rebels and totally pushes back.

Be active, not passive. The blank screen therapist creates a blank screen artist in the therapist's own image. Try to be directly helpful. The therapist should always be thinking, What can I do to help my artist, what can I do to save my artist from the bad effects of changing tastes and hostile critics? not, What interpretation is indicated here to resolve conflict and relieve anxiety?

Help the artist change his or her negative environment, when necessary. The artist with the wrong environment is like the weed that would be a flower, if only it were in the right garden. The artist to prevent/cure block, should transplant in the right garden: limit contacts with negative people whenever possible; avoid reading bad reviews (the method of a number of artists); get a whole new set of best friends (the method of Dorothy Parker, meant ironically, but useful literally); or move from place to place—the much discouraged, but often helpful, geographical solution (the method of Beethoven and Tennessee Williams).

Encourage positive identification with the therapist. Positive identification occurs spontaneously in everyday life. According to Toye (1987), Rossini identified with two priests, one who was a "great admirer of Mozart and Haydn" and both of whom had a love for excellent dinners, which the boy assimilated and imitated (pp. 11–12). Artists identify with teachers who urge them on, keep them from throwing their material away, and help them win their struggles with the bad little voices in their heads. As a treatment technique, positive identification is simplicity itself. All that is needed is a benign encouraging therapist who, especially if practicing what he or she preaches, is in a particularly good position to substitute a benign voice for the malignant little voices raging in the artist's head.

Retrain and re-educate, when necessary. It is surprising how often the artist allows him- or herself to continue obvious blockogenic bad habits and how a little guidance can stop the practice. As an example, one bad work habit most artists don't correct is allowing themselves to be interrupted, no matter how much this derails creative thought. They allow themselves to be interrupted out of a sense of responsibility or guilt. They pick up the phone each time it rings because it's a relative with an emergency, or because hope springs eternal, and maybe it's a big agent with an even bigger offer. But of course it's the telemarketer, and the artist gets madder and madder as he or she thinks about being a dupe or innocent victim, or about Xanadu lost.

Teach the artist what he or she has to know to survive. The therapist gives the patient the information needed to get over block. A good model adviser is Samuel Barber's uncle, Sidney Homer. Homer, according to Heyman (1993), told his nephew: "Stick by yourself . . . back yourself up . . . opinions are like the wind and blow from all quarters, and, even when sincere, can arise from inability to understand" (p. 172).

Learning about why critics and audiences mistreat artists can help the artist cope. No therapist can emphasize enough how jealousy is the real reason audiences and critics put artists down; the exact criticisms given are less the aesthetic pronouncements they pretend to be and more the transferential self-statements the critic/audience insists they are not. So often critics devalue an artist's work as part of a process in which they are using the work as a stimulus for their own needs and fantasies already in place, really as an excuse to express a personal dyspepsia already formed. As a simple example, live television audiences boo not to criticize the entertainment but to attract the attention of the camera so that they can wave hello to the folks back home. The message the therapist drills into the artist's head: they are preening, not evaluating you.

Also, teaching is inherently supportive because the very act of teaching says, "I want to help you."

Use manipulation freely. Whatever works, short of bribery, should be considered. Because of the often emergent nature of the problem, almost any means justifies the end.

As an example of a manipulation, a psychoanalyst took responsibility for an obsessional artist. He offered to make decisions for the artist, or to be the one to do the worrying. He pointed out this only worked temporarily. But it was enough to get the artist writing again.

Magical techniques can be useful for patients who believe they will fall ill by magic, such as speakers with stage fright who are convinced that somehow being up on the stage will cause them an almost physical harm. If they believe in magical causes of illness they also tend to believe in magical cures. So they respond well to something like the phobic pass—a piece of paper in the therapist's handwriting that says, "You won't faint during your speech," clutched tight in the hand, so that it can work by osmosis.

Recommend escape routes directly, when available. Most patients respond, at least temporarily, to suggested escape routes from obsessions like, "Take out plenty of insurance on your home and put a copy of your manuscript in your safe-deposit box, then you won't have to worry if you leave the coffee maker on and the house burns down."

Do existential analysis (as well as classical psychoanalytically oriented psychotherapy). The existential analysts have mastered the art of giving insight in a way that goes down well. They have learned to make it sound more upbeat than critical.

A blocked writer moved away from New York and hated the small town to which he moved and the bread-and-butter job he took there. He said of his job, "I feel like I am inside a coiled tube, the world's only tunnel without light on either end." He got a new job in New York, one that, unlike the job he currently had, promised to recognize his potential. The night after the day he got this new job he had the following, revealing dream: he had a New York apartment and was walking to it; the street before him was completely dark. But there, at the end, was the only light, the one coming from the drug store on the corner of the street on which his apartment stood.

While most analysts would stress the patient's fear of the darkness and talk about his conflicts and his anxieties almost as if they were defects, the dasein analyst might talk about the light, in effect congratulating the patient for making a start in the right direction and being able to clearly see where he or she was headed.

Function as a grief counselor as well as a therapist. If block doesn't start with, it eventually ends in, grief, a series of personal and professional losses the results of which have to be dealt with before the artist can comfortably face the intellectual aspect of his or her problem. The damage done by the critics of Barber's *Anthony and Cleopatra*, who suggested that there was more going on between the acts than during them, could have been treated better by Ruth Fox, Barber's therapist. Perhaps if Fox had treated Barber not by putting him in a group, which came between him and the substitute mother he needed, but by seeing him strictly individually in supportive therapy, encouraging him, using her considerable leverage as the expert, and using her considerable personal appeal as the good mother, his wounds may have healed.

Be supportive. The therapeutic situation is a retreat, a respite from the stress of everyday life. The therapist should provide the besieged artist with the equivalent of a quiet, seclusion room, away from his torturers, or a warm healing bath, reducing inflammation. Instead of shaking the artists' "wine bottle" and contaminating it with bottom sediment the therapist should "gently place the artist in a wine cellar" so that the constant temperature and warmth keep him or her from spoiling while he or she mellows with age. The therapist should wrap the patient in an impenetrable, protective cocoon away from the "Butchers of Broadway" and their ilk, the "Butchers from down the Block," the ones from everyday life, who seem to think they have carte blanch (really carte absolution) to sacrifice artists on a pyre of their devising—the ones who tell the painter to "get a real job," and the ones who smile knowingly and suggest to the writer of academic tracts that "you would be much better off writing a harlequin romance."

A supportive approach relies heavily on the placebo effect where the patient improves not from what we think we are doing but from what he or she thinks we are doing. It does nothing to undercut a flight into health even if the patient is getting better just to escape from therapy, avoids uncovering techniques when they stir up strong emotions that preoccupy, deep feelings that flood, and because all insight is critical, cause the artist to have the depressing feeling that he or she is being picked on.

For example, one patient's therapist kept telling her that her cure involved not antagonizing people she needed. All she heard was "you are antagonistic." Not unsurprisingly, this was viewed as more of the same criticism she got from her reviewers. Thinking the therapist was taking the enemy's side, she got depressed, developed severe chronic headaches, and couldn't work at all. When she complained she was getting worse, the therapist interrupted treatment because "you are incapable of insight." To his friends the therapist confided, "She is one of those borderlines who don't get better no matter what you do."

A supportive approach avoids allowing a negative countertransferential attitude toward the patient to build. All artists are depressed because all are the target of negative transference from immature audiences and envious critics. The effects of this negative transference, and the negative feedback to the patient it engenders, is best countered in treatment with positive countertransference/feedback. This is particularly valuable when it comes from the therapist. The best therapist is not merely a remote authority but is also a real person who likes and respects the artist and can say so, giving the artist a second opinion, this time, with weight. Now the artist has not only a seclusion room but an ally in there with him or her.

There has been more success stressing how blocked patients were getting better than excitedly reading the list of problems still to be resolved. The patients take this as a compliment, and it's usually the first one they have received recently. They go around thinking, "someone likes me," and reward the confidence placed in them by improving to the point where it is justified.

Give the patient a positive, corrective emotional experience. A central aspect of my treatment approach is modeled on Erich Lindemann's (1950, and personal communication) approach to the patient with ulcerative colitis. Lindemann noticed that ulcerative colitis patients were so rejection sensitive that they tolerated the conventional insight approaches poorly, reacting with increased diarrhea and bloody stools. Lindemann modified his analytic technique to deal directly with the element of grief and loss (usually of the mother or her substitute) so often found in these patients. He rapidly assessed who was lost and healed the patient by replacing the loss with a substitute relationship. He used a kind of corrective emotional experience where he played the part of the lost object long enough for the patient to get over his or her grief. If the patient lost a brother, Lindemann learned about the patient's brother not merely so that he could detect repeated, self-destructive, brother-transference patterns but so that he could be a "big brother" to the patient, in a way, of course, that did not cross boundaries.

Lindemann's techniques can be adapted for the blocked artist, who predictably feels wounded by life to the point that he "bleeds" easily, especially when wounded again in the transference. The vast majority of what we call terminal blockers fall into this group—artists who, like Rossini and Melville, write little or nothing in the last years of their lives because accumulated insults and losses finally weighed them down and pulled them under.

Artists, like patients with ulcerative colitis, are in effect oozing blood from their wounds. The therapist must not come along and bully the patient or pour salt in these wounds. He or she must help the artist to feel wanted and loved again by being an ally, a benign substitute for malignant people in the artist's life and in the artist's block. He or she must help the artist understand, handle, and countermanipulate the destructive forces that bring on, and perpetuate, artist's block. Artists are in a marasmic retreat, like Rene Spitz's children in the orphanage. They don't need a display of brilliance from an intellectually distant and critical mother, or a veiled emotional outburst from a discouraging father, or a competitive sibling. They need a little hand-holding from a benign big brother or sister, or parent figure.

Use somatic treatments judiciously. Surgeons must not release tendons surgically when a psychiatrist should be releasing inhibitions psychiatrically. Surgeons who treat injudiciously can cripple the computer operator permanently, or reduce the pianist to playing piano concertos for the left hand alone.

Do pharmacotherapy and other somatic therapies where indicated. One message in giving pills is "I care enough to give you something that will help." Except for the implication that "you can't be cured without pills," with all that means, criticism is avoided entirely. The lonely, ignored, grieving artist thinks he is once again snuggling at the bosom, figuratively speaking. And the medications themselves can be very effective. Some anxious public speakers respond to treatment with inderal, and some depressive blockers respond to treatment with antidepressants, particularly depressives who block in the main because of depressive low self-esteem.

A veteran/writer could speak Vietnamese and think up plots when asleep (his wife tape-recorded his speaking Vietnamese but he wouldn't tell her the plots). But in the morning, when he woke up, he couldn't speak a word of Vietnamese nor remember any of his plots. Antidepressants didn't help him speak Vietnamese when awake. But antidepressants did help him become less depressed and down on himself, enough to allow himself to recall, write down, and develop some of his nighttime plots.

APPENDIX

WHEN TO TREAT

Treatment may be indicated:

1. When a primary emotional disorder blocks the creative person and his or her creativity, and/or when it fouls the creative product.
2. When an emotional disorder is the result of the creative process; for creativity itself weakens, exhausts, and depletes the ego. It simultaneously stirs up disturbing strong feelings and thoughts along with unbearably intense memories. The artist must have a strong ego to handle this.
3. When emotional disorder is the result of the creative life, due to the stress all creators undergo, if only because all are, or soon will become, targets of negativity from jealous friends, audiences, and critics.

Treatment may be unnecessary: When creativity heals depression, as Kennedy (1987) throughout his biography implies it did for Elgar, who, at least until the last decade of his life, seems able to have recovered from his depression, and his depressive block, by writing music.

Treatment may be contraindicated: When emotional difficulties enhance creativity, as when creativity is the product of madness, and so, in a sense, the madder the creator the better the art. Authors like Kavaler-Adler (1993) in *The Compulsion to Create*, Rothenberg (1990) in *Creativity and Madness*, and

Jamison (1993) in *Touched With Fire* come close to suggesting something of this sort. Kavaler-Adler asks, "Is creativity a form of compulsive madness, driving artists by an urgent need for contact with their dark, demonic, and usually unconscious selves, or is it an effort to expel or exorcise inner ghosts? Is it perhaps a way of making friends with these ghosts, snakes, and other threatening demons?" (p. 1).

Could James Joyce have written *Finnegans Wake* without an ability to speak in language that resembles the primary process language of schizophrenics? Are poets like Sylvia Plath directly inspired by a psychosis? And if Robert Schumann's *Carnival* was the musical expression of a split personality, expressing now his Florestan and now his Eusebius side, should we have prayed not for his mental health but for his continuing mental destabilization?

By implying that madness can in some cases be a necessary condition for creativity, Kavaler-Adler (1993), and others of like mind, suggest that creative block is not an anticreative result of emotional disorder (my view) but an anticreative complication of emotional *stability*.

ON THE RELATIONSHIP BETWEEN CREATIVITY AND MADNESS

There are several ways creativity and madness seem to be related. Some creators seem unquestionably mad—schizophrenic, or bipolar, or at least "highly neurotic," and their creativity seems to derive at least to a degree from their madness. Others, like Schumann, show signs of madness, yet this madness has little relationship to all but the superficial aspects of their creativity, such as the speed at which it is produced. Still others, like Bach, (this is true of many successful artists) show little or no evidence of madness either in the individual or in that individual's art.

Creativity is more like a neurological than a psychological process, and as such not really capable of being conceptualized/understood in psychological terms, using psychological methods. As Freud (1957) put it in "Dostoevsky and Parricide," "Before the problem of the creative artist analysis must, alas, lay down its arms" (vol. 5, p. 222), and "the nature of artistic attainment is psychoanalytically inaccessible to us" (Gardner 1993, p. 24); as Giovacchini (1984) said, "the sources of creativity are still as much a mystery as ever" (p. 458); as Rank, quoted in Leader (1991), said, "pure psycho-analysis of . . . [creative] types undertaken for the removal of inhibitions . . . help[s not] at all for the psychological understanding of the creative process" (p. 64); and as Graf, quoted in Gedo's *Portraits of the Artist* (1989), said that "while pathography might clarify . . . obstructions of creativity . . . it has no bearing on the primary issues involved in artistic creation per se" (p. 10).

Some (admittedly inconclusive) evidence for these views:

1. The frequent disparity, certainly in music, but also in physics and other creative fields, between an artist's personal madness and his or her creative product. For example, there is not a drop of insanity in Schumann's music, unless we overread a kind of fatigue toward the end as symptomatic of an emotional disorder.

2. The tendency to create in a trance, where it is as if we have a parting of the psychic waters. One part of the brain in effect steps aside to let another part of the brain come through, one reason why many artists "don't know how they do it" (see below).

3. The very same artists who have endless things to say about their madnesses are unable to intelligently discuss their creativity. They are only able to talk circles around it, without really getting at it. They discuss "words or music first," talk of how they write patterns before notes, discuss their imagery (by which they possibly mean their creative inspiration), reveal how they manipulate twelve-tones and then get their computers to manipulate the manipulations, or speak of their programs ("I tried to make it sound as much as possible like a forest bird I heard on a walk"). But the best they can tell us about the creative process itself is: from Agatha Christie, "A sudden excitement would come over me and I would rush off to write down what I felt gurgling round in my mind" (p. 179); from Saint-Saens, according to a quote widely attributed to him, that he creates like an apple tree produces apples; from Ravel, quoted by Orenstein (1991) (Ravel seems to have had excellent psychodynamic perception), "I possess a melodic tap at a place which you will not permit me to designate more clearly, and music flows from it effortlessly" (p. 36); from Leo Ornstein, a composer, "My creativity is a being flooded with ideas" (quoted in a 1993 lecture from Richard Beaser in Carnegie Hall), that is, "I create because I am creative, and I am creative because I create"; and from Michael Colgrass, a composer, "My inspiration is like a buzz down the middle" (personal communication).

It would seem that creativity is what might be called an extra-psychic phenomenon. As such it is primarily conflict free, and only secondarily, if at all, is brought into the fray of emotions and emotional disorder, as when Beethoven takes back a jolly tune to make it ponderously minor because of a pervasive morality that reflects the age he lives in and his individual guilt.

Suggesting that all artists are mad does psychiatry an injustice and insults artists and hurts their feelings. When this view is repeated, as one artist complained, ad infinitum and ad nauseam, by a knowledgeable and credentialed profession with many widely disseminated publications to its credit, it amounts to little more than a sadistic attack on creators, worthy of standing alongside the familiar kind of artist abuse from nasty audiences and abusive critics. But here the abuse is even more devastating because its source is people who should know better, but don't, and who should be a little more compassionate, but aren't.

BIBLIOGRAPHY

Abse, D. Wilfred. 1959. "Hysteria." In *American Handbook of Psychiatry*, ed. Silvano Arieti. New York: Basic Books, Inc.

Alper, Gerald. 1992. *Portrait of the Artist as a Young Patient*. New York: Insight Books, Plenum Press.

American Psychiatric Association. 1994. *Diagnostic and Statistical Manual of Mental Disorders (DSM–IV)*. 4th ed. Washington, D.C.: American Psychiatric Association.

American Psychiatric Association. 1987. *Diagnostic and Statistical Manual of Mental Disorders (DSM–III–R)*. 3d ed., revised. Washington, D.C.: American Psychiatric Association.

Anchan, Harry S. 1994. Letter to the editor. "Making Good Tapes." *Stereo Review*, May.

Angier, Natalie. 1993. "An Old Idea About Genius Wins New Scientific Support." *New York Times,* October 12.

Bartlett, John. 1992. *Bartlett's Familiar Quotations*. Ed. Justin Kaplan. Boston: Little, Brown.

Bemporad, Jules R. and Henry Pinsker. 1974. "Schizophrenia: the Manifest Symptomatology." In *American Handbook of Psychiatry*. 2d ed., ed. Silvano Arieti and Eugene B. Brody. New York: Basic Books.

Bennett, William I. 1994. "Book Mark." *Harvard Medical Alumni Bulletin* 68 (summer): 13–14.

Bindman, Ellis, and R. W. Tibbetts. 1977. "Writer's Cramp—A Rational Approach to Treatment?" *British Journal of Psychiatry*. 131: 143–148.

Blum, David. 1994. "At a Rustic Retreat, Sibelius Explored His Many Selves." *New York Times*, July 24.

Cancro, Robert. 1985. "Overview of Affective Disorders." In *Comprehensive Textbook of Psychiatry/IV*, ed. Harold I. Kaplan and Benjamin J. Sadock. Baltimore, Md.: Williams and Wilkins.

Carpenter, Humphrey. 1992. *Benjamin Britten: A Biography*. New York: Charles Scribner's Sons.

Chadwick, George. No date. Notes for "String Quartet No. 4." Northeastern NR 234 • CD.

Cerf, Steven R. 1994. "Portrait of the Artist as an Old Man." *Stagebill* (program guide), Lincoln
    Center, Metropolitan Opera. February, 1994.
Christie, Agatha. 1977. *An Autobiography*. New York: Berkley Books.
Condrau, Gion. 1988. "Daseinsanalytic Therapy with a Patient Suffering from Compulsion
    Neurosis and Writer's Cramp." *The American Journal of Psychoanalysis*. 48(3): 211–
    220.
Diamond, Edwin. 1994. "The Last Word: Behind the Mystique of the *New York Times* Book
    Review." *New York Magazine*, January 10.
Dorland, W. A. Newman. 1951. *The American Illustrated Medical Dictionary*. Philadelphia:
    W. B. Saunders.
Downey, Bill. 1984. *Right Brain. Write On!* Englewood Cliffs, N.J.: Prentice-Hall.
Eliot, George. 1872. *Middlemarch*. Reprint. New York: New American Library, 1964.
Ellison, Cori. 1993. *Stagebill* (program guide), Lincoln Center, Metropolitan Opera.
Favazza, Armando R. 1985. "Anthropology and Psychiatry." In *Comprehensive Textbook of
    Psychiatry/IV*, ed. Harold I. Kaplan and Benjamin J. Sadock. Baltimore, Md.: Williams
    and Wilkins.
Feder, Stuart. 1992. *Charles Ives: My Father's Song*. New Haven: Yale University Press.
Federn, Paul. 1952. *Ego Psychology and the Psychoses*. New York: Basic Books.
Fenichel, Otto. 1945. *The Psychoanalytic Theory of Neurosis*. New York: W. W. Norton.
Fox, Ruth, and Peter Lyon. 1955. *Alcoholism: Its Scope, Cause and Treatment*. New York:
    Random House.
Freud, Sigmund. 1957. "Character and Anal Erotism." In *Collected Papers*. Vol. 2. Trans. by
    Alix and James Strachey. London: Hogarth Press.
———. 1957. "Contributions to the Psychology of Love. The Most Prevalent Form of Degra-
    dation in Erotic Life." In *Collected Papers*. Vol. 4. Trans. by Alix and James Strachey.
    London: Hogarth Press.
———. 1957. "Dostoevsky and Parricide." In *Collected Papers*. Vol. 5. Trans. by Alix and James
    Strachey. London: Hogarth Press.
———. 1957. "The Psychogenesis of a Case of Homosexuality in a Woman." In *Collected
    Papers*. Vol. 2. Trans. by Alix and James Strachey. London: Hogarth Press.
———. 1957. "Some Character-Types Met with in Psycho-Analytic Work." In *Collected
    Papers*. Vol. 4. Trans. by Alix and James Strachey. London: Hogarth Press.
———. 1953. "Three Essays on the Theory of Sexuality." In *Standard Edition of the Complete
    Psychological Works of Sigmund Freud*, ed. James Strachey. Vol. 7. London: Hogarth
    Press.
———. 1950. *Totem and Taboo*. New York: W. W. Norton.
Friedman, Bonnie. 1993. *Writing Past Dark: Envy, Fear, Distraction, and Other Dilemmas in
    the Writer's Life*. New York: HarperCollins.
Frosch, William A. 1992. Review of *Charles Ives: My Father's Song: A Psychoanalytic
    Biography*, by Stuart Feder. *The American Journal of Psychiatry*. 149(12): 1741–1742.
Gammons, Peter. 1992. "The Throes of Tossing a Baseball." In *The Best American Sports
    Writing*, ed. Thomas McGuane. Boston: Houghton Mifflin.
Gardner, Howard. 1993. *Creating Minds*. New York: Basic Books.
Gedo, John E. 1989. *Portraits of the Artist*. Hillsdale, N.J.: Analytic Press.
Gibbon, Edward. 1776–1788. *The Decline and Fall of the Roman Empire*. Reprint. London:
    Viking Press, 1980.
Gibson, H. B. 1972. "Writer's Cramp: A Behavioural Approach." *Behavior Research &
    Therapy*. 10(4): 371–380.
Gill, Gillian. 1990. *Agatha Christie: The Woman and Her Mysteries*. New York: Simon and
    Schuster.

Giovacchini, Peter. 1984. *Treating Character Disorders*. Northvale, N.J.: Jason Aronson.

Gross, Ruth Belov. 1991. *Your Don't Need Words*. New York: Scholastic.

Gussow, Mel. 1994. "Elusive Playwright." *New York Times*, February 27.

Hayman, Ronald. 1993. *Tennessee Williams: Everyone Else Is an Audience*. New Haven, Conn.: Yale University Press.

Heyman, Barbara B. 1992. *Samuel Barber: The Composer and His Music*. New York: Oxford University Press.

Hendrick, Ives. 1958. *Facts and Theories of Psychoanalysis*. New York: Alfred A. Knopf.

Henning, Lawrence H. 1981. "Paradox as a Treatment for Writer's Block." *The Personnel & Guidance Journal*. 60(2): 112–113.

Holland, Bernard. 1994. "After a Long Absence, Perahia at Carnegie Hall." *New York Times*, April 11.

Hugo, Victor. 1862. *Les Misérables*. Reprint. London: Penguin Classics, 1982.

Jamison, Kay. 1993. *Touched With Fire*. New York: The Free Press.

Jones, Ernest. 1953–1957. *The Life and Works of Sigmund Freud*. 3 vols. New York: Basic Books.

Kaplan, Harold I. and Sadock, Benjamin J. 1985. "Typical Signs and Symptoms of Psychiatric Illness." In *Comprehensive Textbook of Psychiatry/IV*, ed. Harold I. Kaplan and Benjamin J. Sadock. Baltimore, Md.: Williams and Wilkins.

Kavaler-Adler, Susan. 1993. *The Compulsion to Create*. New York: Routledge.

Kennedy, Michael. 1987. *Portrait of Elgar*. New York: Oxford University Press.

Kozinn, Allan. 1994. "Bryn Terfel in an All-German Recital." *New York Times*, October 26.

Kris, Ernst. 1952. *Psychoanalytic Explorations in Art*. New York: International Universities Press.

Krueger, David W. 1984. *Success and the Fear of Success in Women*. Northvale, N.J.: Jason Aronson.

Layton, Robert. 1992. *Sibelius*. New York: Schirmer Books.

Leader, Zachary. 1991. *Writer's Block*. Baltimore, Md.: The Johns Hopkins University Press.

Lindemann, Erich. 1950. "Modifications in the Course of Ulcerative Colitis in Relationship to Changes in Life Situations and Reaction Patterns." *Association for Research in Nervous and Mental Disease, Proceedings. 29:706–723*.

Lublin, Joann. 1994. "Managing Your Career: How to Get Around a Boss Who Blocks Your Career Path." *The Wall Street Journal*, August 24.

Ludwig, Arnold M. 1994. "Mental Illness and Creative Activity in Female Writers." *The American Journal of Psychiatry*. 151(11): 1650–1656.

Mack, Karin and Eric Skjei. 1979. *Overcoming Writing Blocks*. Los Angeles: J. P. Tarcher.

Malcolm, Janet. 1993. "The Silent Woman." Parts 1–3. *The New Yorker*, August 23 and August 30.

Marsden, C. D. and M. P. Sheehy. 1990. "Writer's Cramp." *Trends in Neurosciences*. 13(142): 148–153.

Meissner, William W. 1985. "Theories of Personality and Psychopathology: Classical Psychoanalysis." In *Comprehensive Textbook of Psychiatry/IV*, ed. Harold I. Kaplan and Benjamin J. Sadock. Baltimore, Md.: Williams and Wilkins.

Melville, Herman. 1851. *Moby Dick*. Reprint. New York: Bantam Books, 1981.

Michener, James A. 1991. *The Novel*. New York: Random House.

Minninger, Joan. 1980. *Free Yourself to Write*. San Francisco: Workshops for Innovative Teaching.

Nelson, Victoria. 1985. *Writer's Block and How to Use It*. Cincinnati, Ohio: Writer's Digest Books.

Nemiah, John. 1985a. "Obsessive-Compulsive Disorder (Obsessive-Compulsive Neurosis)." In *Comprehensive Textbook of Psychiatry/IV*, ed. Harold I. Kaplan and Benjamin J. Sadock. Baltimore, Md.: Williams and Wilkins.

———. 1985b. "Somatoform Disorders." In *Comprehensive Textbook of Psychiatry/IV*, ed. Harold I. Kaplan and Benjamin J. Sadock. Baltimore, Md.: Williams and Wilkins.

Nimet. 1995. Radio announcement on January 8, 1995, New York City Radio Station WQXR.

Orenstein, Arbie. 1991. *Ravel: Man and Musician*. New York: Dover Publications.

Perez-Pena, Richard. 1994. "Nine Years of Resolve." *New York Times*, November 1.

Perlmutter, Donna. 1994. "A Little Night Music." *New York Times*, March 3.

Perry, J. Christopher. 1992. "Problems and Considerations in the Valid Assessment of Personality Disorders." *The American Journal of Psychiatry*. 149(12): 1645–1653.

Pinsker, Henry and Martin Kantor. 1973. "Musical Expression of Psychopathology." *Perspectives in Biology and Medicine*. 16(2): 263–269.

Plaskin, Glenn. 1983. *Horowitz: A Biography*. New York: William Morrow.

Popper, Charles W. 1988. "Disorders Usually First Evident in Infancy, Childhood, or Adolescence." In *American Psychiatric Association Textbook of Psychiatry*, ed. John A. Talbott, Robert E. Hales, and Stuart C. Yudofsky. Washington, D.C.: American Psychiatric Press.

Prigerson, Holly G., Ellen Frank, Stanislav V. Kasl, Charles F. Reynolds III, Barbara Anderson, George S. Zubenko, Patricia R. Houck, Charles J. George, and David J. Kupfer. 1995. "Complicated Grief and Bereavement-Related Depression as Distinct Disorders: Preliminary Empirical Validation in Elderly Bereaved Spouses." *The American Journal of Psychiatry*. 152(1): 22–30.

Ross, Alex. 1994. "Worlds Lost in Seas of Sorrow." *New York Times*, June 12.

Rothenberg, Albert. 1990. *Creativity and Madness: New Findings and Old Stereotypes*. Baltimore, Md.: The Johns Hopkins University Press.

Ramey, Phillip. n.d. "A Talk with Samuel Barber." *Barber Songs*. Album notes. Germany: Etcetera Compact Disk, KTC 1055.

Schildkraut, Joseph J., Alissa J. Hirshfeld, and Jane M. Murphy. 1994. "Mind and Mood in Modern Art, II: Depressive Disorders, Spirituality, and Early Deaths in the Abstract Expressionist Artists of the New York School." *The American Journal of Psychiatry*. 151(4): 482–488.

Schonberg, Harold C. 1992. *Horowitz: His Life and Music*. New York: Simon and Schuster.

———. 1981. *The Lives of the Great Composers*. New York: W. W. Norton.

Schuman, Elliott P. 1981. "A Writing Block Treated with Modern Psychoanalytic Interventions." *Psychoanalytic Review*. 68(1): 113–134.

Schwarz, K. Robert. 1994. "Composers' Closets Open for All to See." *New York Times*, June 19.

Silva-Garcia, Jorge. 1988. "Discussion of the Case of Otmar Presented by Dr. Gion Condrau." *The American Journal of Psychoanalysis*. 48(3): 229–234.

Simon, John. 1994. "This *Lady* Is for Burning." *New York Magazine*, January 3.

Solomon, Seymour R. 1985. "Application of Neurology to Psychiatry." In *Comprehensive Textbook of Psychiatry/IV*, ed. Harold I. Kaplan and Benjamin J. Sadock. Baltimore, Md.: Williams and Wilkins.

Stone, Evelyn M. 1988. *American Psychiatric Glossary*. Washington, D.C.: American Psychiatric Press.

Storr, Anthony. 1992. *Music and the Mind*. New York: The Free Press.

Stravinsky, Vera, and Robert Craft. 1978. *Stravinsky in Pictures and Documents*. New York: Simon and Schuster.

Tavris, Carol. 1993. "Beware the Incest-Survivor Machine." *New York Times*, January 3.

Tchaikovsky, Modeste. 1973. *The Life & Letters of Peter Ilich Tchaikovsky.* New York: Vienna
    House.
Thompson, Oscar. 1964. *The International Cyclopedia of Music and Musicians.* New York:
    Dodd, Mead.
Toye, Francis. 1987. *Rossini: The Man and His Music.* New York: Dover Publications.
Weinberger, Jerome L. 1964. "A Triad of Silence: Silence, Masochism and Depression."
    International Journal of Psychoanalysis. 45: 304–308.
Zinsser, William. 1985. *On Writing Well.* New York: Harper and Row.

INDEX

Memory defects, and inhibition block, 107
Mendelssohn, Felix, 22
Merging, as cause of writer's cramp, 9
Meyerbeer, Giacomo, 86–87
Michener, James, 140; Michener block
 (variation of partial block), 126
Minninger, Joan, 110
Missed block, 117–126. *See also* Covert
 (hidden) block
Moby Dick, 43, 142. *See also* Melville
Models of creative block. *See* Paradigms
Mother, loss of unique status with, 30–31.
 See also Death of mother
Motherwell, Robert, 28
Motor aphasia, and inhibition block, 107
Motor block, 59
Motor damping, paradigm of block, 109
Mozart, Wolfgang A., 6, 29, 32
Multiple Personality Disorder, 77. *See also*
 Dissociative block
Myxedema madness, and inhibition block,
 106

Narcissism, 31
Narcissistic Personality Disorder, 89–90
Narcissistic transference to artist, 144, 145
Negative symptoms of schizophrenia, 12,
 17–18
Nelson, Victoria, 19–20, 42, 107
Nemiah, John, 56, 63, 91
Neurological disorders that can cause
 block, 106–108
New York Times: Cleopatra, review of, 143;
 Perahia, Murray, 15; Schulhoff, Ervin,
 dependent block in, 91; traumatic neuro-
 sis, real or imagined, 77
Nightmares, and block, 74; as paradigm of
 block, 111
Nonartistic block, 117, 121–122

Obsessive-Compulsive Disorder block, 13,
 63–71, 120
Obsessive-Compulsive Personality Disorder block, 91–92
Obstinate (obsessive-compulsive) block,
 67–68
Occupational cramp, 10. *See also* Performance cramp; Writer's cramp; Pianist's
 cramp; Violinist's cramp
Occupational inhibitions, 152

Older people, block in, 123–124
Oppenheim, Meret, 80
Orderly/perfectionistic (obsessive-compulsive) block, 65–67
Orenstein, Arbie, 12, 74–75, 165; anger, in-
 trojected of Ravel, 28–29; grandiosity,
 disappointed of Ravel, 32; spontaneous
 creation in Ravel, 179
Ornstein, Leo, 179

Paganini, Nicolo, 40
Paradigms (models) of creative block, 105,
 109–112
Paradoxicality, paradigm of block, 110
Paranoid Personality Disorder block, 24–
 26, 84
Paranoid transference to artist, 145
Paraphiliac block, 79–82
Paresthesias, and block, 59
Parker, Dorothy, 171
Parkinson's disease, and inhibition block,
 107–108
Partial block, 45–47, 126
Passive aggression, use of as weapon, 31
Passive aggressive personality disorder
 block, 92
Passivity, 31
Pears, Peter, 79
Pedophilia (pedophiliac block), 81
Perahia, Murray, 15, 94
Perez-Pena, Richard, 39
Performance cramp, 23. *See also* Occupa-
 tional cramp; Pianist's cramp; Violin-
 ist's cramp; Writer's cramp
Perlmutter, Donna, 153
Perry, Christopher, 5–6
Persecutory delusions, 23
Personality Disorder block, 13, 83–97
Pharmacotherapy: of block, 175; of obses-
 sive-compulsive block, 71
Philistinism, 142
Phobic Disorder block, 12–13, 45–54
Physical causes of block, 105–112
Pianist's cramp, 9, 22, 46, 107. *See also*
 Occupational cramp; Performance
 cramp; Violinist's cramp; Writer's cramp
Pinsker, Henry, 18, 19, 69, 167
Plagiarism, 15, 87, 117, 124–126; benign,
 125; malignant, 125–126. *See also* Deri-
 vativeness

ABOUT THE AUTHOR

MARTIN KANTOR is a psychiatrist who has been in private practice in Boston and New York. Kantor has been active in residency training programs, including those at Massachusetts General and Beth Israel in New York. He has written five other books including *Distancing: A Guide to Avoidance and Avoidant Personality Disorder* (Praeger, 1993) and *Human Dimension of Depression* (Praeger, 1992).

ISBN 0-275-94905-2

HARDCOVER BAR CODE